Vocation and the Politics of Work

Vocation and the Politics of Work

Popular Theology in a Consumer Culture

Jeffrey Scholes

LEXINGTON BOOKS
Lanham • Boulder • New York • Toronto • Plymouth, UK

Published by Lexington Books
A wholly owned subsidiary of The Rowman & Littlefield Publishing Group, Inc.
4501 Forbes Boulevard, Suite 200, Lanham, Maryland 20706
www.rowman.com

10 Thornbury Road, Plymouth PL6 7PP, United Kingdom

Copyright © 2013 by Lexington Books

All rights reserved. No part of this book may be reproduced in any form or by any electronic or mechanical means, including information storage and retrieval systems, without written permission from the publisher, except by a reviewer who may quote passages in a review.

British Library Cataloguing in Publication Information Available

Library of Congress Cataloging-in-Publication Data

Scholes, Jeffrey, 1971–
Vocation and the politics of work : popular theology in consumer culture / Jeffrey Scholes.
pages cm
Includes bibliographical references.
ISBN 978-0-7391-7890-4 (cloth : alk. paper) — ISBN 978-0-7391-7891-1 (ebook)
1. Vocation—Christianity. 2. Work—Religious aspects—Christianity. 3. Consumption (Economics)—Religious aspects—Christianity. 4. Christianity and culture. I. Title.
BV4740.S315 2013
261.8'5—dc23
2012046617

∞™ The paper used in this publication meets the minimum requirements of American National Standard for Information Sciences Permanence of Paper for Printed Library Materials, ANSI/NISO Z39.48-1992.

Printed in the United States of America

Contents

Introduction		1
1	Theology of Vocation and the Role of Work	19
2	Theology at Work	49
3	Consumer Culture and Its Effects	83
4	The Purchase-Driven Life	109
5	Towards a Political Vocation	141
Bibliography		171
Index		181

Introduction

Studs Turkel's popular 1972 book, *Working*, recounts the testimony that Nora Watson, a staff writer for an institution that publishes health care literature, gives about the meaning of her job. She laments, "A job like mine, if you really put your spirit into it, you would sabotage immediately. You don't dare. So you absent your spirit from it. My mind has been so divorced from my job, except as a source of income, it's really absurd."[1] Later, Nora adds, "I'm coming to a less moralistic attitude towards work.... I don't think I have a calling—at this moment—except to be me. But nobody pays you for being you, so I'm at the Institution—for the moment. When you ask most people who they are, they define themselves by their jobs. 'I'm a doctor.' 'I'm a radio announcer.' 'I'm a carpenter.' If somebody asks me, I say, 'I'm Nora Watson.'"[2]

Nora's testimony expresses a familiar need: to locate life's activities in a broader, deeper context in order to gain satisfaction through their performance. She is also conveying the difficulty in connecting a fundamental activity for most (work) to a deeper, fuller context, or as she calls it, a calling or a vocation. Stating that her calling, for the moment, is just "to be me" betrays the problem that arises when work and a vocation are decoupled. If one's spirit has vacated and one's mind has divorced from an activity as crucial to satisfaction with life as daily work can be, having a calling that only requires Nora to be herself may not be enough to endure the daily grind.

This need to couple daily, remunerated work with a serious purpose for doing it draws on a five-hundred-year history of the Protestant concept of vocation. Since Martin Luther, *all* work, not just priestly work, holds the potential to be godly or to be a response to God's call. This democratization of vocations has mercifully elevated the status of lowly jobs, yet it has also burdened work with the duty to be meaningful and satisfactory. As Max Weber famously pointed out over a century ago, even though vocational work may have lost a connection to any divine metaphysical truth, it is still pursued with a kind of religious vigor.[3] Whether a vocation is considered to be a response to an actual call from God or it is used to satisfy the need for life's activities to be greater than the sum of its parts, it still holds immense societal value.

Andrew J. Weigart and Anthony J. Blasi express the importance of vocations in even stronger terms:

> Much of the change and resistance to change in social life takes the form of the long-term commitments that people have and which they experience as transcending callings. Vocations are not the total explanation for history—i.e., for change and resistance to change; one can cite alienation, disaffection, greed, lethargy and conventionality as well. But vocations surely fill out a major part of the picture.[4]

In terms of work, it is these long-term commitments manifesting in the form of a career that feed off of the satisfaction with one's work to sustain themselves. Satisfaction with work is, of course, measured differently depending on the worker and on the context of the job. It is safe to say that for most workers in the West today, job satisfaction entails much more than the meeting of basic needs such as food and shelter. Whatever factors lead to job satisfaction, if a vocation is to retain any cultural currency in the world of work, it must align itself with these. Alternatively, whatever factors lead to job dissatisfaction, one's conception of his or her own vocation should be able to oppose these.

So when work is not living up to the demands that a vocation can place on it, a divide between work and a vocation opens up, as Nora's testimony exhibits. This divide, especially for those who expect their work to be vocational, invites several responses. If the jurisdiction of a vocation has been overextended to include *all* types of daily work, then the expectation that any job should be able to deliver on a kind of spiritual fulfillment needs to be lowered, or the jurisdiction of a vocation needs to be narrowed. Or if paid work and the activities that would befit a calling are mutually exclusive in reality, then the project to integrate the two should be abandoned once and for all. Or work must produce a certain level of emotional or psychological satisfaction in order for it to be vocation, and then we should cease expecting the work itself to be "calling-worthy." Or finally, perhaps the problem lies not with the lack of agreement between a vocation and one's *feeling* about oneself at work but with the current inability of vocations to engage work and the material and political factors that lead to satisfaction or dissatisfaction.

The twofold purpose of this book is to elucidate the causes of this latter "vocation problem" and in so doing, suggest the conditions that allow for solutions. To get at the problem, I first show that the abstraction of the Protestant concept of vocation from actual work by theologians over the last five hundred years contributes to its inability to engage the concrete work world. These gradual moves towards abstraction have often been made, sometimes consciously, sometimes not, in response to changes in the socioeconomic environment as it involves the meaning of work. Thus, I follow this analysis with a companion piece to the theological history that demonstrates the effects of culture on the nature and comprehension of daily work. I pay special attention to the shift in the twentieth century West from societies organized around production to those now organized around consumption. It is this transition that also contributes to the abstraction of vocations from concrete work, yet it does so by converting work from that which produces to that which is consumed.

The effects of this shift show up in popular self-help and business motivation literature that aims to guide readers into fulfilling work lives. In many of these texts the idea that a job is like a consumer item merges with the idea that a vocation is that which generates a kind of consumer satisfaction with work despite working conditions. I will show that the fleeting nature of this type of consumer satisfaction, as delivered by the vocation language used in these texts, function to benefit the employers over the employees or capital over labor. Again, an ephemeral concept of vocation is pushed onto readers, which, for those who are rightly considered "workers," prevents a clear-eyed view of their own working conditions and the cultivation of a strong will to alter them. These theological and cultural strands intertwine and are woven together particularly well in Rick Warren's bestseller, *The Purpose-Driven Life*. I show that Warren's purpose-*qua*-vocation is a profoundly influential exhibit of a theology of vocation packaged in a culturally relevant, hence consumer-friendly, form. Consequently, Warren only aggravates the "vocation problem."

If the problem is that vocations are being abstracted and distanced from the messiness of actual work, then the solution must involve a more politically charged concept of vocation that is grounded in the material workplace. The burgeoning field of political theology that situates itself in a postsecular context lights a path for theology to interact with politics by revealing the conditions that are currently in place for such an interaction. This can allow a vocation to enter the political space of the workplace as a valuable normative challenge to the norms of the corporate power elite that rely on an ideology of capital growth no matter the human cost.

The "political vocation" that I gesture towards is not necessarily a corrective to attenuated concepts of the past, nor is it a reclamation project that aims to excavate an older, more pristine concept that should now be used. It also does not embody a direct, detailed commentary on business ethics or even on specific political arrangements that result from the relationship between labor and management. Rather, by highlighting relevant aspects of the Protestant concept of vocation and while attending to democratic modern norms that can move the relationship in a positive direction, a path can open up for a joining of the two.

i

An extensive 2006 survey of private-sector U.S. workers that focused on "what workers want" suggested three main findings. First, a large gap exists "between the kind and extent of representation and participation workers had and what they desired." Secondly, the survey revealed that "workers preferred cooperative relations with management to adversarial ones, where a cooperative relation meant both mutual respect and some degree of power sharing." And third, "workers were open to different paths for increasing their representation and participation at their workplace."[5] In other words, what workers really want is *political* in nature. Emotional and psychological satisfaction with work may or may not be felt more immediately than the political kind. But suffice it to say that the presence of certain political arrangements at work is the necessary if not, at times, the sufficient condition for satisfying desire in a working life.

So if a vocation is to be tied to satisfaction at work, it must have something to say about the workplace politics. But does a vocation have the capacity to inform a political situation? Protestant theologians from John Calvin to Karl Barth to Miroslav Volf have inquired deeply into the meaning of vocation with the aim of squaring what it means to live out a vocation with the God who is calling. At the risk of over-generalization, most theological analyses of vocation or of work tend to look first to transcendent truths about God, then at times to actual work for insights into what a vocation is and should be. Hence both the role that workplace politics has played and continues to play in the meaning of work have been historically minimized or ignored when formulating a concept of vocation in order to safeguard God's character. Ken Estey states the problem in terms of theologies of work:

> The voices and experiences of workers are ignored in favor of theological categories that describe idealized visions of work. The social and historical realities that shape the daily lives of workers are neglected. Most theologies of work assume that theological discussions of work can occur without sustained attention to the power dynamics that deeply affect workers and the structure of the workday. Theological or ethical reflection alone cannot cause lasting alterations to the power dynamics that govern the work world.[6]

The theological component of vocation (that it is believed to be a divine call) will not and should not go away—it provides a gravitas to the purpose of work in the form of a divine call for many that cannot be replicated by labor theorists. Yet mere reflection on the relationship between a vocation and God hovers above the world that all vocations engage.

How are we to grasp these power dynamics at work in order for a vocation to address them if theology alone cannot help us? Tracking developments in culture helps us attend to the changes in the relationship between vocation and work. In particular, paying attention to the effects that consumer culture has had both on the meaning of work, a job, or a career is crucial to my project. These effects are especially evident when consumer culture is pitted against its predecessor, producer culture. Because work is more self-evidently tied to that which we produce rather than that which we consume, the association between vocations and consumer culture may, at first glance, seem strained. However, as Rick Fantasia and Kim Voss point out, any discourse involving producer culture where the value of the worker is emphasized must take serious account of consumer culture too.

> The virtual disappearance of the Worker, at a symbolic level, along with the simultaneous symbolic elevation of the Consumer, who has emerged to become the supreme subject and object of economic practice. . . . This shift has been expressed, on the one side, by a steady inflation of the social rights granted to the Consumer (for example the "freedom" to choose . . .). On the other side, this has taken place at the expense of the systematic dissolution of the rights of the Worker (for example, the spread of contingency, wage decline, overwork . . .). It is not just a matter of these spheres standing in inverse proportion to one another, but that they are reciprocally generating conditions: on the other side of the smiling face of endless consumer "convenience" is the stern regime of coerced labor "flexibility."[7]

When the factors leading to the "disappearance of the worker" reinforce those that result in the "elevation of the consumer" and vice versa, any discussion of flagging worker's rights must be informed by an analysis of consumer culture.[8] Indeed, vocations today, as they, themselves, get caught in the flow of consumer culture, demonstrate that they are less and less concerned with the rights of the worker by stressing the individual's right to choose and consume. Hence, in order to better understand current uses of the concept of vocation, its relation to the waning symbolic power of the worker must be seen in conjunction with its acquiescence to consumer culture.

One primary indicator of the relationship between consumer culture and vocations is the language of some of the best-selling literature currently on the market: self-help books and business motivational literature. Finding purpose in life, which often involves one's work life and always involves oneself, has been and is still the central activity trafficked in these books. And when work is invoked as a medium through which to find purpose, the concept of vocation is often trope of choice.

The consumer cultural component to these self-help messages, as it regards a vocation, has to do in part with the "commodification of work." The freedom to choose at a shopping mall now extends into the search for work and its experience, where a job bears the responsibility of satisfying a worker as a purchased commodity is expected to do. And once one is stuck in a less than desirable job, a consumer mind-set, as touted by many self-help books, dictates that searching for that which corresponds to one's passion will attract good things at work or even a more desirable job down the road. Therefore, these texts tempt workers to dovetail their idea of a vocation with the belief that if they carry the right attitude towards work (or even towards joblessness or poor working conditions), their work can be vocational once they make the correct "purchase." Consequently, having a vocation now has less and less to do with what you actually do at work but how you do it. If you have a problem with your job, the problem is you.

On the other side of the labor/capital divide, companies are increasingly encouraging employees to think of their approach to work in terms of consumer-friendly concepts like "purpose" or "mission" to foster efficiency and productivity on the job.[9] Again, consumer culture tailors the idea of a vocation as a palliative for the employee soul but also for opportunistic deployment by an employer. When deployed as such, a calling serves the interests of the employer when it loses the capacity to frame and then expose the ideology backing employer interests. Likewise, the effects of this parasitic usage have a depoliticizing effect on vocation, albeit for non-theological reasons. Not only can such a domesticated version of a calling render inequitable work conditions bearable, but it can also sell out its capacity to make working conditions more just.

When vocations provide work with meaning through emotional and psychological compensations, as pushed in self-help literature or through a vague notion of God's will being done, the question of whether working conditions are the primary cause of job dissatisfaction may not normally figure into one's "vocational calculus." Job loss based on corporate restructuring or outsourcing, the receipt of less than a living wage, miniscule or nonexistent decision-making power on the job—all are realities to an increasing number of employees who make up the majority class in America.[10] In the entrenched battle between labor and management, the latter typically blame these unfortunate states of affairs on inviolable market forces, while the former must resign themselves to a less-than-desirable working life.[11] A workplace democracy, most corporations are not. All the while, the question of whether the employee's vocation, not the employer's, should be informing, even challenging, the lack of democratic power is rarely if ever asked.

Therefore, we see that both theological and popular cultural treatments of vocations distance them from work and its political context at the expense of the worker. Either a vocation derives from a God who infuses a vague purpose into work no matter the job, or a vocation is enlisted to legitimize or delegitimize a career choice based on whether the choice matches desire. In both cases, a vocation has become an idea that has little traction in the concrete work world. And such a disengaged, depoliticized and dematerialized, and free-floating vocation is predisposed for use by self-help authors who prefer to push more palatable, less contentious concepts for popular consumption.

ii

How, then, does a theological concept get politicized today? In the case of vocation, if a transcendent God is doing the calling, how can that call translate into the language of the immanent work world in order to address the concerns of the worker? Working through the answers to these questions involves two moves. One, the admission that theology is inextricably linked to its cultural context provides at once a road map for how theology becomes depoliticized in culture as well as the clues for disentangling a theological concept from depoliticizing cultural movements. I discuss this part of the equation as it relates to work and vocation in chapter 2. Two, the conditions necessary to allow the engagement of theology and politics must be established, which I discuss briefly in what follows.

The burgeoning field of political theology, a branch of both political philosophy and practical theology, claims, amongst other things, that the religion that was formerly private and at arm's length from politics but is now ready to enter the public light of the political environment. In reciprocal fashion, the State or more generally, the *polis*, has also undergone changes, mostly due to globalization, that make it more receptive to religious norms and values.

Political theologians predicate their claims on the belief that we live in a *postsecular* world—one that results from the process of secularization but has established itself beyond the process that helped create it. For postsecularists, the old binary of sacred/profane or if preferred, religious/secular, that helped secularization theorists in the 1960s, 1970s and 1980s proclaim the eventual triumph of secular institutions over religion, is now defunct, as is the secularization theory that relied on the binary. Postsecularists see the stubborn data (religion has not only stuck around but is growing in many parts of the world) and question whether religion was ever truly separated from secular discourse, despite what secularization theory suggests. Many of the tenets of secularization theory (religion is private and separate; the secular is public and engaged, for instance) have been subjected to serious scrutiny and criticism for the past twenty years. Perhaps the criticism that carries the biggest ramification for religion is that secularization theory defines religion too narrowly, thus stripping it of power that it never really relinquished.[12]

Despite the general movement of secularization in the West over the last several centuries, religions have never been prevented from entering the public realm and offering a contesting normative discourse in contraposition to the dominant secular discourse. This was and is only possible if the boundaries of the public/private and religious/secular split that were defined by secularization theorists were never as fixed as they claimed. Clayton Crockett writes, "[t]he recent and continuing deformation of the line delineating the religious and the secular also demonstrates that it has never been possible to strictly separate the two, although a large part of what we call Western modernity has been predicated on the possibility that religion and secularity can be kept apart."[13] Hence the success of modernity has been predicated on the conviction that not only should the religious and secular be separated, but that they, in fact, are. Yet if this is shown not to be a fact at all, as José Casanova, for instance, cogently demonstrates, then the postsecularist rightly demands a different relationship between religion and the secular to be acknowledged and examined for its implications.[14]

Political theologians operating under this postsecularist assumption admit that some level of secularization has occurred over the last sixty years and that its effects still reverberate. The ascendancy of the scientific worldview and the liberal State has taken place at the expense of religion's cultural power. The persistence of religion at once challenges the prediction and assumptions of secularization theory while undergoing modification wrought by secularization. Political theologians contend that secularization generated the unintended consequence of "ready-ing" religion and theology for entrance into once-prohibited secular, political environments. Jeffrey Robbins states, "One result of this generalized trend is the postmodern return of religion wherein religion has been repoliticized. If modern secularism required the privatization—and thus, the depoliticization of religion—then the postmodern, postsecular is a repoliticization."[15] Repoliticization suggests that religion is able to engage political norms, as it itself is politicized, but what kinds of norms are religion particularly apt at engaging?

On the first point, Robbins warns of the dangers that a political theology encounters when it gets in bed with modern liberalism. Yes, for theology to be explicitly political in the West, it will usually end up buttressing democratic values. But democracy in America has most recently been the expression of our roles as free economic subjects in a capitalist economy rather than as free citizens. The marriage of democracy and a laissez-faire economy does not allow a political theology to be critical of abuses in a capitalistic society if it does not distinguish democracy from modern liberalism. Robbins offers a "radical democracy" that extracts democratic principles from their neoliberal context and works through his political theology in order to critique neoliberalism. He writes that "while getting its impetus from the despair over the perceived failures of modern liberalism, political theology need not, and must not be allowed to, translate into a rejection of democracy as such."[16] This way, a political theology helps a democracy that is divorcing from neoliberalism reimagine itself, as novel political manifestations reciprocally bear on the kind of political theology that is needed.

What, then, of the commitment to theology that, on some level, political theologians must have? In order to engage political norms operating on the ground, religions that enter the public sphere cannot assume either an anti-modern stance, as is often held in conservative circles, or an a-cultural, transcendent perspective. Crockett states it this way,

> If religion and secularity cannot be neatly separated, we cannot fully separate or distinguish political philosophy from political theology. In a postsecularist environment, we possess no absolute or certain criterion by which to claim that any phenomenon is theological as opposed to nontheological. Here theology means theoretical reflection about religious phenomena in general rather than a specific tradition or set of truth-claims.[17]

While postsecularism allows for connections between religion and secularity, it simultaneously prohibits the political theologian's recourse to metaphysics. Ironically perhaps, it is under secularism that theology could stake out its own fiefdom from which universal theological claims could be made, whether honored by secular institutions or not. Under postsecularism, no such private, parochial enclave exists for both theology and secularity. However, the term "theology" is still used by political theologians, so what does it mean and how is it deployed? Crockett again,

> Theology indicates a commitment to certain values, whether these are identified, acknowledged, intended, or deployed. These values may be more traditionally religious or more secular, but we should keep in mind the difficulty of fully distinguishing the two terms. Using the term "theology" would pressure scholars of religion to reflect upon their own commitments, principles such as freedom ethics, dialogue, liberation, and understanding, and certain aspects of particular academic religious, or political traditions.[18]

Theology, instead of being thought of as brokering in transcendent, universal truths, merely designates a type of relationship to values and norms. The fact that these values can be either historically religious or secular reveals the detachment of the theology of political theology from that of traditional theology. However, in a postsecular context, not only is theology's role necessarily circumscribed, it is also able to supply a unique and at times, powerful level of commitment to certain values.

This commitment may be theistic or not. As long as the role of God as the informer and even underwriter of a political theology takes a back seat to the realization of political aims, there is nothing in a postsecularist understanding of religion that prevents God-talk.[19] God, in this way, is prevented from becoming the sole object of theological reflection, and reflection alone is disallowed from being the only activity of political theology. Crockett, in fact, uses one of the cherished values of political theologians, freedom, as a more appropriate way of reflecting on God. For him, "Freedom does not simply substitute for God, but in a formal sense captures the possibility of thinking God as well as thinking anything at all. In this sense a formal theological thinking would attend to what makes concepts available for understanding and articulation."[20] Here, theology and theological thinking are intertwined with the project of political theology. True to postsecularism, theological thinking continues but is utterly inseparable from its cultural context. The task of theology, then, is a cooperative endeavor with culture that lends its voice to worthy political projects.[21] It is exactly this task that I take on with the theological concept of vocation as it circulates in a consumer culture and fights to become politically relevant in the modern corporate workplace.

iii

It is necessary to elucidate some of the terms that I have already been using and will continue to use throughout before laying out the structure of the book. In *Habits of the Heart*, Robert Bellah, et al. provide a useful glossary to parse important terms associated with the relationship between vocation and work. In a chapter intended to locate work within the changing religious landscape, Bellah distinguishes a job from a career from a calling. A *job* is not typically interpreted by his respondents as an end in itself but is performed for material benefits alone and as such, does not provide the means to express the jobholder's deeper interests. A *career* furnishes the worker with the means to transcend mere material benefits of work through advancement within an occupational structure, though salary alone may still be the indicator of advancement. Bellah states that higher social standing, job satisfaction and perhaps self-esteem can accompany a career, but work is still not an end in itself in a career. A *calling*, on the other hand, forges the relationship between one's life and work that renders them inseparable. Work is an end in itself in a calling because it informs all of life; monetary gain and social standing are secondary and even dispensable as the "meaning-givers" of work.[22] However, the point at which a job becomes a career or a career devolves into being merely a job seems less clear than when either become a calling. The different meanings of a job and a career respectively may be helpful to the holder of either, but work is still occurring in each despite the language used.[23]

Raymond Williams's set of definitions of "job" and "career" largely mirror Bellah's, though he contends that "work" can stand in semantically for both terms.[24] Generalized work, which grounds both a job and a career, as Williams defines it, is "the piece of work, the activity you get paid for, the thing you have to catch or to shift or to do, the ordinary working experience."[25] Here, work is a more inclusive term that contains worker experience *and* the thing that one does without getting caught up in whether it is a part of a job or career.[26]

Williams also remarks that the meaning of the word "work" has undergone changes—the most profound being those wrought by capitalism. From the Reformation until early capitalism, work carried more of a medieval character of *toil*.[27] Yet since the onset of capitalism, the meaning of work has been narrowed "to indicate activity and effort through achievement" and to be defined in relation to "its imposed conditions, such as 'steady' or timed work, or working for a wage or salary: being hired."[28] As opposed to effort put into adhering to family roles or even unpaid "work" (despite the often tremendous energy needed to succeed in these endeavors), for practical reasons, I only consider work as defined by Williams when relating it to a vocation in this book.

Richard Sennett's emphasis on the impact of *social relations* on the modern workplace is particularly helpful for locating both the nature and effects of working conditions. Sennett conceptualizes the work world as a network of social relations that determine the environment in which identities on the job are forged.[29] He describes social capital as an expression of individual and/or corporate power saved up and/or exerted at work that defines the social relations. The level of social capital acts as a barometer for the overall health of the work world and as such, indicates the degree of receptivity that a vocation can handle.[30] As noted earlier, I seek to extend the concept of vocation into the political arena of the work world. Lacking a baseline description of the way in which social groups interact in the workplace, a vocation remains individualized, private and unable to alter social structure.

Sennett pares down his task further by focusing primarily on business institutions on the "cutting edge of the economy: high technology, global finance, and new service firms with more than three thousand employees." He is quick to remark that most Americans do not work for such firms. "Rather, they [employees of cutting-edge firms] represent a leading edge of change, an aspiration of what businesses ought to become: no one is going to start a new organization based on the principle of permanent jobs."[31] As a vanguard that may be in a nascent stage but is *the* model for any business desiring to be successful, these "flexible" firms represent a, "small slice of the economy" yet have "a cultural influence far beyond its numbers."[32] Sennett is "unabashedly inferring the culture of the whole from a small part of society, just because the avatars of a particular kind of capitalism have persuaded so many people that their way is the future."[33] Integrating the concept of vocation into workplaces that practice flexible capitalism, then, carries far-reaching implications for the concept. Therefore, as I rely on Sennett's use of social capital to elucidate the relationship between work and vocation, his focus on *this* sector of the business world will be where my focus is as well.

Admittedly, circumscribing my inquiry in this way risks passing over people whose work is not directly or obviously impacted by flexible capitalism. Indeed, Luther is explicit in his inclusion of *all* jobs, including those that stem from social roles as calling-worthy. Work environments vary wildly from those of the forest ranger to the mid-level bureaucrat to the self-employed who work out of the house. While aspects of a political vocation can engage all work, I center my attention on a specific type of work environment so that the concept of vocation retains specificity too. This is not to say that all work cannot be vocational, but to account for all types of work, as Luther does, is a difficult task given the vast difference between say, manual labor and service industry jobs in late capitalism.

In addition, as we will see, there are particular qualities of the flexible corporation that differentiate its workers from manual laborers. As will be explored later, "team-based," intra-business competition and the use of consulting firms in corporations lend themselves to some of the mechanics of consumer culture. Manual, wage labor typically does not participate in such business strategies. Finally, because fewer and fewer corporations are controlling the economy, their actions are felt in some way by more and more American employees. Therefore, if a concept of vocation can engage *this* working environment, its implications can be far-reaching.

Three brief qualifications remain. One, a political vocation has family resemblances to, yet more measured goals than, the concepts employed by liberation theologians. For many who consider themselves to be doing liberation theology, theological concepts must fit into a conceptual whole under the burden of liberating all constraints on the human condition.[34] Or the political and economic liberation of the poor is underwritten by a comprehensive set of theological convictions. The *political* is the *theological* and vice versa in most liberation theologies. A political vocation is an offering that carries the spirit of liberation theology, but, in lockstep with the assumptions of political theology, it claims no totalizing application, nor does it allege membership in a historical theological system.

Two, brief qualifications remain. It should be noted that remunerated work is by no means fully determinative of the meaning of a vocation, both past and present. Purpose in life, even that believed to align with God's call, can find its source in family life, hobbies, and in other activities outside of work to be sure. Yet even these non-work activities, if they are considered to be vocational, are interpreted as such because of the historical relationship between work and vocation that supplies a calling with its primary meaning.

Three, as we recall from Nora's reflection on her calling or lack of one, religion may not play an explicit or conscious role in whether one's work is a part of a vocation. Despite this, as Weber was well attuned, certain theological commitments are causal factors in socioeconomic effects, whether consciously acknowledged or not by those affected. Hence, close attention paid to theologies of work and vocation continue to bear fruit in any analysis of a vocation as it is thought of today.

iv

Chapter 1 draws on a selective theological history of the Protestant concept of vocation. This history discloses that theologies of vocation, far from articulating a static concept, continually bend to accommodate changing work environments. This history additionally charts the gradual rise in the authority of human agency and choice, especially in American writings, at the expense of the authority of a sovereign God to dictate the terms of a vocation. Despite this unmistakable current and with only a couple of notable exceptions, theologians, past and present, typically emphasize the need for vocations to ally themselves with God's will, either despite the changing conditions of work or because of them. Hence the vast majority of Protestant theologies of vocation betray the profound cultural and economic impact on the meaning of the term by lamenting the effects of the "world" on our interpretation of a vocation. Consequently, the relationship between a vocation and the material conditions/political dynamics of a job, while tight in reality, has been neglected in favor of attending to the proper relationship between a calling and a transcendent God who calls. This historical survey supplies us with one of the reasons for the type of concepts of vocation that are now popularized—ones where the nature of work recedes into the background and a mixture of human agency and God's power awkwardly comingle.

Chapter 2 seeks to clear a methodological path for theology to engage the political norms of the workplace by asserting that theologies of work are always culturally embedded. The overall method I employ to relate vocation to the environment of the workplace is not so much an established, programmatic framework as it is a set of assumptions about theological products that reveal a long-standing, yet overlooked, interaction. The idea that theologies are culturally embedded and hence cannot be distilled out from culture is unpacked in this chapter and applied throughout the book. I show that the admission that theological products are culturally embedded is a more honest and effective way of approaching the problematic political arrangements in the workplace. Finally, I utilize these methodological tenets locate my project tentatively within the field of political theology and postsecularism.

Chapter 3 acts as a kind of supplemental piece to chapter 1 as it supplies a cultural explanation for the changing relationship between work and vocations. It does so by tracking a secular or non-theological history of the shift from societies organized around production to that of consumption. Highlighting the implications of this shift will reveal the mutually supporting movements of the vanishing of the producer and the rise of the consumer—both of which bear heavily on the current meaning of a vocation. I look at the writings of sociologists Zygmunt Bauman and Richard Sennett, who couch the shift from production to consumption in terms of the resilience and then a grand slackening of social bonds that hold together each society respectively. The scholars' respective designations, "liquid modernity" and "flexible capitalism," provide useful frameworks with which to view the social conditions that structure the work world and its relation to vocations in a consumer culture.

Chapter 4 looks at a particularly influential book that combines a theology, elements of the self-help genre, and consumer culture to advance a particular concept of vocation. Rick Warren's idea of "purpose," as the functional equivalent of the idea of vocation, can be engaged and realized without reference to one's material or social life; it is merely "consumed" as an idea. I examine the connection between *The Purpose-Driven Life* and consumer culture through its questionable status as a self-help book and as a text that uses seeker-sensitive methods to woo religious consumers. After establishing that purpose is a kind of vocation, I demonstrate that Warren's concept is shorn of any reference to a material world in which one's purpose should be able to engage—if in fact purpose is universal in scope and power as Warren attests. In this way, Warren's version of vocation solicits readers to maintain a "shallow engagement" with the concept that establishes the conditions for Warren to use seeker-sensitive methods to package a book with self-help qualities.[35] Hence it will be shown that *The Purpose-Driven Life* and books like it overlook the mechanics at work that precede and undergird the expression of these qualities.

Chapter 5 explores the means by which religion generally and the concept of vocation specifically can fight through the effects of consumer culture in order to provide an avenue for a political vocation to engage the corporate work world. Before articulating what a political vocation needs to be able to accomplish, I do a reconnaissance of the battlefield between producers and consumers as it pertains to religion. I argue that Vincent Miller, while insightfully describing the dematerialization of religion in a consumer culture, fails to treat the etiology of consumer culture with similar scrutiny. His emphasis on "habits and dispositions" that are instilled by consumer culture serves to de-emphasize the role that human and corporate agents play in the production and sustenance of consumer religion. Lacking a detailed discussion of the real beneficiaries of the commodification of religious products, Miller is resigned to leaving consumers with *tactics* of resistance when a *strategy* is called for. I pit Miller's leanings towards a "democracy of consumers" against the more critical stance of Jeremy Carrette and Richard King. The latter argue that the consumer orientation towards religious concepts and practices is far from innocent; the commodification of spirituality is "corporate-led" and "corporation-served."[36] Their argument simultaneously reveals the distance between commodified religious concepts and actual work conditions as well as exposes the means by which employers benefit by the distance. Here, the "consumer-friendly calling" meets the work world to reveal the limits of such an appropriation of vocation.

Later in the chapter, I explore ways in which a vocation can gain traction and act to redress uneven and unfair power dynamics at work. A political vocation must be able to deploy itself as a weapon that can counter the institutions that maintain the status quo through their use of consumer culture strategies. Yet, as a concept that necessarily traffics in the transcendent and immanent realms (a call from God is interpreted and applied in the world), a vocation, even a political one, must strike a balance between its ethereal roots and its concrete fruits.

For the transcendant portion, I life out elements of John Calvin and Walter Rauschenbusch's respective theologies of vocation that intersect with the political world in order to connect the transcendent and immanent in ways that remain political. Then I draw on some of the implications of postsecularism that point to a new relationship between the religious and the secular that allows for novel ways for religious notions of vocation to dialogue with historically secular environments such as the workplace. A postsecular environment permits the theological import of a vocation to remain intact as it simultaneously utilizes modern political norms to inform itself as well.

My move towards a concept of a political vocation, then, is one that is comfortable in a postsecular world, yet wary of its own commodification that leads to an overemphasis of its transcendence at the expense of its immanence. Only by resisting the pull of consumer culture and the theological tendencies that encourage resignation to it can a vocation ground itself and then challenge certain normative structures of the corporate workplace. Perhaps ironically, it can do so only by remaining faithful to elements within the original Protestant concept that merge with modern democracy and political freedom. It must be said that the political content of a vocation by no means exhausts the entire meaning of a vocation. It merely represents a latent element within the concept whose awakening is sorely needed. Resultant is a concept of vocation that, through an exertion of its political muscle, can promote obedience to God's call by inducing disobedience towards an unjust or merely unsatisfying working life.

NOTES

1. Studs Terkel, *Working: People Talk About What They Do All Day and How They Feel About What They Do* (New York: Ballantine, 1972), 675.
2. Terkel, 679.
3. Max Weber, *The Protestant Ethic and the Spirit of Capitalism* (New York: Scribner's 1958), 182.
4. Andrew J. Weigert and Anthony J. Blasi, "Vocation," in *Vocation and Social Context*, ed. Giuseppe Giordan (Leiden, The Netherlands: Brill, 2007), 13.
5. Richard B. Freeman and Joel Rogers, *What Workers Want* (Ithaca, NY: Cornell University Press, 2006), 1–2.

6. Ken Estey, *A New Protestant Labor Ethic at Work* (Cleveland: The Pilgrim Press, 2002), 4–5. See also Esther D. Reed, *Good Work: Christian Ethics in the Workplace* (Waco, TX: Baylor University Press, 2010), 9. Reed shares the same concern as Estey, but she locates the need for reform in a theology of vocation—a context that Estey would reject as a means to achieving these goals.

7. Rick Fantasia and Kim Voss, *Hard Work: Remaking the American Labor Movement* (Berkeley: University of California Press, 2004), 27–28. Flexibility has been championed by many business authors, but none more than Tom Peters. Peters, who starting in 1982 with his book that is considered to be the best piece of business literature ever written, *In Search of Excellence*, has consistently cited business flexibility as the chief modus operandi of successful businesses. See Thomas J. Peters and Robert H. Waterman Jr., *In Search of Excellence: Lessons from America's Best Run Companies* (New York: HarperCollins, 1982).

8. The elevation of the consumer does not mean that we work less. A Gallup Poll recently found that time spent at work has not changed significantly over the last half century. Alex M. Gallup and Frank Newport, *The Gallup Poll: Public Opinion 2005* (Lanham, MD: Rowman and Littlefield, 2006), 339.

9. Richard H. Roberts, *Religion, Theology and the Human Sciences* (Cambridge: Cambridge University Press, 2002), 63; Jesper Kunde and B.J. Cunningham, *Corporate Religion* (Upper Saddle River, NJ: Prentice Hall, 2002), 8, 64; Carrette and King, 132–37.

10. Michael Zweig, *The Working Class Majority: America's Best Kept Secret* (Ithaca, N.Y.: ILR Press, 2000), 34–35.

11. Michael Perelman, *The Invisible Handcuffs: How Market Tyranny Stifles the Economy by Stunting Workers* (New York: Monthly Review Press, 2011), 25–26.

12. José Casanova, *Public Religions in the Modern World* (Chicago: University of Chicago Press, 1994), 14.

13. Clayton Crockett, *Radical Political Theology: Religion and Politics After Liberalism* (New York: Columbia University Press, 2011), 2.

14. Casanova, 14–39.

15. Jeffrey W. Robbins, *Radical Democracy and Political Theology* (New York: Columbia University Press, 2011), 78.

16. Robbins, 5.

17. Crockett, 2.

18. Crockett, 39.

19. Crockett, 32.

20. Crockett, 17.

21. The vast majority of writings considered to be political theology center on geopolitical matters, not necessarily on the politics of more limited spheres such as the workplace. Hent de Vries suggests as much in his introduction to his almost exhaustive compilation of political theologies: "What has happened to 'religion' in its present and increasingly public manifestation, propelled by global media, economic markets, and foreign policies as much as by resistance to them? How should we understand the worldwide tendencies toward the simultaneous homogenization and pluralization of our social and cultural practices, that is to say, of our individual and shared forms and ways of life?" De Vries and the lion's share of essays that fill his edited volume take this "worldwide tendency" as an opportunity to recast the role of religion as a player in global politics. No doubt flexible capitalism and the workplace politics that follow are products of globalization as de Vries describes it. It must be said, however, that though my project is indebted to the shifting nature of religion in a global setting, I am applying political theological insights to a specific case, the American workplace, with a specific theological concept, vocation. Hent de Vries, *Political Theologies: Public Religions in a Post-Secular World* (New York: Fordham University Press, 2006), 1.

22. Robert Bellah et al., *Habits of the Heart: Individualism and Commitment in American Life* (Berkeley: University of California Press, 1985), 66.

23. Another problem with Bellah's analysis (for my purposes) stems from the fact that his analysis is based largely on work testimonials gathered from workers. These

testimonies cull more of a subjective feeling about work; work is unfulfilling (unworthy of a calling) or satisfying (calling-worthy). But the reasons for these responses are not stated in Bellah's interpretation apart from a down deep feeling that the respondents cite. My concern is not the more subjective reckoning with meaning on the job but the more objective work conditions that help generate these expressions. Worker satisfaction is an important piece of the puzzle regarding the relationship between vocation and work. If the relationship between a vocation and work can be analyzed using workers' interpretations of their working experience alone, the conditions that contribute to such interpretations are downplayed in the analysis, and appropriations of vocation like the one Mims uses can be legitimized (Bellah et al., 67–71).

24. Raymond Williams, *Keywords: A Vocabulary of Culture and Society* (New York: Oxford University Press, 1983), 335–37. It should also be noted that "work" as a verb can include non-paid activity as it is used with expressions such as "work around the house" or "work on my jump shot." And while these activities can be construed as vocational, given Luther's expansive definition, they leave open the possibility that *any* activity can potentially be a part of a vocation—a possibility that this project has not the ability to address fully.

25. Williams, 337.

26. Williams's generalization of work succeeds instrumentally at the expense of an accounting for the vastly different meanings that work carries. I willingly incur this expense for the sake of making my project feasible yet still substantial. No matter how high the amount of meaning or purpose is being extracted from one's work, the concept of vocation can do more heavy lifting.

27. Williams, 335. The difference between Reformation "work" and today's version is important to note when attempting to understand the Reformation treatment of vocations in chapter 1.

28. Williams, 335.

29. Specifically, Sennett argues that descriptive terms like "liquid" or "flexible" define modern capitalistic society. Contrasting today's business world with Weber's "iron cage," Sennett places company demands for worker flexibility and complacence with job volatility under the umbrella of a pervasive consumer culture—an association that I explore in chapter 2. By connecting volatility that accompanies flexible capitalism to the mind-set of the modern consumer, Sennett situates work in the larger cultural setting. As noted earlier, the meaning of vocation is caught up in this setting as well, and hence Sennett's investigation proves doubly fruitful.

30. Richard Sennett, *The Culture of the New Capitalism* (New Haven: Yale University Press, 2006), 63–66.

31. Sennett, "Capitalism and the City," in *Future City*, eds. Stephen Reed, Jürgen Rosenmann and Job van Eldijk (New York: Spon Press, 2005), 119.

32. Sennett, *The Culture of the New Capitalism*, 12.

33. Sennett, 12.

34. The father of liberation theology, Gustavo Gutierrez, writes: "From the outset, liberation was seen as something comprehensive, an integral reality from which nothing is excluded, because only such an idea of it explains the work of him in whom all the promises are fulfilled." Gustavo Gutierrez, *A Theology of Liberation* (Maryknoll, NY: Orbis Books, 1988), xxxviii.

35. Vincent Miller, *Consuming Religion: Christian Faith and Practice in a Consumer Culture* (New York: Continuum, 2004), 106.

36. Carrette and King, 127–32.

ONE

Theology of Vocation and the Role of Work

> Each man has his own vocation. The talent is the call. There is one direction in which all space is open to him. He is like a ship in a river; he runs against obstructions on every side but one, on that side all obstruction is taken away and he sweeps serenely over a deepening channel into an infinite sea. —Ralph Waldo Emerson, *Spiritual Laws*

The question of whether work is properly vocational has historically been answered by consulting two authorities that are often seen to be working at cross purposes: God and the self. God may call us to a vocation, yet how does one know that he or she is answering that call faithfully? Can unfulfilling jobs, as measured by the worker, be divinely sanctioned? How much influence can society have on a career choice before that choice is at odds with God's plan? Can an individual's desire for a certain career merge with God's plan so that both are in sync, or will there always be tension?

If there is a scale weighing the power of these two authorities to shape the meaning of a vocation, it has slowly tipped towards the self over the last five hundred years. Early in the history of the Protestant iteration of the concept, individual desire to choose a career was severely circumscribed both by the will of a sovereign God and a rigid social hierarchy. But with the slow breakdown of patrilineal descent of work wrought by the onset of capitalism and an ever-expanding market came a disentangling of vocation from work and a subsequent entangling of vocation with human choice and agency. "Finding a vocation" began to replace "abiding in a vocation."

Along with the socioeconomic changes that spurred this development, theology followed in kind. Liberal theological conceptions of vocation, as well as those coming from secular societal circles in the nineteenth and early twentieth centuries, tended to deem human volition and desire as *the* determining factors in how one responds to God's call. We then see a reflexive theological response in the twentieth century to the inflated self that is able to craft its own vocation. This conservative rejoinder attempts the restoration of an omnipotent and immutable God who issues a consistent call over and against the dictates of a protean and often cruel culture that feeds the self.

Yet minimized or neglected altogether in both liberal and conservative concepts of vocation is the variable of daily work. Their ideas of a vocation, whether animated by human will or by a call from a wholly other God, are ones that may uphold a certain theological conviction, but they lack the ability to inform actual work practices. And when work is not a primary informant of a vocation, the idea of vocation is ironically more susceptible to cultural manipulation. I say "ironic" because reiteration of God's sovereign power in the matter of our call is meant to subdue the power of worldly culture to design its meaning.

It bears noting that a theological history of the Protestant vocation has rarely, if ever, been undertaken.[1] As such, not only will the history that I offer in this chapter be somewhat of a pioneer effort, but, given the freedom granted by the dearth of predecessors, it will also be a selective, albeit justified, one.

THE DEMOCRATIZATION OF VOCATIONS: LUTHER AND *BERUF*

Martin Luther's novel interpretation of the concept of vocation marks a momentous departure from the established Church position on vocation in the early sixteenth century Europe. This rather famous departure is made evident in many ways, but no evidence is more telling than Luther's translation of the word "vocation" into vernacular German. Vocations had previously referred only to priestly work or to jobs directly related to the Church. Through his interpretation of St. Paul's Greek term *klesis* (calling), Luther equates vocation to *Beruf*, or "occupation." And by not specifying certain occupations, he means that all jobs have vocational potentiality, not just those occupied by priests, monks, and nuns.[2]

Beruf reflects and incorporates Luther's overall theological leanings. He maintains Paul's emphasis that the call from God commands obedience to a godly life, but then Luther extends the means by which one can obey God's call through mundane activities including work. Consequently the Lutheran refrain of "The Priesthood of All Believers" signifies more than the lifting of the status of all believers into that of clergy—his innovative notion also sacralizes the activities of all believers. The pulling of the priest off of his perch not only brings the privileged status of vocation down to the ground, but it also boosts non-priestly vocations to previously unknown heights. Or as Marx puts it, "[h]e turned priests into laymen because he turned laymen into priests."[3]

If one's status, priestly or not, dictates which activities within a job were vocational before Luther, activities themselves, apart from status, fill out a vocation after Luther.[4] And as long as actions follow the biblical mandate to express brotherly love in social interactions, those actions are now properly vocational. This means that any activity, including that stemming from fatherhood or friendship that is motivated by care for others, is a valid means by which to respond to God's call. The requirement that brotherly love serve as the necessary feature of any vocation not only democratizes work (brotherly love can be expressed in *all* jobs) but also forces God's call to interact with the world through all forms of labor. No longer can the cloistered life of the monk be exclusively considered holy in the eyes of God—justification before God requires outward godly living that can only disclose itself through worldly engagement.

And for Luther, it is labor that acts as the primary vehicle for such expression. The way one conducts one's business, not only through the diligence required to perform tasks on a job but also through honorable financial exchanges, must be motivated by care for the other and not exploitation. Or working for self-gain is not a proper answer to God's call.

> The rule ought to be, not, "I may sell my wares as dear I can or will," but, "I may sell my wares as dear as I ought, or as is right and fair." For your selling ought not to be an act that is entirely within your own power and discretion, without law or limit, as though you were a god and beholden to no one. Because your selling is an act performed toward your neighbor, it should rather be so governed by law and conscience that you do it without harm and injury to him, your concern being directed more toward doing him no injury than toward gaining profit for yourself.[5]

"Law" is, of course, God's law mediated by the Bible, and conscience is what translates biblical law into action on a daily basis. The Bible, however, is not restricted to the text itself. The tools of one's work act as a kind of biblical text as well, as Luther states it.

> To use a rough example: if you are a craftsman, you will find the Bible placed in your workshop, in your hands, in your heart. . . . Only look at your tools, your needle, your thimble, your beer barrel . . . and you will find this saying [the Bible] written on them . . . you have as many preachers as there are transactions, commodities, tools and other implements in your house and estate; and they shout this to your face, "My dear, use me toward your neighbor as you would want him to act toward you with that which is his."[6]

The Bible is used metaphorically to convey the seriousness of work; every business transaction and its needed materials are didactic and sermonizing. Hence, the transmission of God's Word is not confined to church or even to a private room in which the Bible is quietly read. God's Word follows the worker and appears whenever the opportunity is present for brotherly love to be expressed. Just as the actions of the Good Samaritan were holy, so is ordinary work.

Yet the lift on the ecclesial restrictions of what counts as vocational work is offset to a degree by societal restrictions that Luther sets down on the kind of job one can have. The priestly estate was considered by the Church to be divinely appointed and hence carried with it certain duties required of the office of its estate. Luther simply expands the number of divinely appointed estates, while maintaining the integrity of their boundaries, to cover all social situations in which believers find themselves. But instead of arguing that a vocation is damaged by the circumscription (because one's estate is divinely assigned), Luther asserts that one's calling can operate *only* with such limitations. Paul Marshall explains, "If some objected that they had no calling, Luther replied, 'how is it possible that you should not be called. You will also be in some estate, you will be a husband, or wife, or child, or daughter, or maid.'" Marshall goes on to elaborate on the relationship between vocation and social estate in Luther's works:

> All work in the world, not just some particular offices, was understood as immediately divinely appointed; one was called to it. The type of work varied according to one's office; one's office was determined by one's estate; one's estate was given by God, and it was one's existing social situation. The calling was hence a definite divine commandment to work diligently according to one's given social position.[7]

The parameters of one's estate help to execute God's will by governing the selfish motives that may entice a transcending of one's lot. If newly found pride in one's work and talents incites a move (or even the desire to move) beyond these parameters, divinely ordained offices are breached. That brotherly love can only be made manifest when work is contained within the social boundaries reveals conservatism in Luther's formulation of vocation. Yet Luther's narrowing of the social and political scope of a vocation is held in tension by a theological liberalism that upholds the democratizing of vocation.

If the freeing of vocation from the jurisdiction of the Catholic Church elevates the status of work in God's eyes, Luther's critical response to humanism helps us see how he can concomitantly place societal limits on a working life. Richard M. Douglas points out that for Luther, in contrast to the kind of vocation that humanism would advocate, choice and human volition play *no* role in the determination of a calling:

> The humanists implicitly defended a principle of utility resting upon the belief that the welfare of the commonweal depends upon the existence of self-determined members, each of whom he has chosen the

course of life which best suits him or which he most enjoys pursuing. The sixteenth-century reformers, on the other hand, explained vocation as the office or station in which God has placed us in the orders of creation or that which God has assigned us for the service of others through love.[8]

While Luther gives non-church occupations divine import in relation to the heavenly kingdom, the sky is not the limit in the earthly kingdom. God's stratified order for creation dictates that a vocation always connotes a "station in life" that is not to be vacated.

Because work for Luther serves as a means to the end of serving others and serving God in the process, he does not take pains to delineate either the substantial differences between jobs or how individualized calls are heard and deciphered. Luther's writing on vocation nevertheless prefigures more contemporary forms of the distinction between a *general* call to follow God and a *special* one to follow the call made to particular individuals. The general calling refers to the broad-based, open invitation to a relationship with God that is universally issued to all. A special calling, in contrast, is delivered to the individual and hence is more closely tailored to the capacities of an individual to perform certain tasks needed to answer the call. Jobs can evoke the talents needed to answer a special calling. Yet because a job is largely chosen for you in Luther's theology of vocation, any special talent or skill is limited in its ability to bring righteousness before God. Or the special call is subsumed by the general call. This is a point that Luther was wont to make over and against those who, in his view, claimed salvation on the basis of works rather than on faith. Gustav Wingren interprets Luther on this point:

> Conscience does not find peace through any work. Here, it is only the gospel which is fully effective. . . . Vocation gives steadiness and strength before men, because righteousness in vocation, according to earthly rules, is real righteousness, which before men we are not able to despise or label as sin. But before God, on the other hand, even the most righteous work is a serious sin, which stands in need of forgiveness, since it proceeds from an evil heart. . . . Only the gospel, not one's vocation, can remove that judgment against the sinful heart and gives peace to the conscience.[9]

So while one's work, however ordinary, is endowed with incredible, society-transforming power, the superiority of the heavenly kingdom over the earthly one reminds the worker that it is God alone who can ultimately redeem all human activity.

Luther's thought marks a watershed in the meaning of work and the vocations that sanctify it. Because one's job is understood by Luther to be part of a preordained and fixed office, switching jobs based on individual desire or whim was out of the question. The fixity of an office during the early sixteenth century was ordained by God and affirmed by a late-feudal society that was based on established class distinctions. Therefore, the work that one performs, no matter how diligently or morally it is performed, does not affect the structure that holds the job in place.

However, since work, as part of vocation, is only a vehicle used to express brotherly love, the actual job performed is relatively unimportant for Luther. Marshall explains, "What he [Luther] usually had in mind when he spoke of calling was a call to service that came to a Christian *within* the midst of his or her sphere of work. Vocation was hence seen primarily as a summons to work for a neighbor's sake. . . . In this sense, a vocation could be distinguished from one's immediate work."[10] This distance between "immediate work" and a vocation permits Luther to write in vaunted tones about vocation while glossing over actual work activity, the material conditions that modify it, and the social station that fixes it. To the extent that Luther's writings valuate jobs, the special calling is more of an extension of God's general call to serve the almighty. Little account is taken of the difference between a magistrate, a merchant, and a lowly seamstress. Consequently, scant attention is paid to whether being fixed in these stations is unfair.

Finally, Luther's subordination of individual desire to God's will leaves little room for questioning, reflection, or analysis of one's calling. Douglas states that Luther's vocation

> does not proceed in some vague way from the self, from a *vocatio interna* by which one responds to a voice of one's own. For the Christian to be certain of his vocation, he must be called to it through the independent, external fact of a calling from God, mediated to him through other men.[11]

One performs daily activities for the benefit of others only because God has dictated thusly. More pointedly, our jobs are unworthy in themselves but are worthy as instruments of God, or as Luther put it:

> All our work in the field, in the garden, in the city, in the home, in struggle, in government—to what does it all amount before God except child's play, by means of which God is pleased to give his gifts in the field, at home, and everywhere? These are the masks of our Lord God, behind which he wants to be hidden and to do all things.[12]

Be that as it may, by merely labeling the job of a seamstress as a role that is just as much a vocation as the job of a priest, Luther sets into motion a transformation in what it means for newly minted Protestant Christians to be called by God. Despite the delimitation of social mobility, daily work for all acquires a backbone under Luther that now holds the *potential* to exert an influence on all aspects of society.

CALVIN AND VOCATION AS WORLD-TRANSFORMING

John Calvin on vocation, as on many other topics, follows a general Lutheran trajectory. In mimicking fashion, Calvin uses the concept of vocation to govern human activity. He explains in *The Institutes*:

> And that no one may thoughtlessly transgress his limits, he [God] has named these various kinds of living "callings." Therefore each individual has his own kind of living assigned to him by the Lord as a sort of sentry post so that he may not heedlessly wander about throughout life.[13]

For Calvin and Luther alike, all work is potentially calling-worthy, yet this does not mean that one can escape the duties that attend to divinely assigned work. Calvin, though, asserts more emphatically than Luther that it is *God alone* who assigns believers to their "sentry post." And when God is the sole legislator and executor of all human life, a distance between God and humanity opens up that allows a surprising freedom of movement in the earthly kingdom. Marshall summarizes the difference between Luther and Calvin on this point: "Calvin's view was not as static as Luther's. One's given social position was not quite so normative, limiting, or all-encompassing. Although he still emphasized that one should stay in a calling, Calvin did not regard this as an iron rule but only as a caution to prevent undue 'restlessness.'"[14]

As compared to the Lutheran accent on the external office or estate that effectively rationalizes immobility, Calvin's reasons for remaining in a station find a more internal justification. If stepping out of the line that a vocation-*cum*-God has drawn means an ill-advised move up the social ladder for Luther, Calvin traces transgression back to our own weak mind.

> The Lord bids each one of us in all life's actions to look to his calling. For he knows with what great restlessness human nature flames, with what fickleness it is borne hither and thither, how its ambition longs to embrace various things at once.[15]

The God-given purpose of a vocation is to keep in check the natural, yet sinful, inclinations to chase aimless pursuits. The problem is not necessarily the political unrest that can result from transgressing that which God establishes in one's vocation, but the human mind run amok. Letting our own desire direct the terms of a vocation is tantamount to disobedience.

> No one, impelled by his own rashness, will attempt more than his calling will permit, because he will know that is not lawful to exceed its bounds. A man of obscure station will lead a private life ungrudgingly so as not to leave the rank in which he has been placed by God . . . [e]ach man will bear and swallow the discomforts, vexations, weariness, and anxieties in his way of life, when he has been persuaded that the burden was laid upon him by God. From this will arise also a

singular consolation: that no task will be so sordid and base, provided you obey your calling in it, that will not shine and be reckoned very precious in God's sight.[16]

So the law that bars movement out of an unpleasant job is one predicated not as much on societal norms but on the need to settle a restless and impulsive human nature. It is the duty of self-protection, not societal protection, with which Calvin charges a vocation with carrying out.

Another way to see this subtle extension of the social boundaries that contain work within a calling is through Calvin's account of the special calling. Again as with Luther, for Calvin, discerning God's will is the means for understanding how to execute our own special calling. However, where the duty to fulfill this calling acts more as a *burden* in Luther's rendering, Calvin sees vocation more as a *gift* from God.[17] This difference is predicated on Calvin's interpretation of work after the Fall. Work was given to Adam as a punishment for the first sin, yet it cannot be reduced down to a mere curse. According to Andre Biéler,

> Calvin points out that the curse does not wholly do away with the blessing that was attached to work in the beginning. "Signs" remain that give man the taste for work . . . The curse that lies heavily on work is of educational value. It is intended to open man's eyes to his real condition and lead him to repentance. So this curse is constantly lightened by God's grace . . . That was already to be seen when Adam, instead of succumbing to the consequences of his error and being crushed under the weight of God's curse, received the power to till the ground and live from his work as a new grace.[18]

If work is an extension of God's mercy instead of judgment, then a vocation is that which governs and channels this gift from God into appropriate expressions. A calling is a kind of follow-up gift from God that ensures that the original gift of work is managed properly. The refusal of the gift of vocation results in the kind of psychological angst that vocations are meant to alleviate. Douglas interprets Calvin's reading of Genesis, chapter three:

> [w]hat Adam once enjoyed as wholly his own came through sin to be redistributed in infinite variety through grace to his progeny. Those who refuse their vocations are condemned to unpurposed confusion, whereas those who accept them confirm their callings by the holiness of the lives they lead.[19]

By interpreting work as a gift instead of a burden and bringing in a burden only as a result of refusing the gift, Calvin permits himself to speak of work as something to be enjoyed as opposed to that which must merely be endured. Appropriated as such, Calvin lessens the instrumental role that work plays in Luther's formulation of vocation. Of course, that work involves care for the neighbor is the defining sign that one's work is vocational for Calvin, too. However, because the enjoyment of work is an *additional* sign of God's will being carried out, work is more self-referential in Calvin than in Luther—though self-referentiality can never be confused for and converted into self-pride.

Finally, Calvin's stern, almost draconian theology has the odd effect of elevating the act of working to a level of higher importance than even Luther's theology. According to Weber, Lutheranism develops in the seventeenth century along pietistic lines that stresses "a feeling of actual absorption in the deity" that indicates the highest level of faith to the believer.[20] The Reformed tradition stemming from Calvin's teachings, on the other hand, rejects the use of feelings to register God's presence. This leaves faith and action as the two primary, albeit severely limited, means of understanding God. Weber explains:

> A real penetration of the human soul by the divine was made impossible by the absolute transcendentality of God compared to the flesh: *finitum non est capax infiniti*. The community of the elect with their God could only take place and be perceptible to them in that God worked through them and that they were conscious of it. That is, their action originated from the faith caused by God's grace, and this faith in turn justified itself by the quality of that action.[21]

Here, faith and action operate in a kind of feedback loop that props up action as an essential component (and sign) of faith. And action that emanates from a faithful stance must demonstrate social utility in order for certain actions to be honored by the object of faith, God.

Where Luther passes over the sheer utility of work in favor of work as a platform for brotherly love, perfecting the earthly kingdom only happens when work is useful, for Calvin. Weber writes that "in Luther we found specialized labor in callings justified in terms of brotherly love. But what for him remained an uncertain, purely intellectual suggestion became for the Calvinists a characteristic element in the ethical system." He continues:

> Brotherly love, since it may only be practiced for the glory of God and not in the service of the flesh, is expressed in the first place in the fulfillment of the daily tasks given by the *lex naturae*. . . . This makes labour in the service of impersonal social usefulness appear to promote the glory of God and hence to be willed by Him . . . [hence] the social activity of the Christian in the world is solely activity *in majorem gloriam Dei*. This character is hence shared by labour in a calling which serves the mundane life of the community.[22]

Weber's larger argument, that of causally connecting the Calvinistic work ethic to modern capitalism, needs this crucial separation of the work world from immediate moral importance in order to succeed. It is the effects of the doctrine of predestination along with Calvin's emphasis on the social usefulness of work that enables an eventual, and no doubt unintended, disengagement of work from a religious calling. Ernst Troeltsch, channeling his friend, Weber, writes that Calvin,

> raised the ordinary work of one's profession (within one's vocation) and the ardour with which secular work was prosecuted to the level of a religious duty in itself; from a mere method of providing for material needs it became an end in itself, providing scope for the exercise of faith within the labour of the "calling." That gave rise to that ideal of work for work's sake which forms the intellectual and moral assumption which lies behind the modern bourgeois way of life.[23]

When work is tied to survival or even to direct care of the neighbor, it is more attentive to human desire than to God's will, Calvin could argue. Yet when work contains within it the means *and* the end regarding these goals, the worker is left with a vocation in which work is honored, yet has only itself to confirm its vocational status. In circular fashion, God is connected to work *through* work. Therefore, work alone becomes the primary expression of faith in a God who demands hard work as a sign of one's faith.

While Calvin's emphasis on the utility of work departs from Luther's focus on interpersonal realm at work, the effects of Calvin's notion of work creates further distinctions. Recall that for Luther, the estate is confined to the sociopolitical parameters that define proper work, which obviates the need for one's work to contribute to large-scale societal alterations. Troeltsch notes that for Luther,

> the vocational system was not consciously designed and developed for the purposes of the holy community and of the Christian Society, but it was accepted as a Divine arrangement. The individual, moreover, regarded his work, not as a suitable way of contributing to the uplift of Society as a whole, but as his appointed destiny, which he received from the hands of God.[24]

Calvin, on the other hand, in effect hides the nitty-gritty of daily work from the surveillance of divine providence so that it can be used in the active construction of a community.[25] When alignment of the will to that of the sovereign God is the goal of work, the immanent power of society and tradition to confine and direct the status of one's labor is greatly diminished in Calvin's system. Society then becomes a kind of blank canvas on which God's plan can be painted by faithful citizens, no matter what they actually do to paint it. A healthy community, or "Holy Community" as he calls it, stands as the outward proof of a people following God's plan for creation and of God's blessing on such a community both financially and spiritually. Only work that is *useful* in the service of this latter goal is able to add value to such a community, thus changing it, as well as worthy of integrating it into a vocation.[26] Calvin and his followers believed that a smooth-running society functioned as a primary sign of a people who are operating according to God's will. In order for the societal machine to run properly, Calvin envisions a kind of division of labor in a community where all individual jobs play a cooperative role in the social health of the community.[27]

To sum, despite a shared desire between Luther and Calvin for a new kind of vocation, the latter's dogged emphasis on the sovereignty of God bears heavily on the relationship between a vocation and work in discriminating ways. Calvin's deviation from Luther on vocation and work finds its source in a radically transcendent and sovereign God who wants human work to create a Holy Community that mirrors divine will for creation. Hence, work (or minimally, human effort) needs to be sufficiently detached from the transcendent realm (practically, not theoretically) in order to realize Calvin's vision. Therefore the relationship between vocation and work, left somewhat to its own devices in constructing a society, begins to loosen somewhat in Calvinist societies compared to Lutheran ones.

It is important to remember that despite the fact that Calvin gives individual work the authority to alter society through its own utility, he always answers the question, "useful for what?" with, "serving God." While his stress on the utility of work can allow space for individuals to reflect more on the nature and purpose of their own work, Calvin nevertheless grants no space whatsoever for the authority of the self to arise in the analysis of one's calling. Douglas notes, "Self-knowledge and vocation are inseparably bound to the knowledge of God and of God's intention; the whole meaning of vocation is to be found in abnegation of the self."[28] So while one's work enacted under a special calling is given more prominence in Calvin's thought, the general call to obey God's commands above all else holds sway. However, some ground is laid by Calvin that, under the right social, economic, and political situations, permits the individual's desire and talents to assert themselves more forcefully within the meaning of a calling.

VOLITIONAL VOCATIONS OF THE PURITAN AGE

For several centuries after Calvin, early Puritan ministers and theologians continued to address the issue of a vocation by playing off the difference between the general and special calling. As with Luther and Calvin, the general call from God always takes precedence (at least nominally) over the particular ways of heeding a special call in Puritan thought. However, we see the special calling beginning to foreground the general calling during this time period. In short, reflection on individual talent and human agency becomes a source for defining what is and is not vocational. As Douglas puts it, "[b]efore Protestantism had entered its second century, a more secular idiom of self-knowledge and vocation began to penetrate the early orthodoxy of Luther and Calvin and to complicate its original clarity."[29] This original clarity was safeguarded by the belief that a vocation is prescribed and authorized by God alone. Hence, the increased role of human participation in the construction of the meaning of one's own vocation starts the process of short-circuiting the relatively uncomplicated connection between Calvin's sovereign God and the call.

Calvin's anthropology that emphasizes humanity's total depravity still resonates in the sixteenth- and seventeenth-century Puritan mind, and therefore, there is a reluctance to give *carte blanche* to the self in vocational decisions. Instantiations of a Puritan idea of vocation hold firm God's sovereignty over an individual's calling, but interestingly, the merits of one's own talents deployed in an inviting new economic world begin to be used as leverage in a negotiation with a more rigid Calvinistic theology of vocation. The tension between divine and human forces is evident in the writings of sixteenth-century thinkers. British theologian, William Perkins (1558–1602), demonstrates this tension thusly:

> By reason of this distinction of men, partly in respect of gifts, partly in respect of order, come personal callings. For if all men had the same gifts, and all were in the same degree and order, then should all have one and the same calling; but in as much as God gives diversity of gifts inwardly, and distinction of order outwardly, hence produced diversity of personal callings, and therefore I added, that personal calling arise from that distinction which God makes between man and man in every society.[30]

What was once guided by purely "outward order" instituted by God alone, a vocation is now informed by "inward" gifts and talents too. The outward order, now reconceived, guarantees and explains that the fact of individual gifts is not haphazard, but intentional. That individuals do not have the same gifts is proof to Perkins that God has designed it so.

And with the splitting of a vocation into one part ensuring that social order is maintained and another part maintaining the differences between individuals, Perkins, unlike Luther and Calvin, places a modicum of power in the individual's hands. "Every man must choose a fit calling to walk in; that is, every calling must be fitted to the man, and every man be fitted to his calling."[31] Here, we find the meeting, albeit logically awkward, of divine and human agency in Perkins's theology: we can choose the fitting calling, but it is already pre-fitted. Douglas states it this way, "Perkins said that we must be permitted to choose what we are born—and what God has called us—to do. Vocation is in one sense imposed, but in another, it is chosen according to one's gifts."[32]

The tension inherent in choosing what has already been chosen tells of an increasing role for human volition in vocational matters, despite its logical inconsistency. If medicine is chosen as a vocation, yet carpentry is where one's gifts are truly suited, a wrong choice has been made. God did not err in giving you gifts for carpentry; you erred in choosing a vocation that conflicted with your gifts. Therefore, discernment becomes a necessary prelude to landing a vocation, and the act of choosing takes on a newly found *gravitas*. Perkins, then, preserves God's sovereignty as the sole giver of gifts while allowing individuals to use their volition to discover the vocation that fits these gifts.

This voluntaristic trend is continued by Richard Baxter (1615–1691), a Presbyterian pastor and civil leader in England. Baxter honors the choosing of a vocation but warns that the wrong choice may have long-lasting effects. In a section of his book entitled, "Directions about Our Labor and Callings," he relies not only on God's law but also on the law of the land to "direct" what kind of work constitutes a calling. While legality is a necessary condition for vocational work, it is not a sufficient one. "It is not enough that the work of your calling be lawful, nor that it be necessary, but you must take special care also that it be safe, and not very dangerous to your souls." He warns, "Some callings are employed about matters of so little use (as tobacco and lace sellers, feather makers, periwigmakers, and many more such) that he that may choose better should be loath to take up with one [of] these, though possibly in itself it may be lawful."[33] Here, Baxter spends most of his time staying in the immanent realm by distinguishing between work that meets given standards (is legal and necessary) and work that is healthy for the soul (is socially useful), while Perkins attempts to justify worldly action by relating it to the transcendent.

Baxter's introduction of legality into the debate about vocation indicates a level of deference to the maintenance of social order. But laws are meaningless without the kind of moral sense that derives from our God-given soul. And for him, what is good for the soul is that which benefits all souls. "The public welfare or the good of many is to be valued above our own. Every man therefore is bound to do all the good he can to others, especially for the church and commonwealth. And this is not done by idleness, but by labor!"[34]

Baxter's means of achieving societal health differs from Calvin's, if only subtly. The status of Calvin's Holy Community as a perfect, yet never realized, embodiment of God's will is never legitimized by human standards or even societal consensus but by God's standards. Baxter agrees that functioning societies reflect God's will, but because he elevates the decision to undertake occupations that are salubrious to the soul and contribute to the common good, the means of legitimizing a godly society rests in part on consensus and in part by means of an appeal to a distant God. Whereas Calvin demurs on the ability of a society to receive God's approval, Baxter does not. When the public good that is desired by each individual soul serves as the primary manifestation of God's will, the door is opened ever so slightly for the authority of societal dictates to modify what a soul (read: individual) desires and consequently what the common good will look like. Labor is still the means of creating a community that accords with divine will, but against Calvin, self-referentiality can result in the legitimization of the self's desire.

Consequently, the relationship between one's estate, one's labor within that estate, and one's vocation that is meant to monitor the first two begins to change in the Puritan era. Marshall remarks that the

> views of Luther and Calvin, which had previously been understood in England in terms of abiding and being dutiful in one's estate, were being combined with an openness towards new developments in the social structure. This latter attitude manifested itself in an individualism which sat uneasily with traditional views. The resulting doctrine was one which stressed individual responsibility in economic affairs but limited itself to recommending quiet labour in one's estate with a strong emphasis on being able to *preserve* that estate. Over time, however, the content of particular callings came less from God's word which challenged social patterns and more from social patterns which themselves reveals God's will.[35]

A reversal of this kind signals a new trajectory for theological understandings of vocation specifically where Puritan writings gain purchase. The inclusion of human decision into the "vocation calculus" began to quiet the divine voice. With this silencing, we begin to see social patterns that both stoke human desire *and* strive to express God's will. Vocations, then, could still presumably align with God's plan, but divine will and/or the call may be more and more difficult to hear over the din of the surrounding culture that stokes desire.

WORK AND A CALLING AT THE TURN OF THE CENTURY

The Calling of the Self-Made Man

In the time that passes between the height of Puritanism in America with Jonathan Edwards in the mid-eighteenth century and the emergence of American industrialism in the late nineteenth century, vocations undergo yet another set of alterations. As the first two Great Awakenings in America bookend this time period, they draw the outlines of the theological development of vocations. During the First Great Awakening in the early decades of the eighteenth century, America was still beholden to the twin Calvinistic principles of the sovereignty of God and the depravity of humanity. Yet a break from Calvinist rigidity was occurring around the second awakening one hundred years later. Arminianism that rejected Calvin's doctrine of predestination in favor of a qualified free will began to assert itself in American theologies as well as an impetus for the Second Great Awakening.[36]

While Calvin's grip was loosening in America by the nineteenth century, daily work and its ethic held its grip. With the slackening of the relationship between a meticulous, omnipotent God and work, the authority of work itself (what it is, what its role should be) began to serve as an invaluable lens through which people understood themselves. Vocations understandably underwent drastic changes too. "This prodigious, high value of work, argued by Marx, which before him, had never known such exaltations," according to Jacques Ellul, "is the result, on the one hand, of the growth of work in the Western world during the nineteenth century, and, on the other, the secularization of the idea of man's divine vocation in work."[37] Work as a fundamental feature of human life does indeed reflect a secularization of daily activity, and its slow distancing from a controlling God allows society to step in and influence the relationship between work and whatever is left of a vocation. What we see is a vocation being used to justify meaningful work after a more secular society has defined the value of work and what makes it meaningful.

This secularization of vocations is displayed prominently in the writings of "success writers" of the American Gilded Age in the late nineteenth century. Cultural historian Judith Hilkey examines the literature of these writers, highly influential authors who played on the ideology of the "self-made man" to inspire those forced to look for work in the cities, as she pays close attention to their interpretation of vocations.

Success writers were not necessarily theologians, but a theology is present in many of their works. Calling language is utilized by them to carry ideas of stability, hard work, and a kind of religious seriousness from the farm to the city where these values may not be shared or easy to find. Success manuals often acted as surrogate parents instructing new urban dwellers on matters foreign to rural life. With a traumatic move such as this, they contend that one's *character* is the hidden weapon smuggled in from the farm that not only acts as a reliable bridge back to one's origins but also holds the keys to success in the city. Character is a new form of capital, according to Hilkey. Or it is men of character—the kind forged only on the farm—that are able to navigate the urban jungle and be truly successful. And a vocation, as realized through the fitting of a job to unique talents, is chosen on the basis of character and values rather than economic exigencies. Hence the self-made man is just that: the one who achieves success based on his own abilities, character, and determination and not on external necessity or luck. The connection of a calling to character provided a psychological function as well:

> It was this compromised idea of "choosing a calling"—buttressed by the doctrine of the "dignity of all labor"—that helped cushion the transition to a world of work in the new industrial order in which hierarchy and inequality were both pervasive and sanctioned. At the same time, success writers' celebration of an idealized past and their antipathy for many aspects of the new world of work constituted an implicit critique of the new industrial order they often seemed to defend.[38]

The calling that is chosen is tied to character in that it acts as a tie to the world left behind as well as a kind of shock absorber for the ride into cities where new and graphic scenes of injustice are in plain view. These writers could tap old calling language to invoke the same God who inhabits the farm and the city. Despite radically different appearances, the reality underlying both environments is the same: God-given character and talent will win the day as long as God's call is answered and followed through.

Vocations take on a different set of responsibilities in the Gilded Age. If they had a punitive, yet cooperative function with Calvin (to reprimand capricious human tendencies to build a Holy Community), vocations were now a vehicle to "wealth, fame, and fortune, while simultaneously providing reassurance, dignity, and self-respect for those whose 'success' might be of a more modest nature."[39] Moreover, if a calling is chosen rather than dictated, its features that traditionally restrained the freedom to switch jobs or start a new career altogether would expectedly be rejected, as Hilkey states.

> Insofar as the Puritan notion of a calling evoked a presumably stable and pious albeit idealized past, it suggested that which was comfortably familiar and accepted in rural small-town America: a view of work characterized by long-standing patterns of father-to-son occupational continuity . . . On the other hand, the modern concept of choosing rather than inheriting one's life work opened the doors to new possibilities. With the proliferation of new kinds of work . . . more and more young men of the late nineteenth century left home in search of work with which they and their fathers had no experience and very little familiarity.[40]

The waning power of institutions such as the family or church to corral the choices that involve work into a vocation allows those choices to dictate the meaning of the concept of vocation. Hence the social and political conservatism that issues from Luther is traded for a more liberal (and freeing?) set of career options that neither a father nor the Reformation-era God has much to offer in terms of guidance.

Yet success writers simultaneously, perhaps contradictorily, located career choices within a kind of determinative framework as well.

> On the one hand, as we have seen, success writers preached self-reliance and self-help and presented a view of the world in which the individual was all-powerful to determine his own fate, to snatch victory from the jaws of defeat, to choose success over failure. On the other hand, success writers preached loyalty, duty, discipline, and sometimes even blind faith in the ultimate beneficence of the established order.[41]

Hilkey emphasizes an established social order here, but success writers often conflated the order that issues from social hierarchy with God's order. In William Mathews's success manual, *Getting On in the World*, Jesus's parable of the talents, in which gifts are either squandered or maximized, is used to promote hard work which will always be rewarded. However, it is unclear whether it is God or the employer who is rewarding the worker.[42] And as Mathews trades the spiritual reward that Jesus likely intends for a monetary one, the tale serves as a tip for employers rather than employees. Hilkey writes that "an employee whose honesty, industry, and initiative multiplied the employer's wealth," in the way that Mathews casts the verse. God as the "grand employer" becomes the reward-bearer *after* the worker shows God that he is deserving in Mathews's rendition. Mathews's theology can be summed up in Benjamin Franklin's aphorism, "God helps those who help themselves."

Implicit in this phrase is a chronological order of events. God responds with help only *after* we put in the work ourselves and show that the investment in our talents was a wise move. Instead of a stubborn divine plan guiding the believer to a pre-established, singular vocation, once the proper job is chosen, it then *becomes* a vocation *post facto*. The power to choose a calling (not abiding by an envisioned pre-arranged plan) and character on the job (not necessarily physical talent) are qualities, according to these writers, needed to ensure a suitable vocation. God's name is invoked in many of these success manuals, but the ability of human agents to find their calling tends to push out the God of Luther who unequivocally dictates the terms of a vocation thus forcing human desires to serve the larger divine plan.

In addition, the type of work that one does is slowly subordinated to more abstract forces such as character, according to success writers. *How* work is done supplants *what kind* of work is done for those aspiring to be self-made men. God can certainly provide strength when faced with obstacles to success, but again, this is a far cry from the God who dictates the how and why of one's work. And when an individual's character and talents are considered prior to the actual work or job that is done and money replaces brotherly love and the common good, vocations begin to blend in with capitalism, with Calvin's God standing on the sidelines.

Rauschenbusch and Sayers

The rise of monopoly capitalism in the West towards the end of the Gilded Age in America (and decades before in Europe) provided a sobering check on the drive to be a self-made success. Many who either left farms for the cities or immigrated to the United States with high hopes were met with crushing factory jobs; success was for the few who owned and operated the factories. The fantasy proffered by success manuals ran up against obstinate reality.

The Gilded Age ideology required a hopeful spirit to feed and sustain it, and the empowering act of choosing a vocation was similarly buoyed by this same spirit. Though industrialization may have dampened this spirit, vocation language did not disappear throughout the end of the nineteenth and the beginning of the twentieth century. By the time of Weber's writing of *The Protestant Ethic and the Spirit of Capitalism* in 1905, he could plausibly claim that a calling was only nominally connected to God. He persuasively argues that the spiritual energy that an individual gains from the *belief* that a calling is divinely inspired fuels a work ethic able to withstand the grind of factory work. But for Weber, the reality of work within a calling belies the belief that allegedly sustains it. He famously paints the situation in stark terms:

> The idea of duty in one's calling prowls about in our lives like the ghost of dead religious beliefs. Where the fulfillment of the calling cannot be related to the highest spiritual and cultural values, or when on the other hand, it need not be felt simply as economic compulsion, the individual generally abandons the attempt to justify it at all.[43]

While industriousness and a strong work ethic remain, the divine power animating a calling (and perhaps economic compulsion too) was no longer present. Thus he calls out God's impending obsolescence at work. Weber's prediction of the abandonment of a "God-authorized calling" helps him make his case for the unimpeded momentum of capitalism—it is an internal "worldly asceticism" that now drives the train and an external, bureaucratic "iron cage" that keeps it on the rails. And while Weber's blunt pronouncement ends his study nicely, the fact remains that theologians resisted omitting the role of God from a vocation during and immediately after the height of industrialism in America and Europe. This may not challenge Weber's argument in any substantial way, but when viewed in the context of his assessment, some modifications of the concept are needed.

The theologian's task of infusing factory work with a God who desires work to be dignified and humanizing is challenging indeed. A reconciliation of work and vocation in the Industrial Age requires either a de-emphasis of the role of monotonous, often humiliating work in one's vocation or a call for the re-structuring of that work at the ground level so that it can meet the standards of a vocation, whatever they are determined to be. Theologians and religious thinkers who were heirs to the liberal theology of the nineteenth century often used Social Gospel theology at the beginning of the century to argue for the latter option. They claimed that work, through a novel conception of God's interaction with creation, can once again achieve the status that befits a vocation. Thus the rescuing of the concept of vocation from a Weberian fate illustrates the extent to which Social Gospel theology relies on a reversal of the roles played out in the relationship between a vocation and work up to this point. The quality of work, because it acts as a sign that God's will is being done, is a substantial and necessary component of God's earthly kingdom, they argue. Hence what one does at a job must rise to a divine standard instead of being merely a mundane, nondescript activity that serves God's more general call to worship God alone.

Walter Rauschenbusch (1861–1918) begins his book, *Christianity and the Social Crisis*, with the following jeremiad:

> One of the gravest accusations against our industrial system is that it does not produce in the common man the pride and joy of good work. In many cases the surroundings are ugly, depressing, and coarsening. Much of the stuff manufactured is dishonest in quality, made to sell and not to serve, and the making of such cotton or wooden lies must react on the morals of every man that handles them. There is little opportunity for a man to put his personal stamp on his work . . . The modern factory hand is not likely to develop artistic gifts as he tends his machine.[44]

He calls for divine redemption of the world, despite (or because of) its deplorable state under industrialism, by marrying the heavenly and earthly kingdoms of Reformed thought. Provoked by working conditions in the American city, Rauschenbusch translates classic theological terms that deal with the transcendent into immanent, societal ones. God is present in his Social Gospel, though it is not to the heavens but to the earth that we look for divine presence. He understands factory work in terms of its distance from the kind of work to be rightly performed in a divine calling. Channeling a Marxian spirit, Rauschenbusch contrasts alienated work with the kind of work that bears a "personal stamp." Unlike Marx, though, Rauschenbusch asserts that the only way to "un-alienate" work is through religion. Meaningful, hence godly, work is that which not only produces that which can be called one's own, but also that which "contributes to the welfare of mankind." Because most factory work neither personalizes production nor furthers the common good, it cannot be the kind of work that God would deem worthy of a calling.

In this way, Rauschenbusch reverses the Reformed approach to the idea of vocation. Rather than beginning with God's will as that which work must align as Luther and Calvin do, Rauschenbusch looks first to the state of work itself. Granted, Rauschenbusch has a strong notion of God's will; namely, it is God's will to effect an equitable social order, and that will is made manifest through the alteration of work itself. In other words, the nature of work in early twentieth-century America *is* the locus of a calling for Rauschenbusch, and through a modification or even removal of the structures that maintain the status quo, a calling can be returned to the average worker. He writes,

> If a man's calling consisted in manufacturing or selling useless or harmful stuff, he would find himself unable to connect it with his religion. In so far as the energy of business life is expended in crowding out competitors, it would also be outside the sanction of religion, and relig-

ious men would be compelled to consider how industry and commerce could be reorganized so that there would be a maximum of service to humanity and a minimum of antagonism between those who desire to serve it.[45]

Religion *is* morality here. Irreligious work that falls outside of a vocation automatically harms another or oneself. A vocation acts as a kind of moral barometer, judge, and guarantor. Its criteria are gathered from perceived societal ills; its authority is underwritten by God through biblical moral precepts.[46]

This formulation informs the relationship between God and society as Rauschenbusch sees it. God's will for creation is reflected back from a community whose work is not alienated and is geared towards advancing the common good, as opposed to God's will manifesting itself in the believer who endures meaningless work for eternal benefits. It is up to Christian soldiers to recognize true theology through a more honest reading of the Bible so that a vocation can once again accord individual work with God's will. Here, the salvaging of a meaningful vocation must take its cues from a dehumanizing work world in order to overcome it.

Dorothy Sayers (1893–1957), writing thirty years later and in Britain, writes in a Social Gospel vein, though with some branching. She similarly laments the inability of jobs to rise up to the standards of a vocation in a capitalist system. The problem for Sayers, however, is not that certain kinds of work generate inequality between the rich and the poor, but the simple impossibility of *any* job that is performed strictly for money to become a vocation.

> I think we can measure the distance we have fallen from the idea that work is a vocation to which we are called, by the extent to which we have come to substitute the word "employment" for "work." We say we must solve the "problem of unemployment"—we reckon up how many "hands" are "employed"; our social statistics are seldom based upon the work itself—whether the right people are doing it, or whether the work is worth doing.[47]

Work's value has been reduced to mere employment and the wages earned. Sayers suggests that work will regain its proper relationship to a vocation when work is performed for itself—not strictly for unrelated ends, namely money. Her argument is not as specific or programmatic as Rauschenbusch's. But like Rauschenbusch, Sayers looks to a transformation of the meaning of work that corresponds more closely with what she considers to be that performed by one of God's creatures. When money is downplayed, but of course never eliminated, work is permitted to engage the deeper, more godly parts of the human experience.

For both Rauschenbusch and Sayers, work is not taken as a given to which a calling must adjust. Nor is individual success the sign that a calling is being lived out. To the contrary, success is dependent on socioeconomic conditions that allow for equal opportunity to earn a fair wage at a job that fosters humanizing work. Only by overhauling the ideologies that prop up dehumanizing work (both in terms of wages and conditions) can a calling have any real meaning. And it is in the hands of human agents operating with a biblical/moral conscience alone that have the power to recalibrate the relationship between work and a calling.

The Social Gospel's turn to society for evidence of moral violations, as well as for the remedy, constitutes an instructive stage in the Protestant history of vocation. The elevation of the status of work as one starting point for theological reflection impinges on the role that a vocation could possibly serve in an earthly kingdom. Attention to the meaningfulness of actual work necessarily brings the social relations, class structure, and secular ideologies that reify problematic business practices into the equation.[48]

The question of the *kind* of work that is calling-worthy lingers to this day, yielding varied answers. Yet the overall Social Gospel program comes under assault in the wake of World War I. Neo-orthodox thinkers and later Christian realists charged that a world capable of atrocities is no place for God's kingdom to gain purchase. Consequently the meaning of vocation and its relationship to "worldly" work underwent more changes.

VOCATIONS IN TROUBLE

Barth and Brunner

Troubled by the reliance on the ability of human agents to bring about God's kingdom on earth in the wake of a destructive first world war, Karl Barth (1886–1968) broke with liberal colleagues. Barth's "crisis theology" is predicated on an infinite distance between creation and the wholly other Creator. Efforts to bridge this impossible gap, such as altering society to align with God's will, are always futile given the distance they must truly travel.

In opposition to advocates of the Social Gospel, he asserts that God's call to establish our vocations has been confused with human definitions of vocation. The same ideology of work that encouraged Rauschenbusch to align vocations with just working conditions disturbs Barth. When a vocation is tied to the desire to improve the quality of work, whether on an individual or societal level, it is overshadowed by the heightened value of work and therefore, Barth argues, it loses all of its intended meaning.

> It is a piece with the rather feverish modern over-estimation of work and of the process of production that particularly at the climax of the 19th century, and even more so in our own, it should be thought essen-

tial to man, or more precisely to the true nature of man, to have a vocation in this sense.[49]

Barth is responding to a general orientation to work gone awry. He later differentiates "vocation" from "calling" in order to elucidate his point. A "vocation" refers to the current state of the term which has been corrupted by its reduction to work alone. A "calling," on the other hand, is transmitted through a direct revelation from God and is therefore dictated by the terms of the "infinite qualitative distance" between God and humanity.

A calling is overtaken by a vocation when work becomes the primary, or in extreme cases, the only medium through which to live out God's call, according to Barth. With the divine author of a calling in one ear and society in the other, a dilemma arises, as one cannot listen to and follow two imperatives that are moving in different directions.

> [T]he attempt to listen to a Word of God on the right hand and another word on the left, has always had the unfortunate result, as in Protestantism, that vocation has begun to take and has actually taken precedence over calling, so that the Word of God on the right hand has increasingly and finally to yield before that on the left.[50]

Work is always an endeavor that must be placed in the service of God, but if it competes with God, it will win. If God is to win, the divine call cannot constitute a mere summons to search for and acquire satisfactory work. Such an attribution to a true calling only serves as a temptation to substitute human activity and the ideologies that animate it for the things of God. "That a man's vocation is exhausted in his profession is no more true than that God's calling which comes to him is simply an impulsion to work."[51]

Barth is not arguing for the elimination of work, of course. He is, however, claiming that one must not forget that a calling is from a wholly other God. Whether a calling (or Barth's "vocation") elevates work or compels it, work often oversteps the bounds established by God's call. And when work begins to gain a life of its own, create its own meaning, and gain its legitimacy by attaching the word "vocation" to it, it offers a false security as it is working at cross purposes with God.

Emil Brunner (1889–1966) shares Barth's sentiments.

> Thus it is quite obvious that this idea of vocation ("the Calling") has no more than the name in common with that which is called so to-day. The idea of the Calling has been degraded, so disgracefully, into something quite trivial, it has been denuded of its daring and liberating religious meaning to such an extent, and has been made so ordinary and commonplace that we might even ask whether it would not be better to renounce it altogether.[52]

Brunner similarly predicates his assertion on the ultimate power of God's call to determine a vocation. If understood and applied faithfully, the proper execution of a vocation can never take its direction from society. Yet Brunner laments what he calls the "secularization of the Calling": the process by which vocations have been slowly wrenched from their eschatological significance only to be captured by secular forces and left without a teleology.[53] His reclamation of the idea of a vocation involves a desecularization of work by way of grounding the belief that God calls believers to do God's service alone.[54] When one ceases searching for worldly affirmation for work and looks to God's will for the proper goal of all work, then work regains its true purpose and a calling can be restored.

In line with neo-orthodox skepticism towards liberal theology, Barth and Brunner do not argue for the restoration of work so that it can get in line with God's plan. Instead both criticize the unjustified rise of the value of work. They oppose the ungodly endowment of work with import from the secular world when work already possesses divine import through a vocation. Consequently, both are ready to abandon the role of work altogether in a calling if the trend that they see continues. This trend has less to do with the quality of work at any given time and more to do with the general power that work holds in the lives of Christians. Unlike Rauschenbusch, changes in working conditions or the current economic model should have no bearing on a true vocation for them. Moreover, in spite of their dire judgments, both theologians compensate for skepticism toward the ways in which an ideology of work can corrupt a relationship with God by shifting their entire attention to the revealed Word of God. It is by the situating of one's activities completely within the flow of an unknown yet sovereign divine purpose, as laid out in the Bible, that a vocation can possibly maintain its integrity.

Jacques Ellul and Miroslav Volf

Jacques Ellul's (1912–1994) stance on vocation positions itself at the juncture between industrial and post-industrial society. He echoes Barth and Brunner's refrain that a vocation should never bend to culture, yet like Rauschenbusch, Ellul looks closely at the concrete work that people do to assess what a vocation should or should not be. Ellul shares Barth's concern that culture has exaggerated, even sacralized work, which has led to an undue influence over what it means to have a vocation. Yet, this problem is even more pronounced in the latter half of the twentieth century because much of the work that people do has become less and less autonomous and more and more technical. Ellul, as displayed in his classic, *The Technological Society*, takes pains to point out that "technique" is the dominant quality of work that reduces all work to the application of method alone.[55] One only has to learn and employ certain methods in order to succeed at a job as opposed to engage in real craftsmanship. A how-to manual stands in for in-depth knowledge and skill thus de-individualizing and homogenizing work at the beginning of the post-industrial age of the 1960s. For Ellul, technique, as a means alone, has little to do with the kind of work worthy of a calling because it detaches all work from any higher purpose that comes with work that is a means and an end. Technique is only a means to varied, unrelated ends, but work has come to be synonymous with it. Combine this state of affairs with a bloated ideology of work, and a vocation (that needs depth and height) is in crisis.

Technique alters the social component of work as well. It separates work from any ordered whole by atomizing tasks, placing them under the direction of a *seeming* technological whole, and then demanding only a sanguine attitude towards work and one's co-workers. A vocation gets ensnared in the social machinery of technique on the job. "To become a lawyer by 'calling' represents the expression of good sentiments, a generous will, an idealism, but it means in reality to be the victim of an illusion and to live in ignorance of what is real in our society."[56] Work as technique is thus barred from engaging in the *real* as given by a *real* calling. And for Ellul, bestowing this kind of work with divine significance is sinful.

The predicament of modern work as it relates to a vocation is not one that can be averted by either reconfiguring work or by recalibrating vocations to correspond with God's Word. Ellul is more pessimistic than Rauschenbusch or Barth as to the chances that not only work but also any meaningful vocation can be resurrected. Work as technique cannot function alongside a calling, and so work, along with its ideology, must be permanently removed from any true conception of vocation.

> We must accept the fact that work is condemned in our society; that there is a segment of our life that is "cursed." Hence, we can abandon ourselves to trade our profession which is without any value, without any significance, without any interest, which functions solely to supply us with enough money to survive, and we shall find the main interest for our lives elsewhere.[57]

Ellul draws on the idea that work is punishment for the primordial Fall and is and has always been cursed. Yet it is in *our* era that work has become condemned as opposed to being mere punishment. Yes, "work as punishment" casts it in a negative light, but redemption through work is assumed in this kind of assessment. Instead, "work as condemned" doubles down on the idea that sin was brought into the world at the Fall. Even though Ellul would agree that work can never move us closer to salvation, it used to possess redeemable features. Yet our sin plus technology have rendered modern work utterly detached from God, even as an a measured retributive daily act.

Barth was troubled by man-made ideologies that compete with revelation. Work itself is not the problem; its role in misguiding humans who construct worldviews around it is. There can be a role for work in a vocation, if properly balanced. And while Ellul agrees, he goes one step further than Barth. Work has become so vapid, so unhitched from anything meaningful that it cannot be a part of a vocation at all for Ellul. Hence Ellul's argument maintains the importance of a concept of vocation as a response to a call from God, but what is left in its wake if modern work can never be a part of it?

The place to look is the general call that God makes to all Christians. The special call that enlists individual talents can only now place them into the service of technique. If this development is possible, why was the idea of vocation ever held at the mercy of such a susceptible entity such as work? Work should never have been given such power, Ellul charges, but now that it does grip our collective consciousness, it should be used to point beyond itself. "In reality, we must assume, accept positively, and take upon ourselves, this sign of our rupture with God—to live fully this order of necessity, *in order that* the freedom which is at times granted by God, the calling which we are able to assume, represents *its* true value."[58] The contamination of work divulges our necessary burden, but more importantly, it foregrounds moments of freedom that can only be experienced outside of a working life. A calling constitutes our responsive actions in these moments of freedom—moments given by God that are embedded in God's call which will not be heard in the modern workplace.

Like Ellul, Miroslav Volf (1956–) is keenly aware of the problems that plague modern work. In his 1991 book, *Work in the Spirit*, he writes, "Today we can observe a general crisis of work. It frequently surfaces in the negative attitude of workers toward their work. Many people are deeply dissatisfied with the kind of work they are doing."[59] Volf echoes the Social Gospelers in stating that since the Industrial Revolution, most forms of work are exploitative, destructive to the environment, alienating, and hence dissatisfying. Because of this, we should cease trying to square our work with God's will for us as work now stands. In fact, the term "vocation" is ill-fitted to work today for Volf because it carries a history of justifying unsatisfying work rather than redeeming it.[60]

As such, Volf criticizes the Lutheran conception of vocation as too conservative; it is caught up with the duties required of a certain social position with little room left for the questioning of those duties. The Lutheran calling is beholden to the given-ness of the duties of one's special calling which is mitigated by the security manifest in the general call that soothes discomforts experienced at work. Yet how secure can a calling make us when work is also now more transient and fluid as one is not likely to stay in a job for long? The ability of modern work to convey the kind of stability that Luther demanded is gone.

Moreover, Luther's reliance on the general call that provides solace in God's grace is not fully integrative of the whole of human life, for Volf. In contrast to Ellul, Volf holds that the Garden of Eden story establishes work as an essential human activity, not just that which atones for sin. It has a positive role to play in life and should be performed in "cooperation with God" as opposed to being endured as a form of punishment.[61] Or we work to glorify God and in return, God rewards this kind of work. A vocation, then, is not the result of a unidirectional call from God which is then translated into the form of a command. If a vocation is taken as an imperative, work becomes a burden, and resentment replaces the joy that should result from our daily work.

Alternatively, Volf's theology of work is centered on charisms or gifts from God that flow to humanity. This is accomplished and sustained through the work of the Holy Spirit that acts with us as co-creators of the world. Here, human cooperation with God as expressed through work enlivens our working lives, making us better stewards of God's creation.

> Elevating work to cooperation with God in the pneumatological understanding of work implies an obligation to overcome alienation because the individual gifts of the person need to be taken seriously. The point is not simply to interpret work religiously as cooperation with God and thereby glorify it ideologically, but to transform work into a charismatic cooperation with God on the "project" of the new creation.[62]

Volf's pneumatology is an attempt to avoid both the problems of alienation from a distant God and of an anthropocentric construction of the meaning of work. The Holy Spirit mediates the divine and earthly realms to reattach work to a vocation by at once lifting out and legitimizing one's true talents as well as furnishing the worker with the judgment to find work that cooperates with God's creative action. Work that is infused with the Holy Spirit can accommodate a fluid labor market because it is not the job that the spirit legitimates but individual talents. And talent, despite the kind of job that one has, can and must be utilized in order for work to contribute to a new and better world. At the same time, "work in the spirit" is an act of cooperation with God and is therefore not able to be legitimized on purely secular grounds. If the Holy Spirit is animating work, a vocation is able to administer both the divine imperative to work for God's glory and the worldly context in which work occurs. Thus Volf's concept of vocation sidesteps Ellul's resignation to a future of meaningless work while circumventing Lutheran conservatism by placing no limits on the ability of the spirit to transform the quality of work in the face of societal barriers.

Both Ellul and Volf show an unwillingness to drag the concept of vocation down into the morass of the contemporary work world. Whether it be an exaggerated ideology of work or a crisis in the work world that forces each of their respective hands, it is a deep respect for vocations that motivates their responses. For my purposes, the upshot in both analyses, though to a lesser extent in Volf is the further aggrandizement of God's power over a vocation that is a response to the problem of integrating contemporary work into a genuine vocation. This problem is acknowledged by both with some lamentation and consequently, their efforts to salvage vocations with the help of a divine life preserver stands as a further statement of not only the persistence of the idea of a calling (that it deserves to be salvaged) but also of the increasing impotence of modern work to satisfy the demands of a vocation.

Prompted by a work world that reveals itself to be unresponsive to real human needs, Ellul and Volf both turn to God. The turn from work itself for a clue about what a vocation should be is facilitated in part by the assumption that a gap exists between activity at work and a true vocation. When less-than-meaningful work is coupled with the inflated cultural significance given to work, the move to God is understandable. Yet when work is separated from vocation on these grounds, the cultural environment that molds actual work and its experience is similarly devalued and often neglected in the final verdict on vocation.

Abrupt recourse to God to rebuild the troubled relationship between vocation and work can only occur by overlooking the material causes for the trouble. Ellul and Volf, as well as most of their predecessors, are right. The concept of vocation *is* in trouble. But because the concept is a unique theological concept that must engage the world to earn its meaning, a quick theological fix will not do. Hence the reduction of a vocation down to the God who calls tends to abstract vocations from day to day work. And this move unwittingly gives the predominant culture-makers the license to appropriate the concept of vocation to their own ends. Liability for popular, often careless, uses of the idea of vocation does not solely lie at the feet of theologians who have gradually prevented work and its cultural adjusters from informing the idea of vocation. Culture itself is a culprit as well.

CONCLUSION

This selective theological history of the Protestant calling has disclosed a series of changes in the relationship between the concept of vocation and work. Since the original bifurcation of a calling into its general and special responsibilities during the Reformation, the God-bound and socially insured connection between the two began to loosen during the Puritan era. An emphasis on individual talents and the growing prerogative to choose a vocation that finds its way into Puritan discourse undermines the idea that divine muscle alone can restrain the human desire to align a vocation with the marks of "worldly" success.

The Industrial Revolution, with its suppression of the expression of individual talent and the freedom to choose a calling of one's liking, forced theologians to question whether a calling from God could be expressed under the dehumaninzing conditions of factory work. The Social Gospelers' inability to relate industrial working conditions with the Christian God invited a closer look into the nature of work and the human capacity to alter it. The God whose kingdom would be ushered in with a transformation of the work world demanded that the quality of work rise to a vocation in order to bring about this transformation. The predominant twentieth-century reaction was a retrieval of a "proper" calling from a world in which the cultural authority of individual work, which lent credence to a special calling, was said to have been exaggerated and downright sinful. Excepting the response of the Social Gospelers, Barth and many who followed him established the need for God through a general call to redress the abuses allowed by misapplied individual freedom within the special calling.

NOTES

1. Paul Marshall, *A Kind of Life Imposed on Man: Vocation and Social Order from Tyndale to Locke* (Toronto: University of Toronto Press, 1996), 9.
2. See Romans 11:29, Ephesians 4:1.
3. Karl Marx, "Contribution to the Critique of Hegel's *Philosophy of Right*: Introduction," in *The Marx-Engels Reader*, ed. Robert C. Tucker (New York: W. W. Norton, 1978), 60.
4. The *vita contemplativa*, as articulated by Augustine and Aquinas, was considered to exist strictly within the domain of the life of the priest and monk. One argument supporting such a consideration is circular. Priests and monks were the only members of medieval society who lived the *vita contemplativa*; the job of the priest and monk, alone, affords the luxury of living this life. The valorization of the *vita contemplativa* is accomplished by the subordination of its conceptual opposite, the *vita activa*. This relationship between the two is predicated on a separation between the things of the mind or spirit and the things of the physical world or flesh. In this binary, the active life (and physical activities that fill it out) is a necessary kind of life for all, including priests. However, based on an interpretation of the Martha and Mary story in the book of Matthew, Aquinas clearly favors the contemplative Mary over the busybody Martha. See Thomas Aquinas, *Summa Theologiae*, Part 2 of 2, trans. Fathers of the English Dominican Province, (New York: Christian Classics, 1981), 1923.
5. Martin Luther, *Luther's Works*, vol. 45, ed. Walther I. Brandt, trans. Charles M. Jacobs (Philadelphia: Muhlenberg, 1962), 248.
6. Luther, *Luther's Works*, vol. 32, 496.
7. Marshall, 23.
8. Richard M. Douglas, "Talent and Vocation in Humanist and Protestant Thought," in *Action and Conviction in Early Modern Europe: Essays in Memory of E. H. Harbison*, ed. Theodore K. Rabb and Jerrold Siegel (Princeton: Princeton University Press, 1969), 261–62.
9. Wingren, 76.
10. Marshall, 24.
11. Douglas, 291.
12. Exposition of Psalm 147, quoted by Gustaf Wingren, *Luther on Vocation* (Evansville, IN: Ballast Press, 1994), 138.

13. John Calvin, *Institutes of the Christian Religion,* ed. John T. McNeill and trans. Ford Lewis Battles, (Philadelphia: Westminster, 1967), 1: 724.
14. Marshall, 25.
15. Calvin, 1: 724.
16. Calvin, 1: 725.
17. Calvin, 1: 719-25, André Biéler, *Calvin's Economic and Social Thought*, trans. James Greig (Geneva: World Council of Churches, 1961), 352, 53.
18. Biéler, 354.
19. Douglas, 295.
20. Weber, 112.
21. Weber, 113.
22. Weber, 108–9.
23. Ernst Troeltsch, *The Social Teaching of the Christian Churches,* vol. 2, (New York: Macmillan, 1931), 609–10.
24. Troeltsch, 610.
25. Troeltsch, 610–11.
26. I explore the political implications for Calvin's concept of vocation within a Holy Community in chapter 5.
27. Biéler, 141–45.
28. Douglas, 295.
29. Douglas, 295.
30. William Perkins, *A Treatise of the Vocations* (London: John Haviland, 1631), 755.
31. Perkins, 775.
32. Douglas, 296.
33. Richard Baxter, "Directions about Our Labor and Callings," in *The Practical Works of Richard Baxter* (London: George Virtue, 1838), 377.
34. Ibid, 377.
35. Marshall, 53.
36. See George Marsden, *Fundamentalism and American Culture: The Shaping of Twentieth-Century Evangelicalism 1870 – 1925* (New York: Oxford University Press, 1982), 74, 99; Julius H. Rubin, *Religious Melancholy and Protestant Experience in America* (New York: Oxford University Press, 1994), 170; Randall Balmer and Lauren F. Winner, *Protestantism in America* (New York: Columbia University Press, 2002), 58; Sean McCloud, *Divine Hierarchies: Class in American Religion and Religious Studies* (Chapel Hill, NC: University of North Carolina Press, 2007), 113–14.
37. Jacques Ellul, "Work and Calling" in *Callings!*, ed. James Y. Holloway and Will D. Campbell (New York: Paulist Press, 1974), 26–27.
38. Hilkey, 101.
39. Hilkey, 125.
40. Hilkey, 101.
41. Hilkey, 98.
42. Hilkey, 98.
43. Weber, 182.
44. Walter Rauschenbusch, *Christianity and the Social Crisis in the 21st Century: The Classic That Woke Up the Church* (New York: HarperOne, 2007), 234.
45. Rauschenbusch, 356.
46. Rauschenbusch's formulation resembles Luther's association between a calling and brotherly love. Though because Luther is attempting to define a new term, brotherly love ends up filling out what a vocation is. Rauschenbusch is dealing with an inherited definition. Hence he is able to take aspects of the definition of vocation and apply them to instances where brotherly love is absent.
47. Dorothy L. Sayers, "Vocation in Work," in *A Christian Basis for the Post-War World*, ed. A. E. Baker (New York: Morehouse-Gorham, 1942), 104.
48. I revisit the political implications for Rauschenbusch's insights in chapter 4 as I do with Calvin. Similarly here in this present chapter, I highlight only Rauschenbusch's treatment of vocation that is consequential to a theological history.

49. Karl Barth, *Church Dogmatics* III: 4 (Edinburgh: T & T Clark, 1985), 599.
50. Barth, 645.
51. Barth, 599.
52. Emil Brunner, *The Divine Imperative,* trans. Olive Wyon (Philadelphia: Westminster Press, 1936), 205.
53. Brunner claims that Luther never meant to equate vocation with work. Instead, Luther, according to Brunner, altered the meaning of vocation in order to establish a "good conscience in one's Calling" which can more easily submit to God's dictates, rather than certain activities. God then can enact the fulfillment of God's kingdom via the calling by calling the individual to correct belief, then calling him or her out of the world at the eschaton. Brunner writes, "God takes over all responsibility for our action in the world which in itself is sinful, if we, on our part, will only do here and now that which the present situation demands from one who loves God and his neighbour." Brunner, 206.
54. Brunner goes directly back to Luther for this interpretation of a calling.
55. Jacques Ellul, *The Technological Society,* trans. John Wilkinson (New York: Random House, 1964), 13–18.
56. Ellul, "Work and Calling," 34.
57. Ellul, 34–35.
58. Ellul, 42.
59. Miroslav Volf, *Work in the Spirit: Toward a Theology of Work* (Eugene, OR: Wipf and Stock Publishers, 2001), 35.
60. Volf, 110.
61. Volf, 114, 126.
62. Volf, 116.

TWO
Theology at Work

> The question, therefore, is not whether it is permissible to formulate social doctrines from the standpoint of the churches and of religions in general; all we have to do is to ask whether these attempts have achieved something useful and valuable for the modern situation. — Ernst Troeltsch

We can read through the Protestant theological history of vocation and judge the truth of each thinker's concept based on a host of criteria. One criterion has to do with the level of faithfulness that a concept has to a certain notion of God or to a particular interpretation of the Bible. Does Luther's concept accord with what the Bible says about work, God, and vocation? Is Rauschenbusch's vocation too worldly? Does Baxter's vocation leave too much space for human desire to guide what a wholly other God is calling us to do? Such questions rest on the common assumption that the things of God and the creation are separate and not equal. Yet at the very least, the historical alterations to the meaning of vocation should give the questioners pause when attempting to disentangle God's truth from the world. Because all theological concepts that purportedly capture the true relationship between God and humanity undergo historical modification and our understanding of God is mediated by these concepts, our reliance upon a standard for judgment that stands above history is not as easily justified as it used to be.

This is due in part to the evidence that suggests that no concept, belief, or system of thought can escape its cultural context and retreat into a space that hovers above culture. Such stances take the content and meaning of theological concepts not solely as representational of divine truth but primarily as cultural products. This "cultural turn" or the "turn to culture" made by a growing number of theologians and religious scholars is a key move made to understand theology as plastic, not static and receptive to cultural developments, not dismissive of them. Hence, the cultural turn can help us not only to be more comfortable with the changes that the Protestant concept of vocation has undergone, if indeed this is a source of discomfort, but also to recognize the practical impotence of theology when it does not take culture into serious account. The turn to culture in theology also demands that serious attention be paid to the cultural contexts that shape theologies. A hard look at the cultural *Sitz im Leben* of both work and the concept of vocation is required when making the turn.

It is doubly required in an analysis of vocation because of the unique qualities of the concept. Indeed, Christian theological concepts such as salvation, redemption, grace, and the Trinity are conditioned by the community that negotiates their meaning. But if one so chooses to analyze these particular concepts apart from their cultural context, one can according to the concept's own internal logic. Grace, in Christian terms for instance, is given by God despite individual merit. Hence a theology of grace need only deal with the qualities of a transcendent God who would offer such a gift and not with the specific context in which a person receives and interprets grace. A vocation, on the other hand, even as a call from God, must necessarily traffic in both transcendent and immanent realms because vocations necessarily engage daily activity. Or after God's call is decoded by the listener, the one who hears the call must then engage the world in which callings are lived out. Even in the case of the priestly call, questions of feasibility, family situation, geographical location, and desire enter the equation quickly. Thus, the concept of vocation is always already consulting with the economic, political, psychological, and social domains that modify the types of work available at any given time. For this reason, an analytical method that culturally contextualizes theological concepts is especially equipped to tackle the concept of vocation.

Reading a theological history of the Protestant vocation under the assumption that all theology is culturally embedded accomplishes two primary tasks. First, in one direction, the history of a vocation self-evidently demonstrates the impact of culture on the idea. Not only is the cultural impact revealed through the continual adaptation to the changes in the meaning of work through time, but it is also conveyed in the changing role of God in the vocation nexus. Changes to the meaning of a vocation present little metaphysical problem if theological concepts are always conditioned by culture—cultural conditions are constantly shifting. Second, the cultural turn in theology focuses our attention onto the actual cultural forces that influence the meaning of vocation, not just onto the epiphenomenal differences in theological language over time. And once the mechanics of certain cultural developments have been exposed, the theological concept's complicity with culture can be acknowledged and dealt with in a more forthright manner.

The cultural turn aids in the understanding of a modern vocation in another way as well. Underlying both my claim that vocations have been co-opted by consumer culture *and* that a vocation can and should challenge the political norms of the modern workplace is the tacit admission of political theology that culture and theology flow into one another. Hence the cultural turn in theology can appropriate the concept of vocation in a way that allows culture to inform vocations and vice versa. The question of how theology can be used to bring a normative element into secular arenas once its cultural origins have been traced is a difficult one, but one I hope to answer later in this chapter.

After laying out the substance and some of the primary benefits of this approach to theology and theological analyses, I point out the relative absence of such an approach in several recent theologies of work. This absence, I contend, leaves the twin concepts of vocation and work either in a decoupled state or in a relationship where vocations inform *how* to do one's work, but not what vocational work *should be*. Then I apply the insights of the cultural turn to the reading of the theologies present in Christian self-help literature to reveal both shortcomings and benefits to varied approaches to it. Finally, I locate my project in the burgeoning field of political theology in order to clarify further what a political vocation may entail.

THE CULTURAL TURN IN THEOLOGY

The cultural turn is predicated on the fact that that theology has had to contend with shifting ground underneath its feet.[1] Philosophical, historical, and anthropological findings alike reveal that, despite the protestations of confessional theologians in general, theological ideas are and have always been bound up in their surrounding cultural context.[2] Delwin Brown delivers the hard truth. He remarks that, ". . . there are no self-evident generalities from which to begin these scholarly inquiries and hence from which equally sure conclusions might be deduced. . . . They [objects of religion] have lost their essences. This is especially evident when we speak of religion and religious traditions."[3] Religion and theology are special cases because of their historic relationship with the divine that used to self-evidently stand as the unquestioned starting point for theological speculation. If, however, theology is a human endeavor mediated by human language, a claim that the most strident doctrinaire would have difficulty disputing, it cannot be but constrained by culture. While one may still hold that God transcends our language about God, a statement is still being made about God, and hence is unable to avoid the trap. Increased reliance on historicism (that ideas are contextually modified) and heightened awareness of pluralism (that religious concepts vary widely across the globe) lend credibility to the embeddedness of all worldviews, especially religious ones, in the culture from which they emerge.

Therefore any current usage of theological or religious concepts or beliefs, when no account is taken of the cultural conditioning of the concept, is no longer a viable theological option. Granted, this stance is still a particularly difficult pill for many theologians to swallow because of theology's traditional insistence that it trade in universal concepts and systems of concepts. Yet as Ted A. Smith puts it, the evidence for the intertwining of theology with culture is so indisputable that it is traditional, confessing theologians that carry the burden of proof for their claims instead of the other way around. He states that,

> claims to direct access to revelation or reason above any particularity have become unpersuasive or unattractive for a variety of reasons. If not every theologian has agreed to make a cultural turn, then burden of proof clearly has shifted to those making claims to start with something beyond every particular culture. I take the turn for granted as a power element of contemporary cultures of theology and ethics.[4]

We see the impact of culture in the theological history presented in the previous chapter, which in turn, invites several questions. How are we to adjudicate the differences, say, between Rauschenbusch's vocation and Barth's? One could simply claim that Barth is more faithful to the Bible than Rauschenbusch or that Rauschenbusch's God is more realistic than Barth's. Yet in both statements, no appeal is made to the fact that Rauschenbusch is writing in the midst of Hell's Kitchen, a brutal New York City neighborhood, and Barth is responding to the devastation of World War I, which raised his suspicion about the liberal idea of human progress. Refereeing their respective takes on vocation becomes more difficult when their cultural contexts are taken into account. This is not to say that their theologies can be wholly reduced to culture no more than either has recourse to a theology that stands above culture. Like most theologians, both Rauschenbusch and Barth are referring to transcendent objects and universal principles; a reduction of their arguments down to mundane cultural content is difficult given the incongruence between the two planes. So how do we deal with theology in light of the cultural turn?

When sacred texts and doctrines are the focal points of theological inquiry, theological speculation about God can run without obstacle. Whether appropriate or not, doctrines and sacred texts can be taken as self-referential, hence the theology that reflects on these alone does not have to ask about the culture that informed the production and later interpretations of these sources. Yet when the impact of culture is acknowledged on these and other religious artifacts, the way theology is done and God is discussed changes radically. Smith again,

> Christian speech about God and God's hope for the world became problematic for many theologians and ethicists who became convinced

that all speech about God, even scripture, was culturally or historically conditioned. When this concession joined convictions that God stood genuinely apart from any particular human culture, theologians and ethicists found themselves able to say less and less about God's ways with the world.[5]

In other words, the cultural turn exposes the inability to broker in non-contextual, universal, or *sui generis* concepts when faced with multi-cultural, postmodern epistemologies. This may be bad news for traditional theologians who wish to speak about God's inherent qualities once they have owned up to the impact of culture on all theological utterances. However, it is good news for those who wish to engage theology only through publically accessible, culturally mediated discourse. Not only can a full cultural turn be made here minus "the roadblocks of modernist epistemology," but data for theological inquiry is no longer a "conversation stopper," as Richard Rorty put it.

Postmodernity in general and the cultural turn in theology specifically has spawned everything from reclamation projects devised to recapture original theological meanings,[6] to creative reworkings of traditional theological ideas,[7] to the abandonment of theology altogether,[8] to an unqualified acceptance of historicism and cultural relativism but a refusal to abandon theology. This last option, which I opt for, raises a thorny question, however. When *all* is conditioned by shifting cultural contexts, how are theological concepts able to retain a normative quality that can confront and even critique institutions when warranted? Or if competing claims about God or the Bible are relativized, is the theologian still able to make value judgments or prescriptive statements given the traditional capacity of theology to do just that? Smith confirms that

> [t]he price of verifiability, however has been the question of normativity. How can one move from claims about what people do in fact believe to claims about what is true? How can one move from descriptive claims about the practices of a community to claims about what anyone—even people in that community—ought to do? How can one move from fact to norm, from is to ought?[9]

Lacking recourse to a God who legitimates and guarantees the value of theological claims, culturally embedded claims either must find a new path to normativity or abandon prescription altogether. Furthermore, the inability stand on an Archimedean point relegates theological discourse to merely one amongst all other discourses that *never* enjoyed divine protection. This democratization of discourses signals the potential loss of the vocal distinctiveness of theology.

Despite this, there are varying ways to retain and apply theological norms once the cultural turn has been made. Often level of success hinges on the type of community singled out. For instance, the communities that Ted Smith uses to establish theology's normative trajectory are ecclesial ones, and the theologies lifted out of in order to wield them are drawn largely from Stanley Hauerwas and Delores Williams. The theologies of Hauerwas and Williams spring from what they consider to be the ideal church and are designed to spin back on the existent church as a critique. Smith correctly labels this move as a result of the cultural turn that is able to deploy a critique against that which needs critiquing. The theologies that Hauerwas, Williams, and by extension, Smith put forth are taken from both the real church community, its cultural location, *and* a vision of what an ideal church community should have as a theology.

The ideal theology never strays too far from the material context of the church as it responds to material needs in the now. Yet it does stray at times in the positing of an ideal church that can only function properly when attuned to a God who stands above culture. God in this case is perhaps used instrumentally to push the church to higher plateaus, as the prophets of the Hebrew Bible did. But because the community sample is small and the God they use is still one who is beyond the messiness of culture, Smith's use of Hauerwas and Williams to show how theology can be normative after the cultural turn is not taking into account the fact that the ideal church is still unable to free itself from cultural modification.

Alternatively, Kathryn Tanner's use of the concept of grace reckons with the ramifications of the cultural turn, stays close to the materiality of theology, and hence produces a better example for my own treatment of the concept of vocation. She argues that the exchange of money and all of the cultural signifiers that go along with it stand as the interpretive grid within which grace becomes intelligible in the contemporary world.

> [g]race has everything to do with money. Here divisions in the distribution of grace—religious differences most generally, differences in religious commitment, differences in religious affiliation—are taken to be signs of economic differences, for example, differences in class or status grouping . . . money and class are what should not be discussed in polite society or in the supposedly classless society of the United States, what, indeed, the veil of religion keeps from being mentioned as such. Grace is substituted for money, as money's representation, its representable stand-in or sign.[10]

Here, Tanner deciphers the utilization of "grace language" so that the concept operates as a signifier that mitigates the harsher truth that money acts as the real determinant of social differences and status. For this to happen, grace, as a theological concept, must not only participate in the cultural game that designates winners and losers in a capitalistic society, but it must also take its cues from and be deployed by the culture that executes the rules of the game.

Further, Tanner uses the similarities between grace and money to pit an alternative set of economic exchanges over and against the kinds commonly practiced in a capitalistic economy. Her "economy of grace" takes its cues from noncompetitive economic exchanges on the global level that will result in the mutual benefit for all parties to the exchange. Tanner bases her proposal on the meaning of grace as it was appropriated by early Christian communities in both economic and non-economic exchanges.[11] Her overall argument is that grace can act as a normative concept that critiques the non-zero-sum game played by powerful multinational corporations and developing countries. Here, grace is immersed in the world yet still carries with it the import that can imaginatively restructure economic relations in ways that economic solutions alone cannot.

Even if there is some consensus that the use of universal theological concepts is epistemologically impossible, there is still an open question as to the *functional* aptitude of theology. A-cultural theological claims are legitimized by an abstract divine authority, but the theologians, religious scholars, Christian writers, and most certainly pastors who use them typically tout their practical, concrete efficacy too. Treating theological concepts as culturally embedded products must not only be the more philosophically honest way to deal with theology, but it should also be the way to put theological concepts into a more transparent, actionable relationship with the world as well. Therefore, a vocation must also navigate between its historical theological import and the culture that it is fully immersed in. Only then can the temptation to extract it out of its material context and idealize it be resisted.

In what follows, I examine several recent Christian theological handlings of the issue of paid work that vary in their level of commitment to the role that human agency and its culture-making ability play in the things of God. Each author honors the value of daily work as such—work is necessary—and therefore it demands some kind of theological justification. So if work has ontological weight in and of itself, what is work in relation to God? Is it tied too tightly to human effort, which when cast into the Pauline binary of faith and works, is utterly powerless to effect salvation? Does the value of work need to be weighted more so that workers can be co-creators with God in an ongoing creation? The following theologians are asking one or more of these questions while granting that the current state of work is less than ideal. Moreover, they trace much of worker dissatisfaction back to contentious and often unjust relationships between labor and management. Thus like myself, they are addressing the politics of the modern workplace, and similarly, their task is to articulate the means to increase job satisfaction by overcoming its political obstacles in ways that are theologically warranted.

By dealing with the political environment of daily work, these theologians are getting their hands dirty—a sometimes risky move in theology. It is risky because theologies of work must traverse across the immanent domain of work in order to say something about the transcendent and its relation to work. We will see that making this journey with the use of theological concepts that purportedly stand above history and culture have a very tricky time entering into and meaningfully informing the material world of work and then re-entering the immaterial realm of the divine. This is not to say that doing a theology of work is and always will be a fool's errand. Nor that the following theologies of work are exhaustive of the relatively small number of theologies of work out there. My purpose is to demonstrate the practical difficulty of inserting theological concepts into thickets of culture, such as the political environment of the work world, without admitting of the preexistent and continual cultural entanglement with theology.

THEOLOGY AND WORK

Theology of Work as Response to God

Darrell Cosden begins his book, *The Heavenly Good of Earthly Work*, with a report on the current status of work.

> Dissatisfaction with the day-to-day reality of our work is an increasingly common phenomenon in societies influenced by western values and ways of doing things. Longer working hours and higher performance expectations have led to a stress-out workforce. Depersonalization, allowing little room for self-expression and personal development; under-use of our skills and abilities; the pressure to cheat or cut corners—these are just a few of the negative realities that cause many of us to question whether our work is really worth the investment of so much of our lives.[12]

The next sentence tells us the real reason for our dissatisfaction.

> Of course, worker frustration is not new. It is an experience common to all—even Christians. It is bound up with the fallen human condition.[13]

Because the negative reaction to work cannot be traced to the work itself, Cosden looks inward and upward. Our view of the truth about work and about the world, for that matter, is clouded by our limited perspective which is the consequence of original sin.

To further complicate the matter, our confusion regarding the varying degrees of satisfaction with work has to do with the status of certain kinds of work in God's eyes. As Cosden puts it, Christians often confront a "hierarchy of callings" that slots the helping professions (ministry, education, many non-profit work, health care, etc.) above strictly for-profit jobs. Those who work in the latter group of jobs may feel like "second class Christians" which further contributes to the disappointment with one's work.[14]

Because all of us are flawed, we are tempted to replace God's will for our lives with our own will. Yet when we examine God's will for our work lives, we see, with help from Luther, that there is biblical and theological warrant for considering *all* jobs as holy. Cosden argues that the bodily resurrection of Christ means, amongst other things, that "matter matters" to the point that all of creation will be redeemed, not just the spirit or even just human beings, at the *parousia*.[15] Hence earthly work including "second-class" jobs, not just the people who perform it, is able to be saved.[16] In addition, because the cross puts us in right standing before God, we are able to work with God instead of against God which valorizes human work even more.

> Our work does not save us, nor does it build God's kingdom for him. Only God can build his kingdom and bring about his new creation— whether in people, on earth now, or in the new heaven and the new earth. But justification does restore us to fulfill our original purpose— to be God's growing and ever more skillful co-workers.[17]

Work, then, is homogenized (*all* is potentially savable), which allows Cosden to center on how we see our work instead of on the differences between jobs that generate a hierarchy of callings. Is work thought of and performed in a way that makes it worth saving, worthy of redemption? Or is it approached as merely a job? If approached as a job alone, working will frustrate Christians and non-Christians alike. It is the attitude with which we engage our work (are we dour or joyful?) and carry out our work (are we cutting corners or working diligently?) that is emphasized over the job itself.

Cosden ends his book with fictional vignette that helps us understand more fully how his theology intersects with concrete problems in the world. Jason and Jack work at the same company that manufactures computer chips. Jason has the monotonous job of testing component parts; Jack has the more exciting job of designing the parts that Jason tests. And while a hierarchy is present, Jack notices that Jason seems "despite the monotony and obvious frustration in his [Jason's] work, to find meaning within it. He treats it as more than just a way to get a wage."[18] Jack is moved to question the centrality of his own work by asking if work plus salary plus consumption is all there is to life. When Jack presses Jason further on the reason for Jason's enviable attitude, "Jason tries to explain to Jack that he is not just working for himself, although given his personality he does find a degree of satisfaction in his work. Rather, Jason explains, he works with others and even with eternity in mind."[19] Soon Jack not only recalibrates his orientation towards his own work by attempting to align it with God's will, but he also is moved to cross workplace political boundaries and ask Jason for design input. Cosden ends the story (and the book) with the following:

> Jack asks Jason if he might explore with him how their team might use their influence on those above to obtain more "meaningful" projects. Jack also asks if Jason might be willing to help him to understand more about the kind of beliefs that would suggest that somehow their projects could be part of God's purpose for the world . . . [20]

Consistent with his theology, Cosden suggests that if work is carried out with the goal of pleasing God clearly in sight, then monotonous jobs will not be too frustrating, which is the primary problem with work, as he sees it. Moreover, this expansive attitude towards narrow, possibly insignificant work can be infectious and serve as a tool for evangelization. Jason's viewing of his lower-level job in a heavenly context makes Jack aware of the relative lack of meaning in his higher-level, exciting job. In both cases, the work itself as well as the status within the company is irrelevant to the ultimate meaning of the work.

Indeed, while Cosden repeatedly asserts the heavenly good of earthly, material work, there is little development of the nature of this relationship between the two realms. Cosden provides us with general statements about the creation still being "an object of God's love," and that "we are now, and forever will be, genuinely God's co-workers."[21] Yet he does not flesh out these rather thin declarations with concrete ways in which the material world of work is good in heavenly terms. However, with his emphasis on our sinful reaction to unsatisfying work, he protects himself from getting too concrete. A similar theological conviction is shared by David Jensen, who, like Cosden, first recites common complaints about modern work.

> We live in a world where work often becomes drudgery, where many who desire paid employment are denied access to meaningful work, where some control and own the labors of others, where white-collar workers become addicted to work while others languish in unemployment lines, where job satisfaction deteriorates, where backbreaking and exhausting work eclipses Sabbath.[22]

Echoing Cosden, Jensen follows this passage with a lamentation but then a qualification: work is fallen, but it can be redeemed.[23] However, Jensen locates the expression of the fallenness of work within the status of modern work itself rather than in our discouragement about it. In particular, Jensen takes pains to emphasize the deleterious impact of the interminable battle between management and labor on the meaning of work for human beings.[24] His theology of work can be seen, in one respect, as a way of structurally refashioning the terms of disagreement between labor and capital in order to guide both towards good, godly ends. Jensen's goals are more attuned to the unsatisfactory political realities in the workplace than Cosden's, whose response to the divide is more conservative theologically.

Yet Jensen, in almost Barthian fashion, deems the problem so severe that only a transcendent, sovereign God can solve it. As opposed to Cosden's hope that co-working with God will help overcome worker malaise, Jensen claims that human work is redeemed through God's pre-existent work on our behalf, not cooperation with it.[25] God's work, which is the redeeming of the world in Christ and through the Holy Spirit, is the real work that is accomplished. Our work, if it is to be meaningful or as Jensen calls it "good," is relativized by God's overarching work and can only be an expression of our God-given gifts. But because our work is related to God's work, it must involve the whole person, be humanizing, and serve as an act of gratitude to God's primal effort. He writes, "[g]ood work, in and of itself, is an expression of thanks: a finely crafted chair, a graceful gymnastics routine, a sound medical diagnosis, a brightly waxed car, all involve work that employs gifts and gives thanks for them."[26] If a chair is made simply for the wage received or for the profit made upon its sale, the labor that went into making the chair does not come from the whole self. Or the chair itself is in the service of human need or to the market but not to God's work performed through Trinitarian dispensations.

Jensen gives several examples of the kind of work that is unable to elicit the proper response to God's work.

> Mind-numbing work, for example, smothers thanks instead of giving it voice. Work owned by others squashes individual gifts rather than fostering them. Taylorist assembly line methods, which compartmentalize work so rigidly that one worker is given the task of fastening one screw in the same place—widget after endless widget—deaden the heard and our capacity for giving thanks.[27]

It is impossible to show true thanks through work when it gives you little of value. What is there to be thankful for, exactly? Or what, then, are the qualities "work-as-thanks" or good work for Jensen?

> Recent attempts to integrate assembly line workers into factory governance decisions, for example, recognize that all workers express gifts and thanks. At best, they recognize that those closest to machine work provide distinctly needed voices in framing the work of the factory as a whole. In these models, the assembly line worker is always more than the particular task she or he is summoned to do. One criterion for whether work is an expression of blessing, then, is whether it allows for the expression of more than one isolated task. Blessing, as it envelops all of life, elicits a response of the whole person.[28]

When workers are given tasks (always plural) that correspond to the varied abilities and needs of each worker, more of their personhood is affirmed at work just as God affirms the whole person. It is "responsive labor" that can produce beneficial political outcomes for lower-level workers as a holistic conception of the worker is now in play.

Going further, Jensen expands the effects of good work, when practiced by both management and labor, to cover all aspects of the modern company.

> If workers and management recognized that the good of their work increased through sharing and collaboration, then perhaps corporate governance would see unionization less as a threat and more as a voice for the continued flourishing of work, the products of good work, and the profits that stem from good work. The interest of both management and labor, after all, is the creation of good products and services; the maintenance of a decent standard of living that comes, in part, from good labor; and the continued ecological sustainability of work practices.[29]

Here, if all parties are responding to God's redeeming, gracious work in the creation, work is done on behalf of others, shared across working-class lines, and most importantly, is more productive and profitable than the work that comes out of competitive, antagonistic relations. Yet beneficial political outcomes are not the goal—they are simply the natural by-products of good work. Jensen's theology of work is one that relates God to work through mimesis. Good work takes its cues from God's work, and the salutary effects of good work follow from this flow downward from God's larger work.

Both Cosden and Jensen consider the problems of modern work under the presupposition that the stuff of work, as a type of human effort, is unable to resolve its own problems—God alone can. Sin, which has thoroughly infected the world, is that which keeps the world of work at permanent distance from God. Yet they both acknowledge that work is worthy of theological reflection despite its limits. So while they, to varying degrees, take culture seriously by acknowledging the real problems with modern work, their theology of work rests on the separation of the things of God and culture—a stance which ultimately strains the feasibility of their solutions to the problem of modern work.

Further, with Cosden, because the dissatisfaction with work is so quickly reduced to worker frustration with work and then to the frustration as a consequence of sin, he is unable to account for people who may not experience work in this way. There are radically different forms of work as well as radically different kinds of reactions that people have towards their work. For instance, if Jason was treated poorly by Jack and then let go unceremoniously, would he be able to maintain his sanguinity towards work? If not, how would Cosden interpret the role of work in his theology when Jason is not expressing a godly attitude? And what to do with those who are not frustrated with work *because* they are in positions of power? He seems to assume that a lack of ultimate meaning found in and through work will be self-evident to or at least intuitively grasped by those who are working for secular purposes, but what in his theology ensures this? We are all sinners and God is in control, according to Cosden, so in Calvinist fashion when he implores us that God's ways are mysterious but work honorably anyway, he leaves himself unable to answer these questions.[30]

These questions are important because they disclose realities in the work world. Cosden's interpretation of work may be able to make sense to those whose work is already seen as aligning with God's will or to those who are predisposed to want God infused in their work. But for others who are simply looking for satisfying, humanizing work, God does not have to factor into finding it. Therefore Cosden's broad statements about work in general are inapplicable to many workers and ultimately detached from the material conditions of work that can humanize it.

Jensen's answer to the problems with modern work gets at their material/political roots more quickly and thoroughly than Cosden's. The attention that Jensen pays not only to the labor/capital battle but also to details of certain working environments, both real and hoped for, shows the value he puts on actual work as he constructs a theology of work. His work-as-response to God's work in and through Jesus Christ is an inventive means of breaking through the thick wall between labor and management in order that political injustices can be addressed.

However, Jensen's theological way out of the impasse is too reliant on a God that stands above culture to be as effective in culture as he would like. In most working environments, the meaning and value of work is limited or expanded, damaged or enhanced by the political relationship between employers and employees, as Jensen admits.[31] If God's work is the model for the kind of "good work" that can ameliorate the effects of the labor/capital problem, then God's work needs to address the divide between the boss and worker on some level. Yet Jensen's God understandably has no boss that supervises divine handiwork. Moreover, the work that God does is that of "creating, sustaining, refining, and redeeming, nearly every trade of ancient society," but not of conveying how those trades operate under the duress of a market economy. God's work presumably does not change in its essence, hence its a-cultural quality that allows it to be applied to ancient and modern societies alike.

In order to link the work done on both sides of the labor/capital divide to the universal impetus of God's work, Jensen has to blur the line between labor and management when it comes to each of their intentions and desires. That the "interest of both management and labor, after all, is the creation of good products and services" may be true on some level. But as long as labor and management exist, the way that the creation of products and services will be understood by each will *always* be informed by the power differential between the two groups.

God's work may provide the inspiration for both employees and employers to perform work more industriously and/or ethically. But a biblically based, theologically informed notion of God's work that addresses the root of the problems that Jensen lays out so carefully is not realistic nor practical. A biblically based theological response to modern work in capitalist societies, if this is even advised at all, needs to be more nuanced and culturally sensitive (even admitting of its own cultural indebtedness) if it is to address the problem of power in the workplace.

Theology of Work as Co-Creation with God

While both Cosden and Jensen find a prominent place for work in their respective theologies, each downplay the ability of work to make any real theological headway. God's work is more than that which provokes us to do good work—it animates work by providing the foundation for any work to be good. We respond to God's work, but Cosden and Jensen seem to say that God is already working in and through us before we even respond. Hence, our own work is derivative of God's work at best, a poor imitation at worst.

When work is instead considered *cooperative* with God's ongoing act of creation or as an act of *co-creation* with God, as Volf desires, it is not as much a reaction to God as it is an action that carries its own ontological and theological gravitas. The Papal encyclical, *Laborem exercens* delivered by Pope John Paul II in 1981, serves as a seminal text for the development of work as co-creativity. The document commemorates the ninetieth anniversary of Pope Leo XIII's encyclical *Rerum Novarum* that first stated the Church's official position on the state of labor. Entitled, "Rights and Duties of Capital and Labour," *Rerum Novarum* responded specifically and critically to working conditions under industrialization.[32] In the 1981 document, Pope John Paul II seeks to maintain the spirit of the original encyclical while updating the Church's concerns in the face of the current state of labor. The latter encyclical does this by first establishing the Church's stance on what human work is in general. It quotes a statement from Vatican II that positions the status of human work in relation to God:

> Far from thinking that works produced by man's own talent and energy are in opposition to God's power, and that the rational creature exists as a kind of rival to the Creator, Christians are convinced that the triumphs of the human race are a sign of God's greatness and the flowering of his own mysterious design. For the greater man's power becomes, the farther his individual and community responsibility extends.[33]

Human work is not toil, nor is it antagonistic to God's work—it is a manifest expression of the latent power in God's creation. Hence human work is connected to God not through its denigration (our work is a poor imitation of God's work), but through its elevation as a continuation of God's work.

> The word of God's revelation is profoundly marked by the fundamental truth that *man*, created in the image of God, *shares by his work in the activity of the Creator* and that, within the limits of his own human capabilities, man in a sense continues to develop that activity, and perfects it as he advances further and further in the discovery of the resources and values contained in the whole of creation.[34]

This suggests that human work is, in a way, separate from "the activity of the Creator." "Man" bears God's stamp in the form of the image of God, but the encyclical implies that the *imago dei* does not drive godly or good work as much as it allows for cooperation with God in the ongoing creation. A division of labor is articulated that leaves the creation of the universe along with all of its resources to God who still shares in the act of creating by ceding the exploration and modification of those resources over to humanity. God and humanity do not share the same task in the endeavor of perfecting the creation; they are uniquely contributing to the goal of perfection, hence are working together towards this end.

Armand Larive develops a theology of work that is predicated on *Laborem exercens'* interpretation of work as a co-creating activity with God in his book, *After Sunday*.[35] He writes, "the human cocreator, the *homo conservans*, has a freedom to do well or poorly with the creation, implying a weight of considerable responsibility."[36] Human work as co-creative activity must certainly be good work in order for it to participate in the act of creation. Yet unlike Jensen's notion of good work here, work is less a reaction to the work that God does than that which responds to an innate font present in all people. He writes that "good work is often animated with a holy vigor well known to working people, a vigor that can be called out of working people just as Socrates called principles of geometry out of a slave boy in the *Meno*." And, "[t]his knowledge, which working people seem to possess innately, can be articulated in the way work is served by the Trinity. There is, in other words, a very familiar aspect to work that can be related respectively to the Father/Mother, the Son, and the Holy Spirit."[37] The Trinitarian God serves to familiarize the worker with what is already there within each person, yet needs to be awoken.[38]

God's role in defining and even directing good human work is one of an exemplar rather than a puppeteer for Larive. Good work is familiar, even natural, because the inborn "holy vigor" that motivates it is articulated and then confirmed by the interaction of the persons of the Trinity. God as co-creator with good workers instills all with the capacity to join in the act of creation as well as provides instruction on what good work is through the example of the Godhead.

Larive, like Cosden and Jensen, admits that poor working conditions often prevent our innate desire for satisfying work from being tapped. Specifically, he highlights the political dimension of workplaces and maintains that democratic ones where workers participate in decision making are much better facilitators of good work than workplaces where employees have no decision-making power.[39] Larive then discusses different kinds of power that upper management uses to control and disempower lower-level employees.[40] From the threat of layoffs to de-unionization to internecine competition to convoluted chains of command that are characteristic of bureaucratic organizations—all of these render employees politically powerless on the job and unable to perform good work.

The person of the Trinity that can help explain how workplaces have become so undemocratic as well as give guidance on how to redress these situations is the Holy Spirit. But just as workplaces can be undemocratic, spirits can be harmful too. Worker disrespect, oppressive surveillance of employees, cutthroat competition, job insecurity, office communication breakdowns and impersonal bureaucratic chains of command in modern workplaces are traced back to the presence of injurious spirits. But it is the Holy Spirit that can act like a force field that parries the blows of bad spirits and helps to unify warring parties that are squared off on both sides of a workplace divide. The Holy Spirit is not a brute force that steers us towards good action but a field that is invited into human relationships in order to create a healthy rapport between parties. It is not necessarily waiting on our invitation to act, but is given the opportunity to act by us. "Not to say that the Holy Spirit can be invoked, or manipulated, or made present for selfish ends, but the structure of human relations can be instituted that will make this Spirit welcome."[41] Then once the Spirit has entered into these human relations, it can further coax healthy relationships or a "holy rapport" between employers and employees. In the end,

> a holy rapport comes in to existence when people devote themselves to a teacher-disciple relational paradigm, rather than one of master-slave, and look forward to a relation of respectful and mutual servanthood, where quality of product and honor of worker share the "bottom line" that makes profits possible. Into such a working arrangement the Holy Spirit comes like a force field, giving energy and life to a working community.[42]

Again, Larive is giving more weight to the role that human agency plays in the affairs of God than Cosden or Jensen. We are responsible for "setting the table" before the Spirit can sit down and do its work. But the Spirit, like an ever-present force field, is lying in wait, and once working relationships display "respectful and mutual servanthood," it is called up for service. In relation to *Laborem exercens*, our work that is conditioned on the types of political relationships we forge in the workplace shares in

God's act of creation by using resources in humane ways. We co-create with God when work stems from just political arrangements at work. This work is then confirmed as co-creative through the invigoration given by the Holy Spirit.

Larive's formulation, though, leaves one question that is answered unsatisfactorily: who or what is responsible for the undemocratic workplaces? His answer that harmful spirits are to blame seems *ad hoc*—there is no previous mention in his book of anything other than a benevolent spirit that affects human dealings nor any mention of bad spirits after he is through discussing undemocratic workplaces. At least Cosden and Jensen have the Fall. Nor is there any articulation of the relationship between good and bad spirits or the relationship between harmful spirits and the third person of the Holy Trinity—just that bad spirits exist.[43] Moreover, Larive uses bad spirits as the sole reason for maltreatment of workers in the workplace with no acknowledgment of the role that capitalism and its culture has played in disputes between labor and management. This reduction of complex workplace politics down to the machinations of spirits conveniently allows Larive to enlist the Holy Spirit as the lone hero.

This raises another problem as the Holy Spirit needs the structure of human relations to be in the kind of state that welcomes the Spirit. But if the political workplace environment is not welcoming, harmful spirits are to blame. And what are the qualities of a welcoming workplace environment? Skill and rapport, he says, which are fruits of the Holy Spirit. The Holy Spirit is needed to create the appropriate relations in the workplace through skill and rapport (if in fact harmful spirits are overcome) so that the same Spirit can be tapped to remedy unjust and unsatisfactory working environments.

Both Larive's circular argument and his reliance on harmful spirits to explain detrimental workplace relationships means that spirits, both good and bad, are the cause and solution to problems with modern work. His elevation of the human component of work as a contributor to an ongoing creation could go a long way to looking for humanly constructed reasons for the cause and solution to the problem of undemocratic workplaces, as Volf attempts to do. But Larive departs from *Laborem exercens* here, which emphatically lays the problem at the feet of unregulated capitalism. Instead, his closed spiritual circuit leaves us outside of the rectification process.

With good and bad spirits causing and solving problematic workplace politics, Larive's argument differs little from Cosden's and Jensen's in the end. Purely spiritual answers to questions that involve long histories and complex material machineries are incapable of bringing the kind of changes that Larive seeks. If harmful spirits are responsible for current workplace problems, they should also be to blame for pre-industrial labor problems too, such as slavery. Did the Holy Spirit overcome these bad spirits only to lose the battle, perhaps just for a time, in corporate environments? If so, why? And if not, what brought about the changes in labor politics that we have seen over the last five hundred years? Larive's reliance on spiritual explanations for current political problems would seemingly force him to apply this explanation to all historical instances of injustice at work for the sake of consistency. It also commits him to explain, perhaps awkwardly, the constant push and pull of labor/management in terms of a kind of spiritual warfare. Good spirits get credit for instituting more democratic workplaces; bad spirits get charged with the failure to institute these. Aside from the practical impossibility of ascribing gains and losses in such terms (where does human effort end and spiritual power begin?), Larive's spiritual answer would likely fall on deaf ears. There are, no doubt, some workers who view their job dissatisfaction in spiritual ways. However, they are confronted with superiors who are as likely to view their own success as God's blessing; just as workers view their position of powerlessness as a harmful spirit infecting the workplace.

Hence when supplying spiritual solutions to solve concrete political issues, interpretation is in the eye of the beholder. The *how* and *why* of the problem of modern work, which should encourage an inquiry into its historical/cultural influences, are circumvented by emphasizing co-creation and the authoritative role of spirits in its execution. So while Larive allows good, godly work to be the result of human effort, an allowance that could more feasibly elucidate the human contribution and measured solution to workplace injustices, he relies on a wholly transcendent framework to redress the issue. Again, we are left with an a-cultural solution to a problem that has a history and cannot be disconnected from the cultures in which this history is made.

THEOLOGY AND THE TURN TO SELF-HELP LITERATURE

One way to overcome this predicament is to reckon fully with the changes that move workplaces from being undemocratic to democratic back to undemocratic and so on. This is tantamount to admitting the powerful cultural influence on such changes as well as the cultural influence on whatever theology of work is put forth. One cultural expression that acts both as an indicator of how work relates to vocations for the public as well as a force that seals a certain relationship between the two is self-help literature. The cultural turn in theology prompts a careful examination of this cultural form that informs theologies, not just of the theologies themselves. It forces the theologies present in popular self-help texts to interact with the culture that molds them for mass consumption.

To those who dismiss an academic inquiry into self-help books on the grounds that they are superficial, anecdotal, and poorly reasoned, if reasoned at all, the fact is that these books reflect some of the most powerful cultural movements in America. In particular, the association between self-help books and the type of culture that affects the current meaning of work, consumer culture is especially tight. Wendy Simonds writes that,

> Self-help books must be studied as ideologically powerful instruments of cultural commerce that are linked both with the proliferation of buyable therapy, in which assistance comes to be seen as a purchasable commodity, and with the increasing volume of the marketplace for leisure consumption.[44]

Self-help literature successfully advertises certain therapies as commodities for sale by commodifying the concepts found in the books themselves. She continues, "Self-help books, because they are didactic guides, commodify readers while they read, by urging them to make themselves into objects of analysis and improvement." One of Simonds's participants in her study "talked about how self-help books offer self-conceptions readers can 'try on....' If you don't like it, change it; dress up your assets and hide the ugly parts."[45] In other words, self-help literature fortifies consumer culture by commodifying and marketing salable ideas to the public by demanding that the public commodify itself. And because vocation is a concept that self-help authors frequently ask readers to "try on," self-help literature becomes an invaluable tool in its examination.[46]

For example, Steven Covey, the author of the bestselling business motivational book, *The Seven Habits of Highly Effective People*, asks readers to use the power of the idea of a vocation for improving their potential in the corporate world in his follow-up book, *The 8th Habit: From Effectiveness to Greatness*.

> Perhaps the most important vision of all is to develop a sense of self, a sense of your own destiny, a sense of your unique mission and role in life, as a sense of purpose and meaning. When testing your own personal vision first ask yourself: Does the vision tap into my voice, my energy, my unique talent? Does it give me a sense of "calling," a cause worthy of my commitment?[47]

Covey enlists the power of a calling to legitimize one's own sense of destiny, purpose, and meaning. The self is helped if it can justifiably align a vision and mission with a "sense of calling." The reason for using calling language in self-help and personal motivation books such as Covey's should be clear enough—the endowment of an otherwise mundane life with other-worldly meaning is an appealing, useful addition. Even though he is perhaps parasitic on the original force of Luther's concept of vocation, Covey transmits a theology, however covert it may be, through his writing. And the use of theological concepts in self-help books invites an analysis of the relationship between self-help culture and the theologies present in its books.

An analysis of this kind must move between two typical responses to religious self-help literature. Either self-help books are critiqued with a heavy hand that questions whether they are orthodox theologically speaking. Or alternatively, they are analyzed with no concession that their theologies are semantically relevant for the reader. I examine these two critical takes on the self-help genre in this section that, like the goal of the previous section, will demonstrate their limitations that foreground the advantage of applying the insights of the turn to culture to self-help books such as *The Purpose-Driven Life*.

SELF-HELP LITERATURE IN THE WORLD *AND* OF IT

Self-help books are particularly good indicators of the prevailing cultural winds as they are intended to offer aid to the struggling individual by couching their content in culturally relevant ways. Fortunately, the connection between theology and culture made by many religious self-help books is ready-made for the analyst. Self-help books are often written in response to a perceived gap between the way that individuals are living and the way that they should live. Christian self-help literature typically resolves this is/ought problem by accommodating to prevailing cultural trends in its effort to appeal to a mass audience. For instance, God's omniscience may be invoked—not necessarily to make a theological point but to address troubling issues such as depression, addiction, loss of a loved one, etc.[48] Because Christian self-help authors tend to begin with more immediately felt human issues and end with corresponding solutions, their theological concepts *must* be easily translatable into the wider culture.

Instead of investigating this use of theological concepts for the purposes of understanding the tight relationship between the concepts and culture, many critics of Christian self-help literature condemn it for its perceived collusion with "the world."[49] Christian self-help authors make a Faustian bargain with a materialistic, desire-driven culture, so these critics contend. More book sales often come at the cost of distorting the Gospel in order to accommodate a godless consumer market.

John Eldredge, in *Wild at Heart*, calls for men to recapture their masculinity by returning to a kind of primal "wildness." Wildness comes from a reservoir of latent energy in all men that, when tapped, connects them with their true masculine identity. Eldredge relies on examples of men from the Bible (Adam, Abraham, Samson, Job, David, and Jesus) to support his claim. These figures show that the proper relationship with a loving God uncovers the "masculine heart" in all men, which generates excitement not boredom, courage not fear, wildness not docility. *Wild at Heart* enters self-help territory in several ways.

For instance, on the topic of sin, Eldredge talks of the common practice of men carrying a particularly burdensome version of original sin which limits their relationship with God. Yet instead of casting Original Sin in metaphysical terms, the sinful weight is made up of "old psychological and emotional wounds" that hinder the soul's expression of wildness.[50] Daniel Gillespie, a nondenominational pastor, criticizes Eldredge's treatment of sin:

> Man's personal responsibility for sin is overlooked. Instead of establishing individual responsibility for sin, the author encourages men to shift the blame—seeing sin more as a sickness than a moral choice.... By convincing his readers to blame their behavior on these hidden wounds, Eldredge replaces the guilt of a sinner with the self-righteous pity of a victim. That falls far short of the biblical picture of man's responsibility.[51]

Here and in many other commentaries on Christian self-help literature we find a criticism of a theological concept is legitimated solely on the basis of an "authentic" biblical rendering of the concept. Hidden in Gillespie's comment is a reliance on a Calvinistic human depravity in the face of God. We do not rise up out of our depravity by attending to contingent psychological scars—such a suggestion smacks of Pelagianism. For Gillespie, it is either God who dictates the terms of sin or fallen creatures who mistakenly attempt to define sin for themselves. And it is *culture* that is designated by Gillespie as the primary culprit that tempts Eldredge into modifying and diluting the theological concept of sin. After citing Eldredge's use of masculine movie icons, in addition to biblical figures for more examples of expressions of wildness, Gillespie remarks,

> Quotes from secular song writers, poets, and philosophers also line the pages of *Wild at Heart*. From the Dixie Chicks to the Eagles to Bruce Springsteen, Eldredge seems enamored by the thoughts of worldly men.... Is Hollywood where Christians should go to find out what God expects for men? Should movies form the foundation, or furnish the role models, for true masculinity? Since when does the church develop its spiritual ideals from the on-screen imaginations of unsaved directors?[52]

Gillespie answers these questions with a predictable "never." The culture that produces worldly men can never serve as the template for the church's ideal for its male congregants. The Bible stands above culture from where it alone can provide the true foundation for men's lives.

Authors like Gillespie who employ this kind of strategy so clearly stray from the method of investigation employed by those who view theological concepts as culturally embedded that it is difficult to engage them as serious interlocutors. More complex analyses of Christian self-help literature that operate with a historical seriousness when addressing theological concepts in culture are more useful. One such scholar, David F. Wells, has embarked on such an investigation of the historical and cultural forces that help account for the corrosion of evangelical theology in America. Wells's approach differs from Gillespie's because he does not separate culture from theology absolutely. Rather, he admits of the power of culture to transform the relationship that humans have with the objects of theology. By identifying Christian self-help literature as a product of American culture, Wells brings secular culture and the theological ideas contained in self-help literature closer together, though the closeness is bothersome to him. A brief examination of Wells's argument, which extends over a three-book series, will reveal some merits of the claims he makes about Christian self-help literature while at the same time exposing some of the shortcomings of his interpretive framework. Attention to these shortcomings will serve to bolster the claim that the cultural influence on theological concepts is material as well as ideational.

These three books, *No Place for Truth or Whatever Happened to Evangelical Theology?, God in the Wasteland: The Reality of Truth in a World of Fading Dreams,* and *Above All Earthly Pow'rs,* attempt to explain the failure of the evangelical church to hold true to its principles. Throughout this self-proclaimed trilogy, Wells focuses attention on the secularizing tendencies of the Enlightenment to usher in a radical change in the tasks and goals of theology in general. "The Enlightenment worked its dark magic by seizing such Christian motifs as salvation, providence, and eschatology and rewriting them in humanistic terms, offering their substance in this-worldly ways."[53] For Wells, the secular humanism that emerged from modernity failed in its attempt to replace pre-modern values and virtues that he holds dear. And now postmodernism easily blows down the house of cards that was built on humanistic principles without building anything substantial in its place. In other words, postmodernity helpfully reveals the vacuousness and impotence of secular humanism.

> It is thus that modernity has brought forth its own intellectual conquerors in the post-moderns. They are eviscerating its hopes while having to leave its structures—urbanization, capitalism, technology, telecommunications—in place. In effect, they are producing a version of modernity bereft of its beliefs, stuck in despair. On the one hand, postmodern authors have made the Christian critique of modernity easier, but on the other hand their virulent attack not merely on Enlightenment meaning but on *all* meaning has made Christian faith less plausible in the modern world.[54]

This comprehensive damage to all grounded meaning (not just the Christian kind) permits the rise of false prophets of all kinds to capture our attention, direct our activities, and most importantly for Wells, alter the task and substance of evangelical theology.

According to Wells, the principles of correct evangelical theology are threefold: "confessional elements, reflection on this confession, and the cultivation of a set of virtues that are grounded in the first two elements."[55] In its most traditional form, confession is substantive and expresses exactly what the church believes. It has a specific trajectory with regards to what the church is to confess and what guides confession itself. "Churches with roots in the Protestant Reformation confess the truth that God has given to the Church through the inspired Word of God."[56] When the Word of God is understood as the guide for the church's confession, it is always geared towards the truth. Yet the truth of these confessions can be negotiated and argued for because of our limited ability to arrive at the truth. It is this negotiation and argumentation that form the primary task of theology for Wells. Nonetheless, he maintains that there can be *no* disagreement that statements of a proper confessional nature are attempts to get at objective truth about God. Therefore, confession is a means to coalesce biblical truths that both maintain continuity of proper belief across time and orient communities of faith to the truth about the Truth.

Wells blames the gradual loss of the evangelical church's maintenance of the confessional edifice on the fracturing of authority brought on by modernism and the subsequent permanent destruction of meaning effected by postmodernism. With the rise of multiple sources of authority after the Enlightenment, not only has the Bible been forced to compete with non-biblical sources of authority, but the actual capacity of confession to connect the church to the truth about God has been severely compromised as well. The destruction of biblical foundations created a vacuum that other cultural authorities have stepped in to replace.

It is here that Wells points to commercialization and consumerism as the primary movements that have stepped in. As opposed to a secular culture that the church could absorb while still preserving the essential integrity of its confession, consumer culture has altered confession itself. He emphasizes this new power of culture by contrasting H. R. Niebuhr's simplistic interpretation of culture with that of today: "Culture, he [Niebuhr] argued, is what human beings made of nature; it is what we impose upon nature by way of cities and transportation systems, or what we make of it by way of artistic artifacts. . . . What Niebuhr did not ponder is the stunning commercial success that industrialization has brought, and this is what has begun to change the meaning of culture."[57]

No longer is confession directed externally towards objective truth about God but rather towards the church's own inner theater and to the inner theaters of individual members. Wells elaborates, "as the nostrums of the therapeutic age supplant confession, and as preaching is psychologized, the meaning of Christian faith becomes privatized. At a single stroke, confession is eviscerated and reflection reduced mainly to thought about one's self."[58] When the self is the focus, God's commands, moral direction, and proper action are first and foremost subject to human desire, feeling, and intuition, which are amplified and then manipulated by consumer culture. Not only has the need for external direction and truth that confession used to supply dwindled, an ersatz authority in the form of self-help gurus has entered that satisfies needs that are primarily internal and psychological in nature.

Wells has much more to say about the allegedly shameful state of the evangelical church, but it is his method that is used to analyze the relationship between religion and culture that is particularly instructive. Admittedly, there is much to be commended in Wells's project. His claims about the "rise of the therapeutic" in American culture are well documented,[59] and his association of the therapeutic model of self-help books with the diminishment of the power of a traditional confession in the church is plausible. In addition, Wells, unlike Gillespie, establishes his case on an interpretation of American cultural history instead of strictly relying on biblical orthodoxy. Instead of dismissing secular culture as utterly tainted by sin to have any real authority, Wells grants that culture can substantively alter the meaning of theological concepts, albeit lamentably so.

His argument's merits notwithstanding, two questions remain. How does culture function in Wells's analysis, and does his interpretation of culture at large further our understanding of a theological concept such as confession as it is appropriated today? While Wells admits of the power of culture, he clearly rejects the claim that confession is *essentially* given and modified by culture. His claim, rather, is that the meaning and function of confession have been corrupted by culture, and the evidence for corruption is the substitution of psychological contentment for the truth about God—the objective of confessional activities.

To support this claim, Wells reduces the culture that is to blame for the failure of the evangelical church strictly to its *meaning*—primarily that the rise of the authoritative self means that confession is shorn of its ability to connect believers to God's truth. Wells's focus on the meaning of modern confession alone downplays the ways that evangelicals have been interacting socially and materially that have generated that meaning.[60] Wells gives short shrift to material causes of the failure by collapsing culture, which must include the social relations that communicate culture, and the meaning of that culture into each other. This kind of meaning can be more easily manipulated for Wells's purposes without the messiness of social reality getting in the way. Hence, Wells is able to integrate the meaning of the rise of the therapeutic self and self-help literature into a bounded cultural whole. The therapeutic self then cleanly serves as an affront to Wells's biblical view of humanity.

Such a stance on unchanging biblical truths and changing culture entrenches his position that culture *only* corrupts. But it also prevents him from allowing for the possibility that the meaning of confession has *always* been subject to cultural negotiation. In fact, Wells is unwittingly a part of this negotiation. For his reclamation of the "true" meaning of confession is informed so heavily by the cultural forces that he perceives to be undermining confession that culture is involved in his own project.

Additionally, one can rightfully ask of Wells, when does the impact of culture on the nature of the confession itself end and the object of confession, God's objective truth, begin? To concede so much to culture in the construction of the therapeutic self and its confession but then to pull back and restrict the power of culture when it comes to the object of confession is a more difficult task than Wells implies. It is easier and more honest to acknowledge that both the confession and the object to which the confession is directed are subject to cultural modification to some degree. Wells may be correct in the end—God *is* insulated from culture. Yet his argument, while forfeiting more to culture than Gillespie as it interacts with theological concepts, provides little evidence to suggest that the objects of theology are not exposed to the same cultural dynamics. So while Wells is willing to take the cultural impact on theology earnestly, his argument merely detours around the possibility of a culturally embedded theology on his way to a place that more closely resembles Gillespie's argument.

CHRISTIAN SELF-HELP LITERATURE, CONTEXTUALLY SPEAKING

Micki McGee, a sociologist and media studies scholar, is more sanguine towards the self-help genre than Wells. In her book, *Self-Help, Inc.*, she contends that self-help literature is predicated on worthy ideas that have had tremendous political cache in American culture: self-determination and self-fulfillment.[61] Hence this literature and the kinds of people who read it avidly have some of the tools to bring about change when these twin ideas are not being realized. However, McGee is also critical of self-help literature for the simple reason that it is currently not able to engage the political realm. Her critique, unlike Wells's, is immanent as she draws feminist discourse, Weber, and Foucault to arrive at her notion of the "belabored self" that forms the basis of her critique. The belabored self is the real subject of recent self-help books as well as their targeted object. It is the self that is in need; the self that self-help literature rescues through work.

> [T]he belabored self describes an actually occurring phenomenon: workers are asked to continually work on themselves in efforts to remain employable and reemployable, and as a means of reconciling themselves to declining employment prospects. . . . The idea of the

belabored self asks us to reconsider the cultural preoccupation with the self in terms of labor.[62]

Hence the belabored self that endlessly "works on itself" in order to improve job prospects or keep an existent job is most certainly tethered to the concrete working environment.

Yet the material conditions of work are not completely determinative in the formation of the belabored self—this self can certainly manipulate its own surroundings. "Social structures and individual identities are mutually constitutive: interconnected to such an extent that changes in the former necessarily produce changes in the latter, and, some would argue, vice versa."[63] This admission disallows McGee either from evaluating self-help literature from a purely ideological standpoint or with an idea of the self that stands above culture. Because social structure and the individual identity are coextensive, any conclusions drawn about one must use the other to support those conclusions. McGee can still rely on ideals such as self-determination to guide her project normatively even though such ideals are admitted to be cultural products themselves. Her final conclusion may be less audacious than Wells's, but she would probably trade a loud argument for one that accurately analyzes self-help literature.

When McGee discusses examples of religious self-help literature, her analysis does have blind spots that the scholar who is attuned to the intertwining relationship between theology and culture may not have. A considerable amount of pages are used to cover Richard Nelson Bolles's *What Color Is Your Parachute?: A Practical Manual for Job Hunters and Career Changers*, a book that integrates finding the right job with doing God's will.[64] A review of the forty annual editions of the book discloses a waxing and waning cycle of the degree to which God is to be involved in a career search. From the first editions in the early 1970s, Bolles, an Episcopal minister himself, repeatedly implores job hunters to seek God's will in their search or to make sure their job is a divine calling. Yet in the 1982 edition and for several succeeding years, the word "calling" cannot be found in the text. Then in 1988, a high point for the public expression of conservative Christianity (the year that Pat Robertson founds the Christian Coalition and runs for president), Bolles reintroduces religion into the job hunting process in a major way. A line from the 1988 edition reads,

> Your mission here on Earth is . . . **to seek out and find, in daily—even hourly—communication, the One from who your Mission is derived.** *The Missioner before the Mission,* is the rule. In religious language, your Mission here is: *to know God, and enjoy Him forever, and to see His hand in all His works.*[65]

McGee's full comments on Bolles's suspiciously selective moments of religious conviction are as follows:

> Bolles's decision to reintroduce and emphasize the Christian content of *Parachute* during the height of Christian fundamentalism of the late 1980s offers an example of how responsive the advice literature is to cultural trends, yet it also demonstrates the persistence of the traditional idea of calling or mission across two centuries. The seemingly secular literatures of calling and vocation are grounded in longstanding Christian thinking regarding work as a reflection of God's will.[66]

True enough on both of her points. However, left behind are questions that need asking; questions that take Bolles's theology into account. What is Bolles's idea of God, and how does this idea function in his attempt to help readers find jobs or change careers? How is one supposed to reconcile "the Missioner's" grand plan for each individual with the fact that career changes occur rather frequently? What are the theological implications of Bolles dampening the God talk for years and then reviving it at opportunistic junctures? In other words, how does Bolles's theology shed light on his overall self-help message in the book?

In her defense, McGee is a sociologist whose goal for her own book is to illuminate the social and political implications for self-help literature. Theological questions are understandably, perhaps deliberately, avoided by her. Yet asking these questions of Bolles's implicit or explicit theology would add another wrinkle to the belabored self thus expanding the number of factors that contribute to and perhaps assuage the insecurities that self-help books seek to lessen.

The cultural turn approach to self-help literature is better equipped to respond to a concept like vocation as presented in such literature than either the overdetermined theological approach of Wells or the a-theological approach of McGee, though admittedly, it will veer farther away from Wells than McGee. It reckons with the theological seriousness that animates Wells's lamentation of the hijacking of Evangelical theology. Yet it exposes his reluctance to detach certain theological concepts from an immutable divine foundation as unjustifiable. The idea of God, as it impinges on the meaning and function of calling language in certain Christian self-help books, cannot be overlooked in any study of such books. Specifically, the religious content of Christian self-help literature cannot be detached from the meaning and application of concepts like vocation when using them to advance a political argument, as McGee does. But as these two approaches to self-help literature reveal, it is difficult to integrate theology with politics without being ham-fisted or negligent. How, then, do theology and the political come together in a concept like vocation?

POLITICAL THEOLOGY OF WORK

As we saw in the introductory chapter, political theology attempts to establish the conditions for a relationship between theology and politics in a postsecular world. William T. Cavanaugh and Peter Scott enumerate three different ways in which scholars connect the political and theological. With the first approach, the political and the theological occupy separate domains. Augustine's two cities and Luther's two kingdoms exemplify the hierarchical structure that informs it. The state and the political dynamics of civic society are acknowledged as real but separate from theological discourse. Yet while the things of God occupy a different room than those political, both live in the same house and hence can and must talk in order for a political theology to materialize. Given this relationship, "[t]he task of political theology might be to relate religious belief to larger societal issues while not confusing the proper autonomy of each."[67]

The second type of political theology similarly maintains a distance between theology and politics, but that distance is not metaphysical. Here, political theologians come at the stuff of theology and politics from a more Marxist perspective (though it cannot be reduced to this) in that the relationship between politics and religion is mapped onto a base-superstructure schema. Theology is a reflection, at times a reproduction, of the base, which is the political economy. Therefore, political theology is that which recognizes theology as derivative while it tentatively seeks to justify theological assessments in light of just political arrangements or retrofit theological assessments in light of unjust ones. Here, "[t]he task of political theology might then be to expose the ways in which theological discourse reproduces inequalities of class, gender or race, and to reconstruct theology so that it severs the cause of justice."[68]

The third option for political theology is distinguished from the first two by virtue of a lack of distance between theology and politics—they "are essentially the same activities." Or both theological systems and political arrangements are believed to be constructed with the same materials and merely possess nominal differences. Hence recourse to either an apolitical theology (option 1) or to a theology as derivative of the political economy (option 2) is foreclosed. What is left for the analyst is the discovering of ways that "the political" is also "the theological" and vice versa. The task of this type of political theologian "then might become one of the exposing the false theologies underlying supposedly 'secular' politics and promoting the true politics implicit in a true theology."[69]

The first option for a political theology, which relates the theological to the political as ontologically separate discourses, largely ignores the cultural embeddedness of theological endeavors. It takes problems that stem from political arrangements with utmost seriousness but posits a theological response to political and economic matters. For instance, Jürgen Moltmann's theological challenge to ecological degradation at the hands of corporations is proffered only after a thorough reckoning of the situation on the ground. The State plays an essential role in curbing the effects of industry on the environment. However, he claims that good public policy towards the environment is derivative of God's law.[70] So while political institutions are needed instruments for change, the distance between the political and the theological enables Moltmann's God to engage the world from above *and* underwrite any proper political activity. God acts directly and indirectly in the shaping of political arrangements for the purposes of furthering justice in human relations, but Moltmann's God is free from cultural modification. Hence it is difficult to see where Moltmann's theology can gain traction in the fight for economic and political justice when he does not admit of earlier, more formative interactions between all ideas of God and their cultural contexts.

If distance between religion and politics defines the terms of the first option, proximity is the hallmark of the third. Operating on the assumption that "theology and politics are essentially similar activities," the third option leaves little space between the two in which causal relations either descriptive (Weber) or prescriptive (Marx, Freud) can be established. That said, one might justifiably contend that classifying theology and politics as superstructure and base, as is a possibility with the second option, only distorts a much more complex reality. However, if this contention is predicated on the mutual embeddedness of theology and politics, on what ground can one "expose the false theologies underlying supposedly 'secular' politics" or better yet, promote a "true politics implicit in a true theology" without differentiating the two realms in order to reach higher ground? Admittedly, inquiries that look for the theological in political arrangements or for the political in theologies can yield useful insights, as Carl Schmitt's work demonstrates.[71] Yet viewing the stuff of politics and religion as animated by essentially the same sources blurs meaningful distinctions between the two, thus largely eliminating the possibility of mutual critique—a central objective of my project.[72]

Cavanaugh and Scott's second type of political theology cannot but admit of the cultural embeddedness of theology—theology as reproduction and reflection of the material conditions of life betrays its relationship to material culture. Yet political theology need not take theology as wholly derivative and determined by the material base. The first suspicion that theology, like all cultural products, reflects the interests of the materially and political powerful is tempered by the ability of theological products to simultaneously reflect and guide *just* material and political arrangements that make up the base.[73] Here, political theology must recognize the impact of materiality on the content of theology. Yet because of this recognition, theological products are suited to reengage less-than-just material conditions in a critical, albeit measured, way.

This second option for political theology serves my project in two ways. First, in dealing with current manifestations of vocation as expressed through Christian self-help literature, the true beneficiaries of such manifestations can be more readily exposed as well as the meaning of vocation that is being used. In much Christian self-help literature, the meaning and function of vocation language departs significantly from Luther's language. While it is important to bracket off judgment as to whether the change in meaning serves or damages some kind of "true meaning" of vocation, it does not serve us to bracket off causal connections between the interests of those being served by expressions of vocation in self-help literature and the expressions themselves. Recognition of these kinds of ties leads to a clearer understanding of not only the current meaning of the term in popular parlance but also indicates the functional role of the concept of vocation for the readers of Christian self-help literature. Hence connecting the theological component of vocation to the interests of those in power who benefit by the circulation and use of the concept of vocation expressed in this literature is the primary means by which these popular expressions can be comprehended.

Two, with the focus squarely on the material context that produces theological concepts, any reworked concept of vocation will be one that can quickly respond to the material context, if need be. If a vocation is in fact able to confront unjust workplace politics, it does so not by entering the workplace from a privileged position but by closely attending to the conditions that shape vocations in a more ideal context. The theological component of a vocation plays a necessary role in its ability to align just working conditions with God's will, whether the theology behind certain concepts of vocation engages working conditions or not.

Indeed, the Protestant history of the concept of vocation does present us with several instances of direct confrontation with the nature and conditions of work. As stated earlier, these are based on a conception of God and humanity that, when treated as culturally contextualized ideas and then appropriated for modern contexts, carry unique and powerful norms into the workplace where such an ethos for workplace justice is absent or impotent to bring about change. Political theology, in this case, is still bound to a base/superstructure model but one that is not wholly unidirectional. A vocation is necessarily dependent on material culture. Yet it can boomerang back on the political economy carrying with it not a-historical ties to God's call but norms that merge its theological imperatives with liberal conceptions of democracy and justice.

As it stands today, the commonly used concept of vocation is unable to include political considerations in its push to make the working experience satisfactory for those who believe that their work should be vocational. In the next chapter, I look at work and vocation from a cultural, historical perspective as I inquire into one primary reason for vocation's current political impotence: the depoliticizing effects of consumer culture on work and, by extension, vocations.

NOTES

1. This development is now well known, but was introduced by Van Harvey in a well-known article. Van Harvey, "On the Intellectual Marginality of American Theology," in *Religion and Twentieth Century American Intellectual Life*, ed. Michael J. Lacey (New York: Cambridge University Press, 1989).
2. See Kathryn Tanner, *Theories of Culture: A New Agenda for Theology* (Minneapolis: Augsburg Press, 1997), 25–37.
3. Delwin Brown, "Refashioning Self and Other: Theology, Academy, and the New Ethnography," in *Converging on Culture*, ed. Delwin Brown, Sheila Greeve Davaney and Kathryn Tanner (Oxford: Oxford University Press, 2001), 41–42.
4. Ted A. Smith, "Redeeming Critique: Resignations to the Cultural Turn in Christian Theology and Ethics," *Journal of the Society of Christian Ethics* 24, 2 (2004): 91.
5. Smith, 90.
6. For examples see David F. Wells, *No Place for Truth or Whatever Happened to Evangelical Theology?* (Grand Rapids: Eerdmans, 1993); John Milbank, Graham Ward and Catherine Pickstock, "Suspending the Material: The Turn of Radical Orthodoxy," in *Radical Orthodoxy*, ed. John Milbank, Graham Ward and Catherine Pickstock (London: Routledge, 1998), 1–20.
7. For an example see David Tracy, *On Naming the Present: Reflections on God, Hermeneutics, and Church* (Maryknoll, NY: Orbis, 1994).
8. For an example see Don Cupitt, *Taking Leave of God* (London: SCM-Canterbury Press, 2001).
9. Smith, 90.
10. Kathryn Tanner, *Economy of Grace* (Minneapolis: Augsburg Fortress, 2005), 7.
11. Tanner, 2, 26–27.
12. Darrell Cosden, *The Heavenly Good of Earthly Work* (Milton Keynes, UK: Paternoster, 2006), 13–14.
13. Cosden, 14.
14. Cosden, 16.
15. Cosden, 70–77.
16. Cosden, 71.
17. Cosden, 108.
18. Cosden, 147.
19. Cosden, 147.
20. Cosden, 148.
21. Cosden, 113, 122.
22. Jensen, x.
23. Jensen, x.
24. Jensen, 103.
25. Jensen, 41.
26. Jensen, 93.
27. Jensen, 93.
28. Jensen, 93.
29. Jensen, 103.
30. Cosden, 123.
31. Jensen, 99.
32. See http://www.vatican.va/holy_father/leo_xiii/encyclicals/documents/hf_l-xiii_enc_15051891_rerum-novarum_en.html.
33. From Second Vatican Ecumenical Council as quoted in John Paul II, *Laborem exercens*, On Human Work on the Nineteeth Anniversary of *Rerum Novarum*, Catholic-

Pages Website, June 8, 2011, http://www.catholic-pages.com/documents/laborem_exercens.pdf, 52.

34. John Paul II, 51.

35. Armand Larive, *After Sunday: A Theology of Work* (New York: Continuum, 2004), 4.

36. Larive, 105.

37. Larive, 4.

38. Three of Larive's eight chapters are based on Volf's description of the Trinity. The Son is "eschatological," the Father/Mother is "protological," and the Holy Spirit is "pneumatological." These designations help Larive relate the Godhead to human work as an act of co-creation. The Christ-event is a new break in history of the created world that then legitimizes our own work as another "new action" as co-creators in the ongoing act of creation. The Father/Mother is the "Uncreated Creator" who, through the original act of creation, provides the foundation, the working materials and the maintenance of creation for our work to act as co-creation. And the Spirit animates our work on the ground through our use of skill at work and a rapport that is needed between workers in order for co-creation to occur. See Larive, 73–126.

39. Larive, 122–23.

40. Larive, 115–16.

41. Larive, 124–25.

42. Larive, 126.

43. Larive cites I John 4:1–5 that admonishes us to "test the spirits" as his justification to ascribe workplace abuses to spirits that do damage. Larive, 112.

44. Wendy Simonds, *Women and Self-Help Culture: Reading between the Lines* (New Brunswick, NJ: Rutgers University Press, 1992), 7.

45. Simonds, 223–24.

46. Examples this kind of appropriation include Parker J. Palmer, *Let Your Life Speak: Listening for the Voice of Vocation* (San Francisco: Jossey-Bass, 2000); Herbert Alphonso, Sheila Fabricant Linn, Matthew Linn and Dennis Linn, *Discovering Your Personal Vocation: The Search for Meaning Through the Spiritual Exercises* (Matwah, NJ: Paulist Press, 2001); Noel Tyl, *Vocations: The New Midheaven Extension Process* (Woodbury, MN: Llewellyn Press, 2006); Gregg Michael Levoy, *Callings: Finding and Following an Authentic Life* (New York: Three Rivers Press, 1997).

47. Stephen R. Covey, *The 8th Habit: From Effectiveness to Greatness* (New York: Free Press, 2004), 72.

48. See Joyce Meyer, *Battlefield of Your Mind: Winning the Battle in Your Mind* (New York: Warner Books, 1995); Nancy Leigh DeMoss, *Lies Women Believe: And the Truth That Sets Them Free* (Chicago: Moody Press, 2001); M. Scott Peck, *The Road Less Traveled: Spiritual Growth in an Age of Anxiety* (New York: Simon and Schuster, 1978); Stephen R. Covey, *The Seven Habits of Highly Effective People* (New York: Simon and Schuster, 1989).

49. See John MacArthur, *Ashamed of the Gospel: When the Church Becomes Like the World* (Wheaton, IL: Crossway Books, 2001); Nathan Busenitz, "A Sense of Purpose: Evaluating the Claims of *The Purpose-Driven Life*," In *Fool's Gold*, ed. John MacArthur (Wheaton, IL: Crossway, 2004); Os Guiness, *Dining with the Devil: The Megachurch Movement Flirts with Modernity* (Grand Rapids: Baker Books, 1993). For a more nuanced stance towards Christian self-help literature, see Joanna and Alister McGrath, *Self-Esteem: The Cross and Christian Confidence* (Wheaton, IL: Crossway, 2002). Even though the McGraths take a more conciliatory stance on the self-help movement (they cite some therapeutic benefits of it), they conclude their book with the judgment that problems with self-esteem can only be solved with faith in the work of Christ, as detailed scripturally.

50. John Eldredge, *Wild at Heart: Discovering the Secret of a Man's Soul* (Nashville: Thomas Nelson, 2001), 127.

51. Daniel Gillespie, "Roaming Wild: Investigating the Message in *Wild at Heart*, " in *Fool's Gold*, ed. John MacArthur (Wheaton, IL: Crossway, 2004), 93.

52. Gillespie, 82.

53. David F. Wells, *God in the Wasteland: The Reality of Truth in a World of Fading Dreams* (Grand Rapids, MI: Eerdmans, 1994), 47.

54. Wells, *God in the Wasteland*, 47.

55. Wells, *No Place for Truth* (Grand Rapids, MI: Eerdmans, 1994), 98.

56. Wells, *No Place for Truth*, 99.

57. Wells, *Above All Earthly Pow ' rs* (Grand Rapids, MI: Eerdmans, 2005), 18.

58. Wells, *Above All Earthly Pow ' rs*, 101.

59. See Philip Rieff, *The Triumph of the Therapeutic: Uses of Faith after Freud* (New York: Harper Torchbooks, 1966); Christopher Lasch, *The Culture of Narcissism: American Life in an Age of Diminishing Expectations* (New York: W. W. Norton, 1978); David Riesman, *The Lonely Crowd: A Study of Changing American Character* (New Haven: Yale University Press, 1961).

60. An example of such an investigation is ironically where Wells get the title for one his books, *No Place for Grace* by T. J. Jackson Lears. Lears, like Wells, locates some of the sources of the self emergent in the early twentieth century that begins to rely more heavily on self-actualization as the means to "salvation." In contrast to Wells, however, Lears does not conflate the meaning of such a development, such as judging that advertising is inherently manipulative of such selves, with all of the factors that contribute to the development. Hence he refuses to deduce from an emerging therapeutic ethos the whole of the social context that produced it. Lears writes, "Advertising cannot be considered in isolation. Its role in promoting a consumer culture can only be understood within a network of institutional, religious, and psychological changes. . . . The coming of the therapeutic ethos was a modern historical development, shaped by the turmoil of the turn of the century." T. J. Jackson Lears, "From Salvation to Self-Realization: Advertising and the Therapeutic Roots of the Consumer Culture, 1880–1930," in *The Culture of Consumption*, ed. Richard Wightman Fox and T. J. Jackson Lears (New York: Pantheon, 1983), 3–4. The turmoil that Lears refers to is largely the result of grand alterations in both social relations and religious worldviews. "Feelings of unreality stemmed from urbanization and technological development; from the rise of an increasingly interdependent market economy; and from the secularization of liberal Protestantism among its educated and affluent devotees." Lears, 6. All were factors in the formation of the therapeutic ethos around this time in American history and for this reason, cannot be separated from any interpretation of the self, either then or now. See also Lears, *No Place of Grace: Antimodernism and the Transformation of American Culture, 1880–1920* (New York: Pantheon, 1981), 5–6, 32–33.

61. Micki McGee, *Self-Help, Inc.: Makeover Culture in American Life* (Oxford: Oxford University Press, 2005), 24.

62. McGee, 16.

63. McGee, 15.

64. Richard Nelson Bolles, *What Color Is Your Parachute? 2011: A Practical Manual for Job Hunters and Career Changers* (Berkeley: Ten Speed Press, 2010).

65. Bolles, 1988 ed., 295–96. (boldface and italics his)

66. McGee, 120.

67. William T. Cavanaugh and Peter Scott, *The Blackwell Companion to Political Theology*, eds. Peter Scott and William T. Cavanaugh (Malden, MA: Blackwell, 2007), 3.

68. Cavanaugh, 3.

69. Cavanaugh, 3.

70. Jürgen Moltmann, *God for a Secular Society: The Public Relevance of Theology* (Minneapolis: Fortress Press, 1999), 111–12.

71. See Carl Schmitt, *Political Theology: Four Chapters on the Concept of Sovereignty* (Chicago: University of Chicago Press, 2006).

72. Michael Hollerich notes that Schmitt's work "was not to be understood as a form of ideology critique to unmask religious and theological constructs as subservient to and derivative from legal and political ones (or of social and economic ones, either). The connection between the two spheres was 'consistent and radical,' but not

directly causal." Michael Hollerich, "Carl Schmitt," in *The Blackwell Companion to Political Theology*, eds. Peter Scott and William T. Cavanaugh (Malden, MA: Blackwell, 2007), 111.

73. This modification of the second option draws on Antonio Gramsci's concept of hegemony that allows for a two-way street between the base and superstructure.

THREE
Consumer Culture and Its Effects

From the time of the Reformation to the present, the relationship between work and humanity has largely operated under a *homo faber* or a "human, the maker" anthropology. It rests on the idea that human identity is forged through what one produces and how one relates to the materials of production.[1] Likewise, the meaning of Protestant vocations has drawn on a *homo faber* anthropology since Luther. However in the last century, especially in the West, work as that which produces has been replaced by that which prioritizes the consumption of products over the production of them. Consequently vocations, while once engaged with the work that was informed by a culture of production, are now constructed in accordance with the *homo consumens*.

Of course, people still produce things at work, especially if we consider services as a product. The ascendency of consumption represents not so much a grand alteration in the nature of work itself or in the time spent working but more a shift in the way we orient ourselves to work and to a vocation. Because the conceptual structure of vocation is (or should be) supported by the way we view work and how we feel about it, the transition from production to consumption is crucial to the understanding of modern vocations. In fact, a tracking of the movement from a society organized around production to a society organized around consumption is a historical/cultural companion piece to our theological history of vocation. It will show what theologies of vocation had to adjust to when work was centered on production as well as how they operate today in a consumer culture.

It must be said that it is not assumed that consumer culture is the only context that shapes the meaning of vocation today for the simple reason that consumer culture itself is not fully determinative of the contours of the cultural landscape.[2] I choose to examine the impact of consumer culture on work and vocation in part because mine is a conceptual analysis of vocation, and the impact that consumer culture has on the meaning and application of ideas, as plastic and manipulatable as they are, cannot be overstated.

Mike Featherstone identifies three main ways to understand consumer culture. The first is the economic perspective, or more generally, the material perspective. Here, consumer culture is taken to be the result of the expansion of capitalist commodity production. Cheaper goods combine with effective mass advertising to make consumption easy and empowering for the consumer. Second is the sociological view that sees consumer culture as *the* crucible in which social bonds are forged, broken, conceived, and lived through. Not only are personal relationships, both real and imaginary, indicators of the effects of consumer culture, but also institutions that help fasten social bonds. Third is the psychological perspective that focuses on cognitive patterns that shed light on the desires and decision making that feeds and is fed by consumer culture.[3]

I opt for the sociological view because it provides the most appropriate means to connect work and vocations with consumer culture.[4] The strength of a vocation is built and sustained by the bonds that hold an individual to his or her job, to fellow employees, to the boss, and to the kind of work one does. Hence, scholars who are attuned to the means by which consumer culture transforms these relationships add valuable contributions to the study of vocation. This contribution is manifested in two ways. One, the shift from a society organized around production to that of consumption parallels the shift in the meaning of vocation over this same time frame. Two, the casting of consumer culture in social terms supports and helps to explain how vocations became objects of consumption themselves. My use of the socio-cultural perspective is not to dismiss politics, the economy, technology, or psychology as relevant factors; all have been important in the development of a consumer culture and offer valuable interpretative grids. Yet the goal of elucidating the current appropriation of vocation requires an analytical framework that is most closely tied to the form and function of vocations.

CONSUMER INSATIABILITY

Cultural historian T. J. Jackson Lears uses a hyperbolic comment by Virginia Woolf in 1910 in which she claimed that "human character changed." She sensed the beginnings of a breakdown of more stable cultural institutions that was manifesting itself in a fragmented cultural reality. Lears interprets the reasons for Woolf's reaction:

> In the United States as elsewhere, the bourgeois ethos had enjoined perpetual work, compulsive saving, civic responsibility, and a rigid morality of self-denial. By the early twentieth century that outlook had

begun to give way to a new set of values sanctioning periodic leisure, compulsive spending, apolitical passivity, and apparently permissive (but subtly coercive) morality of individual fulfillment. The older culture was suited to a production-oriented society of small entrepreneurs; the newer culture epitomized a consumption-oriented society dominated by bureaucratic corporations.[5]

How the production-oriented society gave way to a consumption-oriented society can be seen in the changing modes of production that greased the wheels for consumption to become a way of life—not just an activity. The question of exactly how this shift occurred needs to be answered before describing the results of the shift and its influence on the concept of vocation.

On a basic level, production and consumption of goods can be thought of as two sides of the same coin. Responding to the market, production feeds consumption, and consumption dictates what and how much is produced in symbiotic fashion. However, capitalistic economies have tended to emphasize one over the other at different times in an effort to grow the economy. And scholars have similarly emphasized one over the other in order to elucidate the current economic milieu. In the mid-nineteenth century, Karl Marx puts forth one such proposal in which he relies on the production of commodities as the foundation for an economy over consumption.[6] Instead of consumption being the result of rational calculation which then influences production (the prevailing classical view), Marx problematizes the relationship between production and consumption through an analysis of the entity that binds both activities: the commodity.

The commodity appears to us as something other than what it really is. The way a commodity primarily expresses itself in the market is through its relationship to the prices of other commodities. Marx claims that the commodity is fetishized in this way. It *appears* as mere exchange value, yet its true value, as given by the social character of the labor that went into the production of the commodity, is concealed.[7] Of course Marx goes on to critique capitalist production after his gambit, yet on a more limited level and perhaps unintentionally, he helps establish a new role for consumption in capitalist societies. With his unmasking of the fetish-quality of commodities, Marx opens up lines of thought that begin to move objects of consumption into the realm of culture; a culture that can continue the fetishization of the commodity by amplifying the added meaning given to it—not just as an object of the satisfaction of needs based solely on the rational calculation of the consumer.[8]

Thorstein Veblen expands on the implications of Marx's analysis to argue for the role of consumption in the construction of social classes. Writing just before the turn of the twentieth century, Veblen claims that "conspicuous consumption" is not simply motivated by the use of a commodity's intrinsic use value, but it is consumption for the purpose of showing wealth, which in turn reflects a higher social status and acts to stratify society on these grounds. The "pecuniary strength," as he calls it, of the consumer is the level of wealth as expressed by the kind and amount of consumer goods purchased. The leisure class is on top of the peak of pecuniary strength as such, the envied class that many strive to emulate through consumption.[9] In other words, keeping up with the Joneses through conspicuous consumption occurs apart from any intrinsic use value of the commodity; the value of the commodity is now primarily symbolic. Hence, the satisfaction gained from the consumption of certain luxury consumer goods adds another variable into the cost/benefit analysis of neoclassical economics. However, the measurability of such a benefit is made more complex because Veblen's commodities have now entered the symbolic world; they are now powerful cultural artifacts.

Veblen's argument further expands the scope of consumption in important ways. He gives language and theory to a burgeoning consumer culture in America. His notion of consumer goods outruns sheer material utility—commodities have the ability to socialize us. Hence, his expansion of the power of commodities to mediate social relations yields more far-reaching social effects of consumption over those of production. Yet the line drawn from conspicuous consumption to the current role of consumption in contemporary consumer culture is not necessarily a straight one.

In his study of the origins of consumer culture, sociologist Colin Campbell cites the contributions of Veblen's work as a needed corrective to the utilitarian calculus of consumer behavior. Though Campbell notes that the placement of conspicuous consumption as the stage following "consumption as satisfaction of basic needs" leaves out some necessary intermediate stages. The sudden appearance of the desire to "one-up" one's neighbor through consumption has more sources than Veblen cites, and more time is needed to develop conspicuous consumption than he allows. In addition, it is unclear to Campbell whether the desire for elevated social status is connected to consumption at all, for Veblen himself does not connect the two satisfactorily.[10]

Campbell's problem with Veblen translates into the problem of connecting conspicuous consumption and today's consumer culture. If consumer desire is reduced to the emulation of others, then this may explain some motivations of the current consumer, but it cannot fully account for how many of today's fashion trends often originate from lower rather than higher social strata, for instance.[11] Neither do the needs satisfied by conspicuous consumption match up with those of our current consumer culture. Campbell alternatively defines the character of contemporary consumer behavior as

> an activity which involves an apparently endless pursuit of wants; the most characteristic feature of modern consumption being this insatia-

bility . . . which arises out of a basic inexhaustibility of wants themselves, which forever arise, phoenix-like, from the ashes of their predecessors. Hence no sooner is one satisfied than another is waiting in line clamoring to be satisfied; when this one is attended to, a third appears, then subsequently a fourth, and so on, apparently without end. The process is ceaseless and unbroken; rarely can an inhabitant of modern society, no matter how privileged or wealthy, declare that there is nothing that they want.[12]

Or as Jean Baudrillard, in an early essay on consumption, states in different terms, if consumption

was a function of the order of needs, we should achieve satisfaction. But we know that this is not the case: we want to consume more and more. This compulsion to consume is not the consequence of some psychological determinant, etc., nor is it simply the power of emulation. If consumption appears to be irrepressible, this is precisely because it is a total idealist practice which has no longer anything to do (beyond a certain point) with the satisfaction of needs, nor with the reality principle; it becomes energized in the project that is always dissatisfied and implicit in the object.[13]

Campbell contends and Baudrillard would agree that consumer insatiability far exceeds (infinitely so) the need to be conspicuously wealthy. Veblen's conception of conspicuous consumption does move consumer goods into the symbolic realm, but it still circumscribes the meaning of consumer goods as supplied by social norms—the Joneses stand as an unmovable embodiment of the final satisfaction of needs, even if those needs can never be met. And in turn, the embodiment constitutes the "home" in which needs ultimately remain needs—that is, desires that are *possible* to satisfy. For Campbell, the circuit of need and satisfaction of need assumed by Veblen remains one that, in theory, is closed and thus is not explanatory of open-ended consumer insatiability.

Campbell locates the origins of consumer insatiability, which spread outward from Europe in the early to mid-nineteenth century, at the nexus of a hedonistic spirit of the Romantic era and the cold, impersonal reality of the Industrial Age. By "hedonism" he means the seeking of pleasure for its own sake. In contrast to the satisfaction of needs realized by the consumption of material goods, Campbell asserts that the realization of pleasure can happen *without* the consumption of material goods. Needs and their satisfaction

relate to a state of being and its disturbance, followed by action to restore the original equilibrium. Hence a state of need is a state of deprivation, in which one lacks something necessary to maintain a given condition of existence, and realization of this leads to exploratory activity in the environment in order to find whatever is capable of remedying this lack.[14]

The satisfaction of needs through consumption has a clear end: a state of equilibrium. In contrast to the satisfaction of needs, pleasure, as the experience of a satisfied desire

> is not a state of being so much as a quality of experience. Not properly in itself a type of sensation, pleasure is a term used to identify our favourable reaction to certain patterns of sensation. . . . [The satisfaction of needs is] being "pushed" from within to act so as to restore a disturbed equilibrium, whilst [the attainment of pleasure] implies one of being "pulled" from without in order to experience greater stimulation.[15]

Being "pulled from without" exposes desire to a virtually unlimited amount of sensations from which to derive pleasure.

The upshot of the hedonistic spirit in the industrial era is that consumption now relies less and less on material items as mediators and more on the anticipation of their future consumption.[16] These experiences provide a different kind of satisfaction. Untethered to material objects or even the external world, consumption can now be self-perpetuating as it is beholden only to the boundless individual imagination and desire. Campbell sums it up:

> The inexhaustibility of wants which characterizes the behaviour of modern consumers has to be understood as deriving from their permanent desiring mode, something which, in turn, stems from the inevitable gap between the perfected pleasures of the dream and the imperfect joys of reality. No matter what the nature of the dream or, indeed, of reality, the discrepancy between them gives rise to a continuing longing, from which specific desires repeatedly spring.[17]

In order for consumer culture to fuel consumer insatiability, it must be able to transcend the kind of consumption with measured ends or the consumption that can actually satisfy once and for all.

LIQUID MODERNITY

The sociologist Zygmunt Bauman crafts a useful metaphorical dynamic that conveys the social ramifications of consumer insatiability. He describes the social bonds that hold consumer society together as *liquid* and the bonds of the society organized around production as *solid*. Solid modernity refers loosely to what most call "modernity" that begins with the Enlightenment and ends around the mid-twentieth century. Liquid modernity is a later stage of modernity beginning roughly in the mid-twentieth century up to the present.[18] The bonds that were solid but have melted or are in the process of melting are

> the bonds which interlock individual choices in collective projects and actions—the patterns of communications and co-ordination between

individually conducted life policies on the one hand and political actions of human collectivities on the other.[19]

Generally speaking, the solid social bonds that have melted are ones that *used* to tie individual choices and desires to traditional social institutions such as the family or church or even ideologies, such as Marxism, nationalism, Fordism, phallocentrism, colonialism, or the ideology of the self-made man. Hence solid societies were able to lock individuals into long-term projects and stable belief systems through institutions, thus making the choices and desires that related to them more permanent, durable, and with an end in sight. Alternatively, liquidity suggests malleability, speed, and weightlessness. Hence, liquid social bonds are able to adapt to given social environments by "spilling into" social spaces as well as "flowing around" obstinate relics left over from solid modernity.[20]

Bauman claims that, on the surface, solid modernity could well be understood as a self-destructive project because it undertook a grand melting of the old solids, such as institutional religion, monarchies and dictatorships, remnants of feudalism, and rigid class structures. However it then quickly replaced these with new solids. Marx's famous line that under capitalism "all that is solid melts into air" was not meant to assign a destiny for capitalism that allows it to melt all things for all time. Communism was a replacement solid intended to be fire-proof. As such Bauman uses the term "solid" to describe this phase of modernity because the melting of solids was meant "to replace the inherited set of deficient and defective 'solids' with another set of 'solids,' which was much improved and preferably perfect, and for that reason no longer alterable."[21] More specifically,

> [m]elting the solids meant first and foremost shedding the "irrelevant" obligations standing in the way of rational calculation of effect; as Max Weber put it, liberating business enterprise from the shackles of the family-household duties and from the dense tissue of ethical obligations . . . leaving solely the "cash nexus" of the many bonds underlying human mutuality and mutual responsibilities.[22]

A new sense of liberation emerged with the loosening of the grip held by traditional institutions which was then followed by the strengthening of capitalism's grip. The new re-embedded arrangement that individuals found themselves in was, "more 'solid' than the orders it replaced, because—unlike them—it was immune to the challenge from non-economic action."[23] Therefore, the motivations of the revolutionaries that ushered in solid modernity were not iconoclastic alone, but constructive too—this time with better building materials.

The new edifices were believed to be able to parry the blows of old solids with reinforced social bonds. The bond between the society and the state that would supposedly occur when social classes are no more (as promised by communism)[24] or the bond forged between the rational bureaucracy and employee (under Fordism),[25] served to assemble stronger bonds between people, and institutions are reinforced in the process. According to Bauman, solid modernity engaged its members in their capacity as producers, and the time needed to produce a product as well as the actual finished product itself act as tangible entities which set parameters, benchmarks, and norms for life.

> Life organized around the producer's role tends to be normatively regulated. There is a bottom line to what one needs in order to stay alive and be capable of doing whatever the producer's role may require, but also an upper limit to what one may dream of, desire and pursue. . . . Whatever rises above that limit is a luxury, and desiring luxury is a sin.[26]

The space that the producer moves in is delimited normatively by what are considered proper needs. Bodily needs that must be satisfied in order to produce goods establish the lower limit. To not satisfy these needs constitutes a violation of one's identity as producer because one cannot produce if they are not met. The upper limit is drawn by a producer culture that encourages the transcending of the mere means of survival via desires and the consumption that can satisfy them. Producer culture is hemmed in on the lower level by the concrete means to produce, and consumption is limited at the top by necessity. To consume beyond what is needed to produce is sinful because luxuries are unnecessary for production. Desire is subordinated to survival.

In contrast, liquid, consumer society puts desire first, which means that the norms that monitored the upper limits in producer society are ineffective and/or removed altogether. Generalized desire, without solid boundaries to keep it in check, flows like liquid into all spaces and expects satisfaction that can come only from consumption. Reaffirming Campbell's notion of consumer insatiability, Bauman writes:

> Life organized around consumption . . . must do without norms: it is guided by seduction, ever rising desires and volatile wishes—no longer by normative regulations. No particular "Joneses" offer a reference point for one's own successful life; a society of consumers is one of universal comparison—and the sky is the only limit.[27]

While solid replaced solid in societies organized around production, in liquid or fluid modernity, melted social bonds remain liquid.

> The solids whose turn has come to be thrown into the melting pot and which are in the process of being melted at the present time, the time of fluid modernity, are the bonds which interlock individual choices in collective projects and actions.[28]

In the culture of liquid modernity, the "interlocking" bond between individual choice and collective projects has been melted, leaving individual choice unhinged from any binding authority. The insatiability that drives consumer culture is permitted to flourish in this environment. Liquid modern society is consumer society.

> Liquid life is consuming life. It casts the world and all its animate and inanimate fragments as objects of consumption: That is, objects that lose their usefulness (and so their luster, attraction, seductive power and worth) in the course of being used. It shapes the judging and evaluating of all the animate and inanimate fragments of the world after the pattern of objects of consumption.[29]

Bauman does not restrict these fragments of life to inanimate objects of consumption that relate to the basic needs of producer society. "Animate fragments" include other people, belief systems, and life projects that have become objects of consumption. All of these animate objects can be consumed like inanimate ones: decide on the fitting object, consume, discard waste, and then begin the search anew.

When individual choice fueled by desire is the primary source of decision and action in a society, life projects, worldviews, and even personal relationships cannot be restrictive so as to eliminate the ability to choose a more enticing alternative. Liquid life, as it were, runs around obstacles, settles on appealing situations, consumer goods, and worldviews only to stream out quickly in search of newer and better versions of what was just left behind. This pattern of consumption is able to continue without challenge in a consumer culture because of a lack of social accountability.

> What sets the members of consumer society apart from their ancestors is the emancipation of consumption from its past instrumentality that used to draw its limits—the demise of "norms" and the new plasticity of "needs," setting consumption free from functional bonds and absolving it from the need to justify itself by reference to anything but its own pleasurability. In the consumer society, consumption is its own purpose and so is self-propelling.[30]

As opposed consumption being the means to another end, the act of consuming is a never-ending end in itself.

If liquid lives can pour themselves into any social space and vacate when consumer desire gives the signal, is critique of it or any feature of consumer culture possible? If ideas are now commodities, from where can a critique of consumer culture stand, if anywhere? Bauman, throughout his numerous books on the social implications of consumer culture, rarely offers value judgments; consumer culture just is, as producer culture was.[31] If we are all now mere interpreters of culture, our fate seems sealed. The integration of Bauman's general contention here and his assessment of liquid consumer culture gives the appearance of a total foreclosure of the possibility of cultural transcendence.

Yet in several of his works on consumer culture, Bauman expands his matter-of-fact description of consumer culture into a discussion of the social effects of such a culture. Here, Bauman contends that the benefits of consumer culture, that of individuals being able to choose from an infinite number of options, does not extend to all equally. A precondition of full participation in consumer culture is the minimal requirement that it is *possible* that desire can be satisfied under the terms given by consumer culture. For the poorest classes in the West, this is not possible. They are "flawed consumers," not so much because of financial inability to consume but because the poor are unable to choose freely amongst consumer items.[32]

> To meet the social norm, to be a fully-fledged member of society, one needs to respond promptly and efficiently to the temptations of the consumer market; one needs to contribute to the "supply-clearing demand" and in case of economic trouble be part of the "consumer-led recovery." All this the poor, lacking decent income, credit cards and the prospect of a better time, are not fit to do. Accordingly, the norm which is broken by the poor of today, the norm of the breaking of which makes them "abnormal," is the norm of consumer competence or aptitude, not that of employment. First and foremost, the poor of today are "non-consumers," not "unemployed"; they are defined in the first place through being flawed consumers, since the most crucial of the social duties which they do not fulfill is that of being active and effective buyers of the goods and services the market offers.[33]

Unable to participate as functioning consumers, the poor are true outcasts. In a producer society, employment was the ticket for entrance into the game played by functioning members of that society. In a consumer society, it is the ability to consume that qualifies participants. Again, because the object of consumption is subordinated to the ability to choose itself, it is the fact that the poorest in a liquid society are barred from choosing freely that draws the real dividing line between classes.

While both refusing to view the distribution of class status through an ethical lens and avoiding offering a remedy, Bauman concludes that until the market is dislodged as the predominant cultural framework, classes will continue to be divided along these lines. The problem of the poor in a consumer culture is real, and nothing short of a complete cultural overhaul is warranted.

Bauman's idea of "good" and "bad" consumers suggests that living in a consumer culture is neither a zero-sum game nor one in which the inexhaustibility of consumer desire necessarily translates into inexhaustible political power for the ordinary consumer. However, Bauman's reluctance to get specific on the causes of the class division between good and bad consumers can be partly explained by his commitment to the idea that the shift from solid, producer culture to liquid, consumer culture is *complete*. Is Bauman right, or does production still have residual effects on a consumer society? If so, work is surely caught up in the production/consumption back-and-forth that is most certainly situated in a consumer culture.

CONSUMING THE ALL-CONSUMING JOB

As we have seen in the overall thrust of the history of theologies of vocation, work has been gradually displaced from its place as a fundamental facet of a vocation. The shift from producer to consumer society explains some of the reasons for this displacement. Bauman frames the nature of the shift regarding work:

> It is from this central place that work is being gradually dislodged, as capitalism moves into the consumer phase of its history. Into the vacated room, individual freedom (in its consumer form) has moved. First, perhaps, as a squatter. But more and more as the legitimate resident . . . work has been progressively "decentered" on the individual plane; it has become relatively less important compared to other spheres of life, and confined to a relatively minor position in individual biography; it certainly cannot compete with personal autonomy, self-esteem, family felicity, leisure, the joys of consumption and material possessions as conditions of individual satisfaction and happiness. Work has been, however, "decentered" also on the social and systemic planes. On every level, consumer freedom moves into its place.[34]

How did consumer culture alter the meaning of work so drastically? And how is consumer culture manifested in the corporate work world today?

Hannah Arendt argues that the Industrial Revolution drastically altered the relationship between labor and work. Labor, for Arendt, is "the activity which corresponds to the biological process of the human body, whose spontaneous growth, metabolism, and eventual decay are bound to the vital necessities produced and fed into the life process by labor." Work is "the activity which corresponds to the unnaturalness of human existence, which is not imbedded in, and whose mortality is not compensated by, the species' ever-recurring life cycle."[35] Labor is cyclic, yet exhaustible with every cycle; work is punctuated, yet durable. Labor self-perpetuates in as much as one is alive, hence its necessity; work is creation in negotiation with the world, hence its contingency. The products of labor are consumed or used up in the service of sustenance, whereas the products of work are used (or not used at all), suggesting their durability.

Work of the *homo faber*, as expressed in pre-industrial craftsmanship, was performed for the purpose of the production of durable products and consumption based on the use-value of the products. The use of these products fed the cycle of survival demanded by labor, yet a space was carved out for work to have social legitimacy as it helped provide for a family. The division of labor mandated by industrial jobs conjoined with Marxian alienation signals the moment that labor came to replace work. The labor of *animal laborans*, with its cyclical "goal" of mere self-sustenance and survival to work another day, *is* the end to which factory work is designed. This, in turn, modifies the appropriation of the products of what used to be work and is now labor.

> The industrial revolution has replaced all workmanship with labor, and the result has been that the things of modern world have become labor products whose natural fate is to be consumed, instead of work products which are there to be used.[36]

Work, in Arendt's terms, has an end in the production process, and therefore, the use of products has a directed end as well. Production by labor, even though its products may not be directly consumed by the laborer, has no real end, which can only be sustained by endless consumption of the products of labor.

> The endlessness of the laboring process is guaranteed by the ever-recurrent needs of consumption; the endlessness of production can be assured only if its products lost their use character and become more and more objects of consumption, or if, to put it in another way, the rate of use is so tremendously accelerated that the objective difference between use and consumption, between the relative durability of use objects and the swift coming and going of consumer goods, dwindles to insignificance . . . we must consume, devour, as it were, our houses and furniture and cars as though they were the "good things" of nature which spoil uselessly if they are not drawn swiftly into the never-ending cycle of man's metabolism with nature.[37]

Sociologist Richard Sennett extends Arendt's connection between consumer culture and work by using consumer culture as a means to talk about new social arrangements at work but not as an end to which all work activities are directed. The flexibility with which businesses must currently employ and the reciprocal flexibility that employees must adopt is the means by which Sennett ties the workplace to consumer culture.[38] It should come as no surprise that flexible, pliant political structures at work contrast with the authority structure in workplaces embedded in a producer culture.

Sennett calls our attention to the "Weberian triangle of bureaucracy" to describe the early twentieth-century geometry of the flow of authority. The boss at the top of the triangle dispenses commands to an expanding bureaucratic chain of command, which is then relayed to the lower-level employees that make up the base of the triangle. The triangle's expansion outward from the boss necessitates more employees, more production, more profit, while the number of people at the top of the triangle can remain small. In order for the boss to be able to control the production process as labor was increasingly being divided, and the number of employees was being multiplied, individual jobs needed to be fixed. "The chain of command within this triangle operated on the principle that each niche had a distinctive function; efficiency dictated that there be as little duplication as possible."[39]

However, twenty-five years ago, businesses began to shed the Weberian triangle model. They

> sought to destroy the practice of fixed-function work, substituting instead teams which work short-term on specific tasks—teams which are shuffled when the organization embarks on new projects ... instead of each person doing his or her own particular bit in a defined chain of command, you have duplication of function, many different teams compete to do the same task fastest, best.[40]

Or businesses have become more flexible. Flexibility best sums up not only the way businesses must be in order to respond quickly to a rapidly changing market but also the quality that employees must possess if they are to keep a job. Short-term tasks, constantly shifting team membership, and competition that replace an imperative that drives the completion of long-term assignments cannot function under a strict triangle model. Instead of a triangle, a circle with a dot in the center more aptly depicts the new dynamic for Sennett.

> At the center, a small number of managers rules, makes decisions, sets tasks, judges results; the information revolution has given it more instantaneous control over the corporation's workings than in the old system, where orders often modulated and evolved as they passed down the chain of command. The teams working on the periphery of the circle are left free to respond to output targets set by the center, free to devise means of executing tasks in competition with one another, but not free to decide what those tasks are.[41]

How and why does the dotted circle model work? Sennett describes three facets of any business attempting to employ such a model, and flexibility is the thread running through each part: "discontinuous reinvention of institutions" (companies routinely deconstructing ways of doing business and constructing anew), "flexible specialization" (companies producing widely varying products or providing highly differentiated services to cover more and more of the market), and "concentration without centralization" (small units of work groups are networked together and run by a diffuse authority instead of an authority that is delivered down in pyramid/triangle fashion).[42]

All three, when executed faithfully, help a company to adjust promptly to market volatility, but they often occur at a cost to mid- to lower-level employees or to those at the edge of the circle. These workers in a flexible company must forego the relative security furnished by the performance of consistent and durable tasks. They must be ever-ready for change. More drastically, change can mean everything from an unexpected layoff, to a transfer, to a radical alteration of the job. Sennett draws a contrast between the situation of old and the one today. "Career ... applied to labor meant a lifelong channel for one's economic pursuits. Flexible capitalism has blocked the straight roadway of career, diverting employees suddenly from one kind of work into another."[43] In fact, non-flexibility or stubborn loyalty to a company can actually act as a detriment to one's career. Barry Schwartz notes that "job-switching has become so natural that individuals who have worked for the same employer for five years are regarded with suspicion. No longer are they seen as loyal; instead, their desirability or ambition is called in to question . . ."[44]

The work ethic has undergone drastic changes to compensate, as Sennett notes. "The work ethic, as we commonly understand it, asserts self-disciplined use of one's time and the value of delayed gratification. . . . Such a work ethic depends in part on institutions stable enough for a person to practice delay. Delayed gratification loses its value, though, in a regime whose institutions change rapidly . . ."[45] The ethic that Weber described in 1905 took its directive from a clear chain of command, whether it be bureaucratic, religious, or both. As he points out, delayed gratification is possible only when the benefits of a resolute work ethic are underwritten by an unambiguous authority.[46] Lacking a trust in the authority to guarantee a delayed payback, the incentive to apply a resilient work ethic would quickly lose its justification.

Replacing this work ethic is a new ethic that no longer relies on consistent, unambiguous institutional support for its energy and direction. And absent the kind of stability that characterizes the jobs in Weber's producer culture, today's work ethic must apply itself to tasks that are vague and protean. When frequently changing job tasks are coupled with general job insecurity, the lack of a central, binding authority at work tells us why. And with a lack of such an authority, a softer way of maintaining productivity and efficiency is needed.

Instead of a dictatorial, top-down management mediated through a thick bureaucracy, the work of channeling employees towards maximum productivity and efficiency is increasingly being exerted through responsibility to one's team. Individual responsibility that used to correspond to an individual work ethic in the context of a one-to-one relationship is replaced with social responsibility to fellow team members. Sennett describes what is necessary to be successful in such a work situation as well as what it means.

> The modern work ethic focuses on teamwork. It celebrates sensitivity to others; it requires such "soft skills" as being a good listener and being cooperative; most of all, teamwork emphasizes team adaptability to circumstances. . . . Teamwork is the group practice of demeaning superficiality.[47]

As the primary unit of work becomes increasingly team-based, the expression of power and authority in the workplace shifts in corresponding fashion. Power still exists and is wielded in all successful corporations. However, rather than emanating unilaterally from the corporate brass, it is now far less centralized as it is dispensed multilaterally. Arrangements of power, in other words, are delivered more in "shotgun style" than single rifle shot, and deployment of power is more hegemonic than dictatorial. Sennett explains,

> People still play games of power in teams, but the emphasis on soft skills of communication, facilitation, and mediation changes radically one aspect of power: authority disappears, authority of the sort which self-confidently proclaims, "This is the right way!" or "Obey me, because I know what I'm talking about!" The person with power does not justify command; the powerful only "facilitate," enable others. Such power without authority disorients employees; they may still feel driven to justify themselves, but now there is no one higher up who responds. Calvin's God has fled.[48]

The reduction of job success to mere social dexterity in the face of a lack of direction from above serves to minimize the role of a barometer that accomplished tasks used to serve for success at work. When tasks within a job vary from day to day and are dependent on social skills, any semblance of sovereignty, human or divine, is gone.

One could argue that the shift from individuals being at the mercy of a large bureaucracy to that of working within a team in competition with other teams is a desirable one. In terms of social capital, it seems as though there is strength in numbers, and lacking unionization within most corporations, team-based work could provide the opportunity for workers to gain social capital (if their team does well). Yet Sennett answers that social inequality grows in flexible companies as it did in industrial factories.

> In the Weberian triangle of bureaucracy, rewards came for doing one's job as best one can; in the dotted circle, they come to teams winning over other teams—which the economist Robert Frank calls winner-take-all organization; sheer effort no longer produces reward. This bureaucratic reformulation, Frank argues, contributes to the great inequalities of pay and perks in flexible organizations, a material reality of inequality entirely at odds with work-place democracy.[49]

Effort is certainly exerted in team projects, however, team success may be at odds with individual effort within a team. Likewise, actual work done by an individual is not a guaranteed factor in the success or failure of a team; more important is the ability to get along with team members. Most importantly, casting worker success in terms of a winner-take-all reward system allows executives to rely on an all-or-nothing dispersal of perks and pay to only one team. Not only does the disparity grow between the small number of winners and the larger number of losers, but the executives are also insulated from criticism based on the perceived fairness of the game. All is fair in love and war.

Another means of widening the social capital gap is the use of consulting. Sennett provides an instructive example. In the 1990s, the BBC hired the consulting firm of McKinsey to help its organization by streamlining "who reported to whom, what they reported, what they had to report."[50] Hired on a contract basis, yet given a massive responsibility, McKinsey acted as another team within the BBC that was assigned a specific task. But because McKinsey's ultimate allegiance was to McKinsey and not the BBC, problems resulted from implementation of their "winning strategy."

> The McKinsey consultants took too little responsibility, however, for implementing these changes, nor did they deal with the human consequences of change; among these consequences were large numbers of people shifted from areas in which they had developed expertise to areas in which they were driving blind. . . . The consultants were paid, then departed, leaving the organization in turmoil, increasing social distances within the BBC. These human disconnections in the midst of change in turn dramatically increased employees' feelings of anxiety.[51]

The social distance here is the one between the executives who hired McKinsey and the employees who had to abide by the new rules laid down. If employees felt greater anxiety over the changes or worse, the changes did not work, at least the executives' hands are clean, and those arguing for change have vacated the premises.

With the Weberian triangle model, at least there was a known place where or a person to whom worker grievances could be aired, whether they were taken seriously or not. When consultants step in between executives and employees, exercise the power to alter the working environment drastically, and then quickly leave, power concentrates even more at the top without those at the top having to present a crass show of muscle.[52] In an odd twist, power is temporarily ceded to an outside contract group, and when power returns to the executives, it has actually grown. The result, according to Sennett, is an increase in the social inequality of the workplace with those at the top shielded from direct criticism and freed from direct responsibility for the welfare of the employees.

Another effect of team-based business is revealed in the way potential employees search for a job and employers search for employees. When soft skills needed for ensuring a winning team are desired, the context of the job is secondary. Potential ability *is* the item sold by the prospective seller and what is sought by the buyer.

> The search for talent, in particular, focuses on the people with a talent for problem solving no matter the context, a talent which skirts becoming too ingrown. Potential ability emphasizes the prospect of doing things one has yet to do; achievement and mastery are self-consuming, the contexts and contents of knowledge used up in being used. Consumption of goods plays a key role in complementing and legitimating these experiences.[53]

Because the job that many apply to will morph and individual success is largely determined by team success, the qualifications needed to get a job in a flexible business need not be intimately connected to the actual work that one would do. Hence consumption, rather than production, is the activity that complements and legitimates the experience of searching for a job and for employees.

It is here that Sennett's use of consumer culture diverges from Bauman's. Sennett seems to agree with the idea of consumer insatiability and liquid modernity in principle,[54] but he is more inclined to emphasize the end game of the consumption of individual items instead of the desire that fuels continual consumption. Or the "self-consuming" passion, while being stoked by unlimited desire and imagination, is one that through perpetual dissatisfaction can tire.[55] Consumer inexhaustibility is never fully extinguished as desire is always active, as Sennett concedes. Yet he implies that consumer desire goes through ebbs and flows, starts and stops as opposed to Bauman's "always-flowing" liquid consumer culture.

Sennett's more measured assessment of the punctuated power of consumer culture is reflected in his interpretation of the relationship between consumption and the workplace. Consumption "complements and legitimates" the experiences of working in a flexible capitalistic economy and the tactics employed when looking for a job and searching for job talent. Yet if consumer culture serves to complement and possibly legitimize workplace experiences, then consumer culture merely works with pre-existing structures of the workplace as opposed to pre-figuring them. In other words, the demand for unlimited choices may animate the approach to work and certain experiences of it, but as Sennett argues, consumer culture is unable to empower the employee *qua* job consumer in terms of social capital. Or consumption acts as a cultural mediator that aids in authorizing not only the elevation of team-based skills but also the way in which jobs are approached.

Bauman would probably agree with Sennett's assessment. However, in Bauman's description of the shift from societies organized around production to that of consumption, he leaves little room for social relations of production to remain. It is as if liquid society has been successful in melting all solids permanently. If we force Sennett into using Bauman's metaphor, liquid is certainly flowing and melting some solids. But despite the appearance of a liquid society, other solids are unable to be melted. The liquid modifies the way that we appropriate work in the way that the lack of choice will frustrate; the expansion of choice (or at least the appearance of it) keeps us going. Despite our approach to work via consumption, the power relations forged under solid modernity have remained relatively solid.

WORKING TO WORK ON ONESELF

One final domain that consumer culture infiltrates—one that affects modern conceptions of vocation—is the self. As was discussed in chapter 1, vocations in the Gilded Age characterized by a weakening of Calvinist proscriptions operated under the ideology of the self-made man. Though attenuated, remnants of a moral ethos of self-control and temperance still patrolled the perimeter of the self by maintaining a clear distance between humanity and God.[56] Disillusioning factory work at the American *fin de siécle* helped complete a disenchantment of the world which led to a breakdown of the autonomous, more unified self so emblematic of the self-made man mythology.

According to Lears, the conditions of work, not only in the factories but also in bureaucracy-driven, white-collar jobs, combined with the waning authority of traditional religious institutions to render the reality of the "industrial self" discontinuous with past self-experience. A sense of "unreality" became pervasive. Fortunate or not, disorienting feelings of unreality were mitigated by a burgeoning therapeutic ethos that promoted self-reflection on and treatment of one's own health, mental state, and success. This helped, albeit temporarily, to bring life under control.[57] And an increased sense of self-control helped to create an internal reality that could insulate itself from jarring external conditions—at least experientially.

In this way, the self slowly became a project for itself—an object to be gauged, judged, and finally, improved. Ironically, increased control that an individual could exert in self-creation resulted in a less rigid core of the self, as Lears observes.

> As success became more dependent on evanescent "impression management," selfhood lost coherence. The older ethic had required adherence to an internalized morality of self-control; repressive as this "inner-direction" had been, it helped to sustain a solid core of selfhood. The newer ethic of "other-direction" undermined that solidity by presenting the self as an empty vessel to be filled and refilled according to the expectations of others and the needs of the moment.[58]

Utilizing David Riesman's archetypes of "inner" and "outer" direction, Lears argues that the softening of the self's core left the individual with no choice but to look outside of itself for replenishment for durability.[59] As the "needs of the moment" began to be satisfied through the purchase of consumer goods, the modern consumer is born.

This new orientation to the self as a project to be fixed was cultivated by a deluge of advertising messages scripted to play on the resident insecurity by claiming cure-all promises. With the increased consumption of everything from advertised material goods, both for utility and luxury, to advice that contributed to overall salubrious health, individuals began to look to consumer goods as the building blocks of their identity. Lears writes,

> In the embryonic consumer culture of the late nineteenth century, more and more Americans were being encouraged to "express themselves" . . . not through independent accomplishment but through the ownership of things. It was a far different and in many ways diminished sense of selfhood from that embodied in the image of the headstrong self-made man.[60]

If "embryonic consumer culture" is marked by the self's identification with owned consumer goods, the "fully birthed" consumer culture feeds a self that constructs its identity not so much in the ownership of things but in the process of consumption.

Lears avers that the deterioration of the self's core has only continued up to the present time. Its waning precedes a waxing number of products and services claiming to make up for the loss. Yet Lears avoids the accusation of advertiser manipulationism by asserting that the origins of consumer culture are found in the self that is confronted by a sense of unreality, not from advertisments. It is this diminished sense of selfhood that advertisers exploited. Needs were not *created* in this exchange between the self and advertisements. However, the discontinuity between the promise of a new self and the absence of a pre-existent one creates a gap that cannot be bridged—except experientially through the reigning power of consumer choice.

> As self-fulfillment and immediate gratification have become commodities on the mass market, calls for personal liberation have begun to ring hollow. The quest for alternative values gradually has become a casual choice among "alternative lifestyles". . . . The effort to re-create a coherent sense of selfhood seems fated to frustration. Every failure inaugurates a new psychic quest, until the seeker is embroiled in an interminable series of self-exploration. This continually frustrated search is the logical outcome of antimodernism in America: the vision of a self in endless development is perfectly attuned to an economy based on pointless growth and ceaseless destruction.[61]

Important is Lears's emphasis on the endlessness of self-creation in a consumer market that feeds off of the energy of a kind of perpetual motion machine while it simultaneously feeds it. In the absence of a self that can feed itself, everything becomes a potential object of consumption, including self-fulfillment. Durable selves need durable goods; ephemeral selves need the kind of ephemeral goods that satisfy the self that it nourishes.

Revisiting Micki McGee's notion of the belabored self, we can now see how she plugs self-help literature into the support system for the self-creation industry. It does so by playing on insecurities stemming from a shaky job situation or family life that are purported to be minimized by actions such as positive thinking or finding the true you. Her problem with this tactic employed by self-help authors is that it maintains the political status quo by emphasizing the endless need to work on oneself instead of working on the fight for political justice in the workplace.

> The appeal of this literature is understandable: the tremendous growth in self-help publishing parallels an overall trend of stagnant wages and destabilized employment opportunities for American workers. . . . To manage this anxiety, individuals have been advised not only to work longer and harder but also to invest in themselves, manage themselves, and continuously improve themselves.[62]

The success of self-help techniques is dependent on the severity of uncertain and unsettling working conditions. When projects at work are situated in such a tenuous context, working on oneself is never finished but will also never go away.

How is the self able to do this, exactly? For McGee, the belabored self works off of a bifurcation of the self into an ideal or authentic self that puts the inauthentic or tainted self into relief.[63] This project, with its momentum guaranteed by a protracted battle between the authentic and inauthentic self, can even insulate itself from social exigencies, such as those that stem from work. "The imperative of inventing the self that is found in the literatures of self-improvement is often cast in the form of discovering or uncovering an authentic, unique and stable self that might function—even thrive—unaffected by the vagaries of the labor market."[64] In fact, the vagaries of the labor market can fuel the drive to work on oneself in that a constantly changing job situation provides new opportunities to re-make oneself through work. If the tasks within a job changes or a job is lost altogether, while frustrating on one level, when enlisted in the service of the project of the belabored self, these situations are fodder for consumption in the building of an identity.

The belabored self that engages self-help literature approaches itself as a project in which consumption of the means to better itself is akin to the consumer approach to work. Consequently, both one's job and one's identity are subject to consumer choice when, at one time, both were subject to certain societal norms that furnished rules and boundaries for the socially legitimate expression of each. Absent such norms, the meaning of work and the self are open to interpretation and creation by the consumer.

Additionally, the job itself must be able to replicate the experience of consumption that is felt in the process of working on oneself in spite of changing labor conditions. A job, if it is to participate in consumer culture successfully, must be able to reproduce consumer satisfaction. Bauman clarifies:

> Like everything else which may reasonably hope to become the target of desire and an object of free consumer choice, jobs must be "interest-

ing"—varied, exciting, allowing for adventure, containing certain (though not excessive) measures of risk, and giving occasion to ever-new sensations. Jobs that are monotonous, repetitive, routine, unadventurous, allowing no initiative and promising no challenge to wits nor a chance for self-testing and self-ascertaining "boring." No full fledged consumer would conceivably agree to undertake them.[65]

When a job is treated as a commodity in a consumer culture, the usefulness of what is produced is in the service of the *experience* of production. The measure of the quality of a job has less to do with concrete work activity and more to do with the kind of stimulation that work spawns. Again, material work is made immaterial, in both senses of the word, when a job is approached as a consumer item.

In the context of flexible capitalism, consumer culture has fully infected working life. The belabored self, which runs on an endless loop of consuming new and better self-images, uses a job instrumentally to provide satisfaction of consumer desire which simultaneously insulates oneself from the disquieting political dynamics of work in a flexible capitalistic economy. And when actual work is rendered immaterial in the push to consume life, working on oneself, pursuing jobs that entertain, and complacence with job flexibility and insecurity can be tolerated so long as the ability to choose is never immobilized.

CONCLUSION

The engagement of consumer culture with work yields several key insights for my project. The cultural ascendancy of consumption over production has had wide-ranging effects on society. The decreasing emphasis on production to act as the basis of one's identity as a worker parallels the evaporation of norms that used to guarantee consistency on the job as well as continuance in a job or trade. The work ethic that internally sustained the society organized around production morphed into an ethic that gets its energy from consumer culture, as shown in various ways by Campbell, Bauman, Arendt, Sennett, Lears, and McGee. Preceded by the unmooring of work from its material context, consumer culture is now able to affect everything from the way we view our job to power dynamics at work to the nature of the job itself. It does so by placing the authority to choose a job and the way to experience it squarely on the individual. Jobs and the work that follows become objects of consumption and are accordingly expected to satisfy individual desire.

Further, as Sennett demonstrates, consumer culture mediates the experience of working in businesses participating in flexible capitalism by translating team-based projects and de-centralized authority into the illusion that employees are making real, consequential choices. Consumer culture expresses itself in the workplace by discouraging dictatorial environments, emphasizing personality over skill, letting teams of workers battle for one prize, and inserting outside agencies to deliver bad news. All of these practices of the modern corporation run cover for those at the top of the corporate ladder as the hierarchy of employers and employees stays intact. Choice and the power that accompanies it for the employee seem to have not been lost in the process.

What is the fate of a vocation when it interacts with work thus construed? Bauman states the problem succinctly:

> What possible purpose could the strategy of pilgrim-style "progress" serve in this world of ours? In this world, not only have jobs-for-life disappeared, but trades and professions which have acquired the confusing habit of appearing from nowhere and vanishing without notice can hardly be lived as Weberian "vocations"—and to rub salt into the wound, the demand for the skills needed to practice such professions seldom lasts as long as the time needed to acquire them.[66]

Generally speaking, terms such as "linear narrative" and "long-term goals" characterized the Protestant work ethic that Weber saw sustaining vocations just one hundred years ago. The consumer ethic can only but deeply affect the current meaning and application of a vocation, as we will see in the next chapter.

NOTES

1. Hannah Arendt, *The Human Condition* (Chicago: University of Chicago Press, 1958), 85, 121.

2. Most literature on consumer culture admits of its inescapability though not of its omnipotence. Wendell Berry suggests lifestyle choices that avoid the pitfalls of consumer culture through non-participatory stances towards the market. See Wendell Berry, *Sex, Economy, Freedom and Community* (New York: Pantheon, 1994), 40. Robert Reich argues for a separation between politics and the market that will reenergize a citizenry that, in his view, can stave off the commodification of public space. See Robert B. Reich, *Supercapitalism: The Transformation of Business, Democracy, and Everyday Life* (New York: Alfred A. Knopf, 2007), 209–25. Vincent Miller, in his efforts to curb the encroaching commodification of religion, calls for a return to a "sacramentality" within the Catholic Church where sacramental thinking and action can counter consumer thinking and action. See Miller, *Consuming Religion*, 188–92.

3. Mike Featherstone, *Consumer Culture and Postmodernism* (London: Sage, 1991), 13.

4. The sociological view also alleviates the need to view contemporary consumers as either "dupes" or "heroes." Don Slater remarks that consumers within a consumer culture have typically been seen as unwitting slaves of advertising who bend to their own shallow desires or as supreme human agents who, over and against the consumer in an earlier stage of capitalism, are finally asserting their power to choose goods in a rational manner. Slater argues for neither, based largely on the Foucauldian problematization of the dichotomy between self-identity and freedom, stating that the "dupes" vs. "heroes" argument contains a false dilemma. He, however, relies primarily on an economic model of consumption (whether consumers are acting rationally or not) which, while important, does not elucidate the effects of consumer culture on

social bonds. See Don Slater, *Consumer Culture and Modernity* (Cambridge, UK: Polity Press, 1997), 33–34.

5. Lears, "From Salvation to Self-Realization," 3.

6. This can be seen early on in *Grundrisse*, the work that sketches out a foundation for *Capital*. On the relationship between production and consumption, see Marx, *Grundrisse* (London: Penguin, 1973), 90–94.

7. Marx, *Capital,* vol. 1, trans. Ben Fowkes (New York: Vintage Books, 1977), 163–67.

8. There is, of course, much more to Marx's analysis as he uses the commodity as the starting point for his entire argument in *Capital*. I use his "fetishism of the commodity" only as an early and profound example of an idea of a consumer product that is able to transcend its status as simply an object of consumption. Marx does not develop a theory of consumer culture as he did not live in one. But his analysis of the commodity in a capitalistic economy sets the stage for consumption to take on a greater role in cultural development.

9. Thorstein Veblen, *The Theory of the Leisure Class* (New York: B. W. Huebsch, 1912), 149.

10. Lears also refutes Veblen's description of conspicuous consumption, though more on historical grounds than explanatory ones. Veblen's association of conspicuous consumption with an upper-crust leisure class is problematized by Lears as he cites that the kind of consumption ascribed to the leisure class was being practiced widely by those in the middle class too. Lears, *No Place of Grace*, 37.

11. An example is the popularity of hip-hop clothing styles worn by middle- and upper-class youth.

12. Colin Campbell, *The Romantic Ethic and the Spirit of Modern Consumerism* (London: Basil Blackwell, 1987), 37.

13. Baudrillard, "The System of Objects," in *Jean Baudrillard: Selected Writings,* ed. Mark Poster (Stanford, CA: Stanford University Press, 1988), 24–25.

14. Campbell, 60.

15. Campbell, 60–61.

16. Campbell's assertion has been confirmed most recently by Martin Lindstrom. See Martin Lindstrom, *Buyology: Truth and Lies about What We Buy* (New York: Broadway Business, 2008).

17. Campbell, 95.

18. He uses "modernity" in his term "liquid modernity," which more closely resembles postmodernity, to connect two phases of one large historical epoch. The way to understand what is commonly called postmodernity is to see the distinctive features of solid modernity as melting (or perhaps deconstructing). Hence Bauman still considers these times to be "modern," though the melting of its qualities certainly spells its demise. In addition, Bauman is ambivalent about whether we are really fully in one epoch or another. Solids are still being melted. This use of the word "modernity" is also used by Slater to describe the stretching of the older concept of modernity that occurs under consumer culture. See Bauman, *Liquid Modernity* (Cambridge, UK: Polity Press, 2000), 10–11; Slater, *Consumer Culture and Modernity*.

19. Bauman, *Liquid Modernity*, 6.

20. Bauman, *Liquid Modernity*, 1–15.

21. Bauman, *Liquid Modernity*, 3.

22. Bauman, *Liquid Modernity*, 4.

23. Bauman, *Liquid Modernity*, 4.

24. Bauman asserts, "in the *classes*, the frames which (as uncompromisingly as the already dissolved *estates*) encapsulated the totality of life conditions and life prospects and determined the range of realistic life projects and life strategies. The task confronting free individuals [in solid modernity] was to use their new freedom to find the appropriate niche and to settle there through conformity: by faithfully following the rules and modes of conduct identified as right and proper for the location." See Bauman, *Liquid Modernity*, 5.

25. Bauman writes that "among the principal icons of that [solid] modernity were the *Fordist factory*, which reduced human activities to simple, routine and by and large predesigned moves meant to be followed obediently and mechanically without engaging mental faculties, and holding all spontaneity and individual initiative off limits; *bureaucracy*, akin at least in its innate tendency to Max Weber's ideal model, in which identities and social bonds were deposited on entry in the cloakroom together with hats, umbrellas and overcoats, so that solely the command and the statute book could drive, uncontested, the actions of the insiders as long as they stayed inside . . ." See Bauman, *Liquid Modernity*, 25–26.

26. Bauman, *Liquid Modernity*, 76.
27. Bauman, *Liquid Modernity*, 76.
28. Bauman, *Liquid Modernity*, 6.
29. Bauman, *Liquid Life* (Cambridge, UK: Polity Press, 2005), 9.
30. Bauman, "Consuming Life," *Journal of Consumer Culture* 1 (2001): 12–13.

31. His predilection for a kind of conservative resignation can be traced back to a work that precedes his current preoccupations with consumer culture. In an essay entitled, "Legislators and Interpreters," Bauman consigns current intellectuals to the status of interpreters when legislation occupied their time in solid modernity. Along the general lines of his solid/liquid schema, Bauman argues that the making of laws by intellectuals was possible when solid social bonds encouraged and protected such offerings. Now in liquid society, the only recourse to intellectuals is interpretation of existing phenomena. This is so because the diversity of cultural authorities in a liquid society prevents overarching universal judgments. When these judgments are not permitted and interpretation is the only avenue, critique must be measured and contingent, if any is offered at all. Bauman, *Intimations of Postmodernity* (New York: Routledge, 1992), 1–25.

32. Fred Hirsch makes the same point, but on economic grounds. See Fred Hirsch, *The Social Limits to Growth* (London: Routledge and Kegan Paul, 1977), 71–96.

33. Bauman, *Work, Consumerism and the New Poor* (Berkshire, GB: McGraw-Hill Education, 2004), 112–13.

34. Bauman, *Freedom*, 74.

35. Hannah Arendt, *The Human Condition* (Chicago: University of Chicago Press, 1958), 7.

36. Arendt, 125.

37. Arendt, 125–26.

38. Sennett draws on David Harvey's early use of "flexibility" to describe postmodern culture in general and applies it to the political economy. See David Harvey, *The Condition of Postmodernity* (London: Blackwell, 1991), 121–99.

39. Sennett, "Capitalism and the City," 118.
40. Sennett, "Capitalism and the City," 118.
41. Sennett, "Capitalism and the City," 119.
42. Sennett, *The Corrosion of Character: The Personal Consequences of Work in the New Capitalism* (New York: W. W. Norton & Company, 1998), 47–57.
43. Sennett, *The Corrosion of Character*, 9.
44. Barry Schwartz, *The Paradox of Choice: Why More Is Less* (New York: Ecco, 2004), 35.
45. Sennett, *The Corrosion of Character*, 99.
46. Weber, 170–72.
47. Sennett, *The Corrosion of Character*, 99.
48. Sennett, *The Corrosion of Character*, 109.
49. Sennett, "Capitalism and the City," 119.
50. Sennett, *The Culture of the New Capitalism*, 56.
51. Sennett, *The Culture of the New Capitalism*, 56–57.
52. Sennett, *The Culture of the New Capitalism*, 58.
53. Sennett, *The Culture of the New Capitalism*, 141–42.
54. Sennett, *The Culture of the New Capitalism*, 150.

55. Sennett, *The Culture of the New Capitalism*, 137–42.
56. Lears, "From Salvation to Self-Realization," 10.
57. This idea has its basis in Philip Rieff's 1966 study of the rise of the therapeutic ethos. In fact, Rieff presages consumer culture with language that is strikingly similar to contemporary commentators. "With the decline of a civilization of authority, the therapeutic requirement shifted toward an action which would take place, first within the circle of personal relations . . . A new kind of community could be constructed, one that did not generate conscience and internal control but desire and the safe play of impulse." See Philip Rieff, *The Triumph of the Therapeutic* (New York: Harper Torchbooks, 1966), 52.
58. Lears, "From Salvation to Self-Realization," 8.
59. See David Riesman, *The Lonely Crowd* (New Haven: Yale University Press, 2001).
60. Lears, *No Place of Grace*, 37.
61. Lears, *No Place of Grace*, 306–7.
62. McGee, 12.
63. For Deepak Chopra, attention to nature allows the true self to emerge; for Eckhart Tolle, it is the overcoming of our "delusion of time" that returns us to the authentic self of the "now."
64. McGee, 16.
65. Bauman, *Work, Consumerism, and the New Poor*, 34.
66. Bauman, "From Pilgrim to Tourist—Or a Short History of Identity," in *Questions of Cultural Identity*, eds. Stuart Hall and Paul du Gay (London: Sage, 1996), 24.

FOUR

The Purchase-Driven Life

It's not about you. —Rick Warren, *The Purpose-Driven Life*

Rick Warren wrote *The Purpose-Driven Life* in 2002 as a follow-up to his book, *The Purpose-Driven Church*.[1] *The Purpose-Driven Church* was written specifically for pastors as a guide to recovering and maintaining the health of their existing institutions as well as building new ones. This theme of guidance runs through *The Purpose-Driven Life* too, but here Warren expands his audience to include all people who are seeking to find a sense of meaning and purpose in life. To date, more than thirty million copies have been sold, making it the bestselling non-fiction hardback in U.S. history.[2] My interest in this particular book is understandably piqued by the sheer number of people who have read it and have presumably been influenced by it. Yet my primary task in this chapter is not to analyze why *The Purpose-Driven Life* has generated so much interest, nor is it to investigate who Rick Warren is to find his motivations. The goal, rather, is to locate the book in the realm of consumer culture and then evaluate the book's language in terms of its ability to convey a political theology of vocation in such an environment.

Provisionally, we can say that *The Purpose-Driven Life* is carried by the river of consumer culture that is fed by three streams: self-help literature, seeker-sensitive religion, and the lack of materiality in the content of the book. After laying out the structure of *The Purpose-Driven Life* and situating it in the context of self-help and seeker-sensitive movements respectively, I analyze the merits of the arguments of those worried about Warren's accommodation to the wider culture. Accommodation to the techniques employed by these two movements, while deemed necessary to communicate self-help techniques or adopted as a survival strategy for dying churches, comes at a high price according to its critics. Some claim that the cost is incurred at the expense of a biblical theology that should never bend to culture, no matter the payoff. I will argue that these critics debate themselves into a cul-de-sac created by consumer culture itself and are therefore unable to level a real critique. Instead, a more accurate portrayal of the relationship between *The Purpose-Driven Life* and consumer culture relies on the recognition that Warren's concept of purpose is the functional equivalent of the concept of vocation but in a commodified or "packaged-and-sold-to-consumers" form. And in this form, a purpose-*qua*-vocation lacks the capacity to engage the political environment of the workplace, and this constitutes the real price of colluding with consumer culture.

To support my claim, I use Vincent Miller, who argues that in order for religious products to become consumer items in the West, the packaging and distribution of such products must encounter little resistance. The muddied and jagged history of long-standing religious ideas and practices is such an obstacle because it makes complex the seemingly simple act of religious consumption. Simplicity equals palatability when it comes to consumption in a consumer culture. The commodification of religious ideas, then, is a process that necessarily includes the injury that consumer culture must inflict on religious ideas and their history in order to make them palatable to consumers. Largely drawing on Miller's claims, I problematize certain criticisms of *The Purpose-Driven Life*—specifically those that are based on suspicions of Warren's ability to transmit a "true Gospel" when in fact it is the commodification of the idea of purpose that precedes such suspicions.

The problem with Warren's book, as it relates to my overall project, is neither that it is a Gospel without teeth nor that it is a piece of a slick marketing that Warren and his publisher employ to expand his ministry. The real problem has to do with the internal logic of Warren's purpose that discloses its disconnect from the material and political context of the workplace. Warren's purpose possesses a kind of slipperiness that invokes the spirit of a Lutheran vocation yet at the same time is detached enough from the material conditions of work, both past and present, that have provided and continue to provide the context in which vocations must engage. Shorn of its materiality, consumer-friendly religious concepts, such as purpose, and the practices that result from the adoption of such concepts, cannot inform the unjust practices of work.

IT'S NOT ABOUT YOU *AND* ABOUT YOU

The success of *The Purpose-Driven Life* may tempt the casual observer to attribute its popularity to its self-help qualities. Indeed, the typical refrain of self-help books—namely, that pre-existent forces, abilities, or entities (both internal and external) can be tapped to give meaning and direction to life—is present in Warren's book. Yet interestingly, these themes are veiled by an unremitting worldview inhabited by an omnipotent, omniscient God and powerless, confused human beings. Such a worldview atypically frames traditional self-help books.[3] If God is a part of a self-help book, personal meaning is typically found through a kind of God/self co-operation in which God is more of a warm-hearted friend than austere parent.[4] On the occasions that an omnipotent God is the protagonist in a Christian self-help book or devotional designed for laypeople, any meaning to be had for one's life is gained primarily through revelation, not self-reflection.[5]

Is *The Purpose-Driven Life* in fact a self-help book? Malcolm Gladwell states in a *New Yorker* piece that it does not appear so.

> It is tempting to interpret the book's message as a kind of New Age self-help theology. Warren's God is not awesome or angry and does not stand in judgment of human sin. He's genial and mellow. . . . The self-help genre, however, is fundamentally inward-focused. . . . Warren's first sentence, by contrast, is "It's not about you," which puts it in the spirit of traditional Christian devotional literature, which focuses the reader outward, toward God.[6]

Indeed, Warren himself confirms Gladwell's observations when he states in the book:

> This is not a self-help book. It is not about finding the right career, achieving your dreams, or planning your life. It is not about how to cram more activities into an overloaded schedule. Actually, it will teach you how to do *less* in life—by focusing on what matters most. It is about becoming what *God* created you to be.[7]

In fact, Warren goes on to classify all attempts to discover purpose on one's own as pure speculation. This is so because the true source of purpose and meaning in life is not the self. Accordingly, he rejects self-help books

> because they approach the subject from a self-centered viewpoint. Self-help books, even Christian ones, usually offer the same predictable steps to finding your life's purpose: Consider your dreams, Clarify your values, Set some goals, Figure out what you are good at, Aim high! . . . These recommendations often lead to great success. You can usually succeed in reaching a goal if you put your mind to it. But being successful and fulfilling your life's purpose are not at all the same issue![8]

Hence any hunt for purpose that remains within the borders of the self, nature, or others' advice is literally an exercise in futility. Life's purpose is given only by God's revelation, not self-revelation.[9] Therefore, the individual's task is, first, to cease looking in the wrong place for purpose in life, and second, to turn one's full attention to the revealed Word of God for the answers to life's questions. A circle develops that becomes the basis for the rest of the book: we find our purpose in God's revelation because God created, designed us, and gave us purpose. In Warren's opinion, self-help books misdirect readers inward, where the Creator does not reside.

There is nothing in Warren's theology that is particularly novel or even earth-shattering. Mistrust of the "world" that nudges Christians towards other-worldly truth has been rehearsed since Paul. By drawing on this common exhortation, any self-help quality of *The Purpose-Driven Life* does not have to be explicitly admitted by Warren nor recognized by Gladwell. Accordingly, the desire to fashion a life based on consumer needs and market supply that propels self-help literature is most certainly at odds with Warren's own words. Individual desire for "worldly" success stands in stark opposition to the divinely mandated imperative for humans to live out the purpose that God, alone, has laid out for each individual. Though *The Purpose-Driven Life* does, in fact, divulge certain self-help qualities. It does so by putting forward an ambiguous anthropology that, in turn, permits more of a role for human agency than Warren would admit.

Warren's all-powerful, all-knowing God follows both the "God-as-friend" and the "God-as-distant-legislator" models. Warren alternates between the two Gods with seamless facility and thus leaves room for the self, as the manager of life's purposes, to choose either. With God-as-distant-legislator, we are first and foremost powerless to find our own purpose through our own efforts—this is God's task alone.

> God was thinking of you long before you ever thought about him. His purpose for your life predates your conception. He planned it before you existed, *without your input!* You may choose your career, your spouse, your hobbies, and many other parts of your life, but you don't get to choose your purpose.[10]

Despite his stated hard distinction between what can and cannot be chosen, Warren effectively blurs this line throughout his book. Our life journey progresses due to our participation in a cooperative effort with a God that desires our friendship, happiness, and finally, success in whatever way we define it. Consequently, our own happiness is a sure sign that God's purpose is being lived out.

> How do you know when you are serving God from your heart? The first telltale sign is *enthusiasm*. When you are doing what you *love* to do, no one has to motivate you or challenge you or check up on you. You do it for the sheer enjoyment.[11]

Even though feelings, such as happiness, are dismissed by Warren as human-centered at one point,[12] he often honors them as a sign of God's grace and even as a means of communicating with God.[13]

Human volition is similarly cast. Our life's purpose is written by God without our input, yet somehow living out God's purpose is entirely dependent on our own choice to let God into a relationship with our purpose. "The truth is—you are as close to God *as you choose to be*. Intimate friendship with God is a choice, not an accident. You must intentionally seek it."[14] By contrasting human choice with mere accidents, Warren elevates our choices to the kind of status given to God's non-accidental dictates. The "God-as-friend" model discloses Warren's desire to leave some of the biggest decisions to us. What kind of friend would coerce friendship?

God, though, is a unique friend—one who, once friendship is freely engaged, commands compliance. Expressed in his phrase, "I must choose to obey God in faith," Warren posits a God who demands our obedience but places the onus on the individual to choose to do so. In this way, the authority of the self to make major life decisions based on the choice to be happy is admitted and additionally legitimated by a God that wants just that.

The anthropological ambiguity that issues from humans as free agents *and* dependent beings provides a safe space for the self-creation and self-improvement promoted in self-help books. If Warren unwittingly allows the choices of careers and spouses to legitimate themselves outside of God's determined world, in a consumer culture, there is little to stop the choosing what a purpose-driven life looks like. Then, God's overarching purposes may step in to underwrite those choices after the choice has been made, but this effectively reverses the terms of Warren's written word.

Choice and obedience flow on an alternating current; however it is the lack of control that God exerts over the details of life choices that permits us to pick and choose such details. Or, obedience to God equates to adherence to polysemic imperatives such as "be like Christ," "serve God," and "make God happy."[15] Such admonitions are broad enough to incorporate a wide variety of ways to interpret and satisfy God's commands, including those which originate in individual desire. Hence, the self that is authorized to make the choices that constitute one's own version of purpose on earth faces few obstacles in the manufacturing of oneself, as far as *The Purpose-Driven Life* is concerned. The fact that God has already sanctioned the choices that align themselves with divine general principles only serves to empower such choices.

His anthropology appeals to those intrigued by the promise of self-help books that meaning and direction are within grasp *and* to those who are skeptical of the self's capacity for such grasping. Hence the self-invention that is subtly promoted by Warren should remind us of McGee's belabored self. Recall that "working on oneself" presupposes a bifurcated self in which the inauthentic self is constantly scrutinized and ideally sloughed off to reveal the authentic self below. For Warren, authenticity is found in the part of the self that is created by God; the inauthentic self is that which has taken cultural, worldly cues for the forging of its identity. Yet instead of locating these two selves on opposite sides of an unbreachable wall, as Calvin does, Warren's theology and attendant anthropology sets up a semi-permeable partition between them. The fixed status of each human being in Calvin's thought is traded for the purpose-driven self that, while instructed to reject self-exploration, is simultaneously told to embark on a search for purpose. Even though the final destination of the search is that which God intends the self to be, the difference between the how of working on oneself found in more clear examples of self-help literature and the means to find purpose in *The Purpose-Driven Life* is minimal.

That the stated goal of the purpose-driven life is one that stands transcendent over the self while the means of achieving this goal does not restrict human pluck help explain *The Purpose-Driven Life*'s status as a best-seller. The potential for the pursuit of excavating an authentic self to end in a solipsistic blind alley is averted by Warren. Yet by concomitantly allowing the activity of working on one's self to proceed in reality, Warren is still able to satisfy the needs of the belabored self. In the end, the purpose-driven person is authorized to continually remake herself through the consumption of self-images as long as the effort is conceived of as having its source in God, not the self.

Yet the questions that involve the religious/cultural context in which such a book is such a success are still unanswered. How does the context of *The Purpose-Driven Life* illuminate Warren's words in ways that a textual interpretation cannot do fully? The push to attract seekers to a church has correlates to the incentive to attract consumers to a product. Establishing this correlation in an effort to position *The Purpose-Driven Life* in a cultural context informs the language of the book that will help us down the road.

NAVIGATING THE GOD-STEERED BOAT TO THE SEEKER'S SHORE

Forty years ago, Peter Berger tied secularization to the role of the capitalist market in framing religious decisions. He remarked that consumer freedom to choose suitable commodities operates in the religious marketplace as well. Consumer culture, then, shapes everything from the selection of a denomination, to whether to attend church at all, to the formation of a religious worldview. Yet there is an obstinacy to religious products that may help them resist complete manipulation by consumer culture. "[T]he dynamics of consumer preference does not, in itself, determine the substantive content—it simply posits that, in principle, they are susceptible to change, without determining the direction of change."[16] Yet as Berger remarks, the stability of religious ideas when thrown into the religious marketplace has little slowing-down effect on the expectation that the ideas will move in a direction that conforms to the desire of consumers.

The terms "seeker-sensitive" or "seeker-friendly" currently describe the methods used by many religious organizations that move their institutions in the direction that Berger initially described. Seeker-sensitive churches and pastors often amend their liturgy, building structure and even theology to appeal to needs of religious seekers and the unchurched.[17] These often uneasy amendments are tolerated if the religious institution is not tied too tightly to traditional, institutional ways of doing things. Richard Cimino and Don Lattin write that

> the underlying concept of "seeker" congregations is that churches should meet the wider consumer culture on its own ground. Ideas and practices—however strongly they may be tied to one's denominational tradition—may be abandoned if they stand in the way of drawing new members.[18]

As in Bauman's liquid modernity, consumer culture is able to overcome traditional, solid boundaries within which many churches used to reside. Unbound by tradition, pastors are then free to alter their medium and at times their message to the needs of the religious consumer. This practice is usually defended as being mutually beneficial to seekers and pastors. Seekers are freed from institutional ties to search for a church until a comfort level is reached; pastors are freed up from institutional restrictions to employ wide variety of novel techniques to get seekers in the door.

The seeker-sensitive model has theological consequences as well as practical ones. Robert Wuthnow provides a useful distinction that connects theological conviction with its effects.

> A spirituality of dwelling emphasizes *habitation*: God occupies a definite place in the universe and creates a sacred space in which humans too can dwell; to inhabit sacred space is to know its territory and to feel secure. A spirituality of seeking emphasizes *negotiation*: individuals search for sacred moments that reinforce their conviction that the divine exists, but these moments are fleeting; rather than knowing the territory, people explore new spiritual vistas, and they may have to negotiate among complex and confusing meanings of spirituality.[19]

Habitation within a spirituality of *dwelling* evokes the idea that God lives with humanity in a home with boundaries. "Home" connotes not only the limits that circumscribe the relationship between God and the inhabitants but also the security and reliability that comes with such limits. A spirituality of *seeking* is animated by similar longings for security in the quest for "sacred moments." Yet these moments experienced by the seeker are not lodged in a fixed metaphysical home and hence are always up for negotiation, are potentially fleeting, and are subject to abandonment.

As a result, a long-term commitment to a fixed, unchanging theology is less likely for the seeker. The serial renter of homes is, in a way, homeless and consequently uncomfortable with the kind of religious belief that forecloses other competing beliefs. Wade Clark Roof similarly notes in his study of baby boomers and religion that

> [a] surprising number of people we interviewed, upwards of one half, move easily from a discourse of seeking to one of believing, or vice versa, from believing to seeking. This would appear to be an important characterization of the present religious scene, and clearly strong evidence of how permeable the boundaries between believing and seeking have become.[20]

In other words, permeable boundaries surround not only decisions involving which religion or church to choose but matters of faith itself. Hence, seeking has a strong family resemblance to choosing in consumer culture.

In such a context, many religious institutions must follow the direction given by potential members (for attraction purposes) and actual members (for retention purposes) of a congregation in order to survive. With control over religious content wrested out of the grasp of traditional religious authorities and thrown into the consumer market, the method chosen to sell the religious message becomes paramount.

THE CUSTOMER IS *ALMOST* ALWAYS RIGHT

The method used to attract seekers is usually considered independent of the true mission of seeker-sensitive ministries. The core message, such as the Gospel in Christian churches, is typically the piece of non-negotiable content in effort to appeal to seekers. In fact, the maintenance of a core message amidst quickly shifting consumer preferences can become an asset rather than a liability. In an ironic twist, it is the ability of certain religious ideas to convey unchangeability that makes them appealing to many religious consumers.[21] Warren has adopted such an approach in the structuring of his Saddleback Church in Lake Forest, California, and his ministry. He echoes the need to adapt the medium to the needs of the congregation and his readers as long as the message remains untouched. In an answer to the question, "Do you advocate watering down the Gospel to cater to seekers?," Warren says in an interview, "Absolutely not! . . . The message must never change, but the methods must change."[22] The subtitle to *The Purpose-Driven Church: Growing without Compromising Your Message and Mission* underscores this dynamic.

Warren's own church is uniquely equipped to employ the methods needed to connect the Gospel message to the shifting needs of seekers and of the existing congregation. In an oft-told story, Warren recounts how he began Saddleback. Instead of the "build it and they will come" tactic, Warren began building his church in 1980 on the basis of the needs of the unchurched in the area. When he went door-to-door in the surrounding neighborhoods to announce the young church's presence, Warren asked people what they wanted in a church as opposed to telling them what Saddleback would be. "Why do you think most people don't attend church?," "If you were looking for a church, what things would you look for?," "What advice would you give to me as the pastor of a new church that really wants to be of benefit to the community?," and "How could I, as a pastor, help you?"[23]

All of these questions bestow authority on the people being questioned. Whether Warren took their responses to heart is beside the point; it is the "customer-is-always-right" attitude that transfers a sense of power from the leader of a church to its potential congregants and helps convert them to members. But Warren is careful to not reduce his early ministry down to marketing techniques.

> Even though I know what these people *really* needed most was a relationship to Christ, I wanted to listen first to what *they* thought their most pressing needs were. That's not marketing; it's just being polite. . . . Intelligent, caring conversation opens the door for evangelism with nonbelievers faster than anything else I've used. It is *not* the church's task to give people whatever they want or even need. But the fastest way to build a bridge to the unchurched is to express interest in them and show that you understand the problems they are facing.[24]

In other words, Saddleback was constructed around an Evangelical core, yet in order to grow the church, a kind of bait-and-switch was employed where the power of the minister is downplayed initially, though justified morally.

Saddleback is now a tangible testament to Warren's original impulse to cater to the needs of the unchurched while keeping the Gospel message intact. To counter the feeling of being lost in a twenty-thousand-member church, he uses the cellular church model that encourages small groups to form and perform many of the duties ascribed to the whole church. In addition, the Saddleback campus has five separate houses of worship, each with their own custom-fitted worship setting. For the edgy, energetic member, a heavy metal service is offered. For a laid back atmosphere, a service in an on-campus coffee shop covers you. For the member put off by the massive television screens and contemporary music, a traditional service gets back to basics. Saddleback is an anticipator and deliverer of almost whatever needs exist for its diverse membership.

The Purpose-Driven Life mirrors Warren's ecclesiology. Employing non-threatening methods of Gospel transmission, Warren uses colloquial language such as, "God wants to be your best friend,"[25] and user-friendly biblical translations such as Eugene Peterson's *The Message*. Such wording is justified by Warren as simply an attractive, accessible husk that entices people to find the kernel inside. Marshall McLuhan notwithstanding, Warren's separation of the medium and message is needed to expose unlikely seekers to the unchanging Gospel. And it is polite to do so.

Moreover, purpose itself is a friendly concept. It is general enough to resonate with people of all faiths as well as non-believers. It can be applied to all of life's tasks without recourse to religion. Like the non-menacing entrance to Saddleback, purpose can get seekers in the door. Despite Warren's contention that the difficult demands of the Gospel are the core of *The Purpose-Driven Life*, this does not take away from the fact that purpose, like all other aspects of his overall message, is a piece of cozy furniture housed in a welcoming package for the seeker.

Warren has been successful in retaining members of his church with seeker-sensitive methods. Yet holding readers to the commitment that they are asked to maintain at the start of *The Purpose-Driven Life* is more difficult than keeping congregants in the pews. The sales of the book prove that Warren has largely succeeded in attracting seekers of all kinds. And the context of the seeker-sensitive movement sheds light on the initial impact of the idea of purpose on a general population of seekers/religious consumers. Yet Warren intends that purpose be more than consumer bait. Left unexplained is the actual mechanism that allows one's purpose to remain a commodity long after the initial purchase. Or needed is an explication of how a religious idea is able to engage the religious consumer beyond acting merely as a billboard.

THE COMMODIFICATION OF RELIGION

Vincent Miller examines how consumer culture actually reaches down into the lives of consumers to shape the very substance and function of religious practice and belief. His primary claim is that consumer culture reframes the modern consumer's orientation to religion by modifying not only the meaning of many religious cultural products, but also the underlying habits and dispositions that fuel and maintain consumer activity.[26] These habits and dispositions are the result of the socializing forces of consumer culture and are characterized by an engagement with cultural products, religious and otherwise, that are disengaged from the material context that have historically contributed to their production and use. Because consumer culture promotes such engagement (or, if you will, disengagement), the consumption of the mere symbolic content of religious items, be they ideas or even belief systems, cheats the consumer out of a fuller religious experience by prohibiting the possibility that the "consumed" ideas can actually inform and alter material practices.[27] For Miller, it is this latter effect that establishes the basis of his critique of consumer culture.

Miller's argument is intended to counter other religiously framed criticisms of consumer culture that express dismay at its shallow engagement with religion. Many of these critics (Wells and Gillespie fall into this camp) replace the thin meanings that consumers take from religion with deeper, biblically grounded religious products.[28] The problem, according to Miller, is that fighting fire with a bigger fire, while honorable in spirit, operates under the assumption that it is possible to draw clear battle lines between those engaging the sacred as consumers and those who engage it properly.[29]

Miller invokes Michel Foucault and incorporates Talal Asad's critique of Clifford Geertz to challenge the usefulness of such critiques. Because power mediated through institutions always lurks below any discourse for Foucault, the intended meaning of expressions often deviates from the actual effects of what was said or written.[30] Consequently, the practices that inform and result from discourse are rarely consonant with the meaning of the surface of discourse or what the stated intention of a discourse is. Geertz's "thick descriptions" that rely heavily on the symbolic cache of religion may not actually tell us anything about how a meaning came to be the orthodox or unorthodox one as Asad points out.[31] It is, of course, power that issues from what Foucault calls discursive regimes (primarily institutions) that act behind the scenes to generate different effects than what the intended meaning of a discourse claims to have produced.[32] Hence, a hermeneutic that takes little account of the relationship between the power and the meaning of discourses is severely limited in its interpretative powers.

Foucault's power/meaning/knowledge dynamic serves two primary purposes for Miller. One, because meaning and practice are often at odds, he questions the ability of some religious critics of consumer culture to frame it accurately. Consumer culture is shallow, it fosters greedy materialism, it is undermining "true" religion—all are common complaints registered by critics. First of all, Miller asserts that consumer culture has engendered practices that do not have any of these pejorative qualities.[33] Thus a clean line between consumer culture and crass materialism cannot be easily drawn. Miller is not declaring that the disconnect between meaning and practice obscures our view of consumer culture thus rendering *any* critical statement about it meaningless. He certainly has some substantial and disparaging comments about the effects of consumer culture.[34] Miller simply posits that the discrepancy between meaning and practice disallows transparency in the interpretative process.

This discrepancy guides Miller into a genealogical investigation into how power is wielded in the construction of consumers and the culture that they inhabit. With consumer culture and religion, Miller considers the relationship between power and consumer desire to be the primary locus for socialization of the modern consumer. The power supply for running consumer culture comes from both institutions, such as corporations and their marketing apparatus, and the ideology that promotes unfettered consumer freedom. Miller argues that it is the twin strategies deployed by both seduction and misdirection that stoke consumer desire and direct it away from consumer items themselves and towards the act of consuming.[35]

Consumers are seduced, not necessarily by the product itself, but by images that may have nothing to do with the product. Because the desire evoked by seduction is one that cannot be satisfied through the simple consumption of a material product (i.e., drinking Budweiser will not make you the life of the party), advertising commonly misdirects the specific need to buy a product into a vague desire to consume in general. Desire, when manipulated in this way, loads the act of consumption with so many unrealistic consumer expectations that the act can never deliver on what is promised. Hence the act of consumption is "overdetermined and undecidable" to the point that "the inevitable failure of the commodity's promised synthesis drives us back into the marketplace for endless, futile repetitions."[36] Echoing Bauman, Miller concludes that it is simply the act of consuming for consuming's sake that constitutes the *primary practice* of consumers in a consumer culture. For neither seduction nor misdirection "has much to do with the vulgar attachment to material things; in fact, both militate against such attachments. . . . Individuals become increasingly indifferent to particular wants and objects of consumption" as they focus their attention on the act of consuming itself.[37]

Miller enlarges the scope of Bauman's analysis by including *religious* commodification. The consumption of religious products for consumption's sake follows the overall trajectory of liquid modernity, yet the means by which religious products become commodified differ from their secular counterparts. Miller arrives at the means of religious commodification by way of an analysis of insufficient scholarly approaches to the relationship between religion and consumer culture. He contends that the source of the mistake that many Christian critics of consumer culture make is the reduction of religion to *beliefs* alone. When this happens, orthodox beliefs become the principal weapon against the meaning-making machine that is consumer culture. Such attacks are based on the misunderstanding that one, consumer culture has a moral axe to grind against Christian orthodox beliefs, and two, that religion can be reduced to beliefs. In fact, consumer culture has no moral compass at all. It can and does assimilate abstractions from religious to anti-consumerist ones then packages them as intriguing, salable consumer items. And when religion is expressed only in terms of beliefs, it makes cultural assimilation easy and painless. "Jeremiads against the excesses of capitalism sell quite well as consumer goods," Miller writes, "as do evocative accounts of more properly orthodox ontologies or anthropologies."[38]

The inability of these lines of criticism to do real damage to consumer culture leads Miller to discuss the real culprit: the dematerialization of religious commodities circulating in a consumer culture. Because consumer culture brokers in symbolic exchange that is geared to meet individual desire, the mediators of consumer culture (buyers, sellers and promoters) are able to lift out the marketable elements from the material/political context of any religion and "sell" them to religious consumers. In turn, consumers are suited to complete this circuit of exchange because they have been educated in the ways of choosing and consuming the symbolic content of a consumer good for its beneficial properties. As a result,

> consumer culture encourages a shallow engagement with the elements of religious traditions because we are trained to engage beliefs, symbols, and practices as abstract commodities that are readily separable from their traditional contexts. . . . They [elements of religion] are reduced to shallow bricolage, not because such popular cultural production is necessarily shallow, but because members of consumer cultures encounter cultural objects shorn of their connection to traditions and communities and are trained by their consumption of commodified culture to treat them in a shallow manner.[39]

Deeper religious beliefs, for Miller, are always intertwined with the material contexts from which they emerge. And practices that are informed by beliefs and inform the beliefs themselves make up an essential component of any material context. Consequently, the relationship between consumer culture and religion can be seen as one where consumer culture damages religion by cleaving belief and practice then dis-embedding certain elements from religion. Detached, abstracted components of religion can then move freely into the consumer market and land into a host of other, unrelated social contexts with little or no resistance and with little or no edge.

Hence "consuming" the religious symbol is made easy when it is disembedded from its thorny and complex social context. The social context includes not only ethical and political conflicts that help construct religions but also bear the mark of the effects of such constructions. "[T]raditions are pillaged for their symbolic content, which is then repackaged and recontextualized in a way that jettisons their communal, ethical, and political consequences."[40] Hence the lack of ethical *gravitas* in commodified religious products that can only be forged in a material negotiation is accompanied by a lack of muscle needed to inform and challenge existing social norms.

For an example, Miller calls our attention to the "Joseph Campbell phenomenon." Here not only Campbell himself but also the book publishers and the producers of the PBS special that popularized him contribute to the commodification of Campbell's ideas. Campbell's ambitious study of the hero archetype itself represents an abstraction of sorts.[41] In his *The Hero with a Thousand Faces*, Campbell culls the internal character qualities of a variety of figures that fit a hero typology at the expense of ignoring the historical contexts of these figures.[42] Thus Campbell is guilty of decontextualization that then greases the wheels for a full commodification of his idea of the hero later.

The Power of Myth is the culmination of Campbell's initial work. This glossy, illustrated publication comprises Campbell's reflection on the hero archetype and its association to Jungian psychology, as expressed in his interviews with Bill Moyers. A combination of hagiography and motivational speech, *The Power of Myth* domesticates Campbell's ideas and makes them ready for market, according to Miller. And when planted in the fertile ground of a hungry and prepared consumer populace, Campbell's hero is readily consumed.[43]

Because the hero motif has only a superficial connection to any one religious/historical tradition, the idea of the hero can be recontextualized in the lives of consumers across space and time who wish to find the hero within. Miller states, "Campbell's debts to Jungian psychology and the *philosphia perennis* incline him to reduce all traditions to manifestations of fundamental archetypes, all religious figures to another instance of the "hero with a thousand faces."[44] Campbell's hero is not tethered to any one religious context and hence "floats free," leaving it able to be appropriated to individual desires while conveying a universality. In other words, Campbell liberally lifts spiritual ideas and religious figures from millennia of history and then seamlessly intertwines them with pithy admonitions to better one's life. Native American beliefs, Christ on the cross, the Buddha's teachings, and the chivalry of the Green Knight are all enlisted to send the message to "follow your bliss."[45] The differences between these figures, both in historical and geographical location, are minimized, which enables Campbell to crystallize and dispense a particularly pleasing message to the masses.

We see this kind of appropriation often in our culture, Miller asserts. Buddhist meditation is a stress reliever in the high-anxiety business world. Yoga is now a physical fitness regimen, and "What Would Jesus Do?" bracelets become status symbols in high school. These as well as the Joseph Campbell phenomenon suggest that while consumers may be therapeutically helped by such appropriations, a certain kind of violence is done to the ideas themselves. Miller reasons that the sheer symbolic content of religious ideas cut loose from its social context will, in turn, be unable to inform the practices of the life of the consumer of such content. Religious products are then used instrumentally while consumer ways of life proceed unobstructed. "As a result, they [religious beliefs and practices] are in danger of being reduced to abstracted, virtual sentiments that function solely to give flavor to the already-established forms of everyday life or to provide compensations for its shortcomings."[46] Ways of life not only continue unmolested but are also energized through the consumption of commodified religious products.

Exacerbating the problem, Christian self-help books meet the activity of consumption for consumption's sake with a presentation of a self that improves itself through endless consumption as we have already seen. Seeker-friendly religion similarly promotes consumer activity through the encasing of an unchanging message in an ever-changing package geared to satisfy consumer demand. Before applying Miller's ideas to *The Purpose-Driven Life*, it is necessary to critically analyze some of the commentary on Warren's book. These commentators share Miller's general concern about religious accommodation to consumer culture, yet they argue from a very different set of premises. Closer scrutiny into the predominant, yet deficient, literature that takes *The Purpose-Driven Life* head on will serve to reveal the usefulness of Miller's approach over theirs.

LOVE THE PURPOSE-DRIVEN PERSON, HATE *THE PURPOSE-DRIVEN LIFE*

Popularity, particularly that gained by a pastor, often begets criticism. Despite the millions who have bought his book and the thousands who attend his church each Sunday, Rick Warren has received his share of reprimands as well. Everything from his ambitious program to build churches to his invitation of pro-choice then-Senator Barack Obama to his church's AIDS conference in 2006 has been fodder for detractors.[47] Along the same lines of these criticisms, critics of *The Purpose-Driven Life* claim that Warren sells out the Gospel in order to make it palatable to the largest number of potential followers.[48] Some of these critiques are strictly theological—Warren's God is an adulterated God. Some label Warren's theology as a New Age spirituality in Evangelical clothing. His theology, as built on an unsound biblical hermeneutic, is supported by his New Age leanings; his New Age worldview is allowed by his inadequate theology.

A part of the strong reaction to Rick Warren can be attributed to the perception that his seeker-sensitive tactics dangerously mix the things of God with the things of the impermanent, protean, and frivolous world of consumer culture. A revisiting of David Wells's general criticism of seeker-friendly Christianity helps frame the overall argument that most critics of *The Purpose-Driven Life* utilize. Recall that Wells warns that if seeker-sensitive Evangelical pastors and authors adopt the ethos of consumer culture, their God becomes weightless, able to be easily picked-up, shaped, and molded at the caprice of consumer culture.[49] Given that consumer choice must be as unencumbered as possible, the weightless God, after the shaping and molding, is left without the ability to constrain the expansion of human demand for any need to be met.

> What has been lost in all of this, of course, is God's angularity, the sharper edges that truth so often has and that he has preeminently. It is

> our fallenness fleshed out in our modernity that makes God smooth, that imagines he will accommodate our instinct, shabby and self-centered as they so often are, because he is love.[50]

This is the god of New Age religion, and as Wells suspects, for a growing number of evangelicals as well.

> New Agers are very eclectic in gathering bits and pieces of worldviews according to personal preference, and so too are many of the baby boomers fished into evangelical churches by marketing techniques.... New Agers tend to gloss over the realities of sorrow, pain, aging, disease, and death out of a constitutional idealism that disparages the importance of the material world.[51]

Here and elsewhere, Wells makes explicit the connection between seeker-friendly tactics employed by Evangelical churches and those of New Age religions.[52] The New Age God *is* the weightless God that is the handmaiden of human self-actualization made manifest through the satisfaction of desires. And to the extent that Evangelicals have adopted the god of New Age spirituality, Wells foresees the end of Evangelicalism as we know it. It is precisely the association between New Age/self-seeking religion and the group of Evangelicals who bend to consumer culture that Wells uses as a way to judge pastors like Rick Warren. While Wells does not discuss Warren specifically, his suspicions about the New Age trajectory in Evangelicals like Warren are shared by several critics who focus on *The Purpose-Driven Life*.

For example, Warren Smith takes great pains to expose Rick Warren as a closet New Ager who thinly veils his true identity with Evangelical buzzwords. Less careful and more rhetorical than Wells, Smith cites evidence that relies on supposed connections between Warren and New Age Thought. The part of *The Purpose-Driven Life* that Smith uses as his chief piece of evidence to implicate Warren is his usage of the *New Century Version* translation of Ephesians 4:6: "He rules everything and is everywhere and is in everything."[53] Smith charges Warren with promoting a pantheistic worldview with this softer translation as opposed to the King James translation which reads, "One God and Father of all, who is above all, and through all, and in you all." The "you" in the latter translation, according to Smith, refers only to believers whom Paul was addressing. Warren expands God's involvement to all of creation, which Smith claims borders on the kind of pantheism commonly espoused by much New Age literature.[54] Other indictments include the mere mention of the word "force" by Warren,[55] the similarities between Warren's language in *The Purpose-Driven Life* and that of pastor Robert Schuller's *Possibility Thinking*,[56] and quotes from Aldous Huxley and the New Age writer Bernie Siegel used in the book.[57]

More generally, Warren's use of more colloquial biblical translations, especially *The Message*, suggests a watering down of the Gospel to Smith.

Predictably, Smith accuses Warren of slyly encoding older translations into language that is understandable to New Agers. And while Smith may seem hyper-sensitive and reactionary to Warren, he warns us that no element of New Age spirituality can infiltrate the Gospel, lest it be completely contaminated.

> A "little" arsenic can kill any of the possible good that might come from drinking that water. And a "little" leaven can kill any of the possible good that can come from *The Purpose-Driven Life*. And what I discovered is that there is more than a little leaven in what Rick Warren is teaching.[58]

It is this kind of totalizing metaphor that leaves no room for degrees of difference between interpretations of the Gospel. If Rick Warren fails the "true Gospel" test on one count, this peccadillo cannot be forgiven, and his entire ministry is justifiably New Age. Smith's intention is not to explain Warren's popularity, and therefore, he does not explicitly charge Warren with using the purported New Age content to attract religious seekers and/or consumers. Yet important is that Smith's relentless, albeit thin, attack on *The Purpose-Driven Life* is based on the belief that Warren expresses New Age tendencies through a purported straying from biblical truth.

Nathan Busenitz takes a more measured, less conspiratorial tone in his analysis of *The Purpose-Driven Life* than Smith yet manages to link concerns over Warren to the seeker-sensitive, consumer-friendly movement more directly. Busenitz is careful not to label Warren's book as heretical, noting that *The Purpose-Driven Life* puts forward an overall message that corresponds with biblical teaching.[59] Yet Warren makes mistakes by omission that result in a pliable theology that easily adapts to seeker mentality rather than to the God of the Bible.

Warren, Busenitz concedes, does mention themes that could offend seekers such as hell and sin. But unfortunately, Warren's use of harsher themes is nominal and lip-service, as he too quickly turns his focus exclusively to God's loving, merciful qualities. For instance, when grace or salvation is broached in *The Purpose-Driven Life*, the benefits of each are underscored with conditions, such as our sinful nature, that make these benefits more the subject of human need and not as gifts from God. Then our sin, as opposed to having its own weight, is used as a mere instrument to get what we want.

Warren's God is "unbalanced" as a result. A God who relates to humanity by only attracting people instead of by balancing the good with the bad is off balance. Such a God is a part of a theology that Warren can deliver to those who may want a sense of divine purpose but also want to feel good about themselves at the same time. Of course, this theology is attractive to seekers and religious consumers.

> Seeker-sensitive churches tend to minimize the gospel message in order to soften topics such as sin, repentance, divine wrath, and eternal punishment. The goal is to make unbelievers feel comfortable until they are ready to accept Jesus.... By embracing *The Purpose-Driven Life*, some readers and churches may become unwittingly entangled in the seeker-sensitive movement—a philosophical system that is inherently unbiblical.[60]

Again, the tight association between Warren's God who does not interrupt the comfort of believers is, like Wells's weightless God, one that also will not interrupt the exchange between seekers and that which is sought. Like Smith, Busenitz claims that Warren is able to get away with his theology by diverging from an orthodox interpretation of the Bible. Busenitz, though, refrains from accusing Warren of smuggling in New Age spirituality. Warren's theology is problematic enough without going this far.

Finally, Marshall Davis's book, *More Than a Purpose: An Evangelical Response to Rick Warren and the Megachurch Movement,* provides the fullest analysis of *The Purpose-Driven Life* and its place in a consumer culture. Like Smith and Busenitz, Davis mines the book for deviations from orthodox Evangelical theology and correct biblical interpretation. Yet Davis makes more explicit the association of these deviations with the authority of consumer culture than the other two critics.

He begins with a blunt assault on the first words of *The Purpose-Driven Life*. Warren's line, "It's not about you," which is intended to turn our attention away from ourselves and onto God, is never supported in the rest of the book. Instead of de-centering the self and centering God, Davis asserts that Warren places human beings on relatively equal footing with God.

> Warren's world is a man-centered universe. Although God plays an important supporting role, man is the center—or at least one of the centers.... Whereas he repeatedly declares that God is the only true focus, it seems like the *Purpose-Driven* universe revolves around us....
> In spite of statements to the contrary, *The Purpose-Driven Life* is about you. It is all about your life and how you can make it better.[61]

Davis provides several pieces of evidence for his claim. First, lines in the book like "God waits for us to act first," or "[S]piritual growth is a collaborative effort between you and the Holy Spirit," are semi-Pelagian according to Davis.[62]

Secondly, in similar fashion to Smith, Davis ties Warren to New Age spirituality through the supposed family ties with Norman Vincent Peale and Schuller. Peale's "positive thinking" is a known influence on Schuller's "possibility thinking," and Warren has written of Schuller's early influence on him.[63] The influence is expressed through Warren's way of defining such activities as repentance before God. That repentance is achieved by the overcoming of thinking that is self-defeating, which by necessity is God's way of thinking, is enough of an indication that Warren has adopted Peale's and Schuller's model. Davis writes, "Repentance is no longer the biblical idea of turning away from sin; it is simply a change of mind. Warren says that we repent whenever we modify our way of thinking to conform to God's way of thinking."[64] Consequently, if this kind of mind-meld is possible, Davis concludes that there exists no real difference between God and humanity in Warren's theology. And this lack of difference can only occur if there is a "downplaying of biblical theology in favor of self-help techniques."[65]

The downplaying is revisited by Davis in a chapter called "Doctrine for Dummies," in which he more explicitly attributes Warren's elevation of the self over God to a "carelessness in doctrinal matters."[66] Warren leaves repentance out altogether in his laying out of the path to salvation. This goes against biblical admonitions to repent before baptism, as articulated in Matthew 3:7–8.[67] More significantly, Davis charges Warren with advocating a spirit/body dualism as evinced by excerpts from *The Purpose-Driven Life*, such as, "You are a spirit who resides in a body," and "Like God, we are spiritual beings—our spirits are immortal and will outlast our earthly bodies."[68] This constitutes a kind of Gnosticism to Davis. The Chalcedonian formulation of Christ being fully human and divine, and by implication, that all Christians will be bodily resurrected is effectively rendered moot. Warren's doctrinal adulteration enables the advancement of "the lowest common denominator theology" which minimizes theological differences that people (and denominations) have. Warren's intent is not to arrive at a sound theology but to attract the largest number of readers by not scaring them off, Davis concludes.

It is both the psychologizing of the Gospel and the avoidance of doctrine that leads Davis to link *The Purpose-Driven Life* with consumer culture. In the chapter entitled, "The Market-Driven Life," Davis locates two primary forces that work in tandem to build up and maintain consumer culture: the authority of personal choice and the institutional willingness to satisfy customers. Davis rehearses these common themes of the seeker-sensitive movement before applying them to *The Purpose-Driven Life*. Interestingly, Davis traces Warren's tie to consumer culture through his seeker-sensitive language to pragmatism. Pragmatism, to Davis, subjects all religious truths to a test; if they work, they are true. Hence absolute truths, which may register no apparent or immediate benefits, are subordinated to pragmatic ones that do. So if *The Purpose-Driven Life* sells well, makes people happy, and brings people to Warren's version of the Gospel, the content of the book must also be true, pragmatically speaking.

> *The Purpose-Driven Life* does not use the Bible as an authority. It quotes it as a supporting witness when it is useful to do so. When the Bible is

used in this manner, its authority is undermined just as certainly as if its cardinal truths were blatantly contradicted.[69]

Honoring pragmatic success overrides the possibility that inherent truth resides in properly interpreted biblical concepts despite the consequences of the idea. Moreover, Davis contends that applying pragmatic principles to the truth permits Warren to define for himself what consequences are favorable and which are deleterious. Warren has clearly demonstrated to Davis that the satisfaction of religious customers is the desired goal of his ministry. Hence pragmatism in the service of seeker-sensitive methods wins out over absolute truth. The coupling of *The Purpose-Driven Life* with consumer culture by Davis, then, is forged solely by the *means* by which Warren reinforces the underpinnings of consumer culture. Though Davis mentions that the clever marketing of *The Purpose-Driven Life* plays a role in yoking Warren to the desires of consumers, he, like Smith and Busenitz, look to Warren's distancing from the true Gospel as the tie that binds.

What is at stake for all three of these critics of *The Purpose-Driven Life* is the Gospel itself. It is one thing if a New Age author twists God's Word inappropriately, but when a powerful Evangelical such as Warren commits similar errors, the damage is catastrophic. Important for my study is not whether these critics are standing on solid theological and biblical footing when they launch their critiques, but what their grievances about *The Purpose-Driven Life* say about their understanding of the relationship between consumer culture and theology. In all three, the criticisms center on claims that Warren has traded biblical truth for a message that appeals to seekers. This is accomplished by the subtle empowering of the self by means of enlisting God in the self's projects instead of the other way around. Consumer culture then becomes a catch-all term used to draw the battle lines between the things of God and all else. Because consumer culture is charged with the transgression of encouraging individuals to authorize their own search for meaning, God is obviated. Despite Warren's expressed protestations, consumer culture provides the environment for *The Purpose-Driven Life* to flourish for these critics. It is the inflation of the powers of the self in conjunction with the enlisting of God's powers in the self's tasks that tips Smith, Busenitz and Davis off to the alliance between Rick Warren and consumer culture.

While there is a connection between the expansive self and consumer culture, the problem is that it is made by these critics based on the premise that Warren and presumably the seekers who adopt a purpose-driven life operate with a flawed theology. Recall that Miller's bone of contention with critiques such as these is that they reduce consumer culture to that which offers a competing set of *beliefs* that then drives the seeker-sensitive movement. Then, only a better belief system built on what they perceive is the true Gospel can legitimately confront books like *The Pur-*

pose-Driven Life. This approach to the relationship between religion and consumer culture is a problem for Miller for the simple reason that beliefs do not drive our behavior.[70]

Miller stresses that there are plenty of devout people who allow their beliefs to inform an anti-consumerism stance yet still act and think primarily as consumers. Simple realignment of beliefs has little effect on the actions of consumers in a consumer culture, in other words. The problem here, apart from the theoretical difficulty of dividing belief systems up into "Gospel-loyal" and "Gospel-disloyal," is that this binary forces the hitching of consumer culture to more clear value-laden ideologies, the primary one being materialism.[71] When consumer culture is reduced to the selfish drive to organize one's life around the acquisition of material goods, it becomes a straw man. Consumer culture, as more of a value-neutral cultural reflex to the interaction between individual desire and marketing, can actually take up an anti-materialism stance, which is in part the result of a desire, and strip it of its moral weight, thus making it a choice amongst others.[72]

This insight is lost on these critics of *The Purpose-Driven Life*. Instead of grounding their criticisms on a consumer culture that works at its base level by brokering in abstracted religious ideas and practices, Smith, Busenitz, and Davis quickly link *The Purpose-Driven Life* to consumer culture by virtue of the book's perceived deviance from orthodox doctrine. Their neglect of this more foundational facet of consumer culture generates two important consequences. One, the underestimation of the power and scope of consumer culture to absorb even the shop-worn stance that they take up—that of the anti-secular, anti-consumerist position—can render their critiques impotent. Anger towards Christians who sell out to the New Age spirituality or towards those who use seeker-sensitive methods can be packaged to compete against other commodified ideas. Or the position of transcendence that these critics claim to be arguing from can be quickly converted into another immanent position quite easily.

Two, when a critique of *The Purpose-Driven Life* stays at the level of belief or theological doctrine, the primary way that the book's message merges with the way in which consumers actually live as consumers is missed. As Miller asserts, consumer life is driven by the ability of consumer culture to abstract and commodify certain religious ideas and practices—not by the establishment of its own competing ideology.[73] Hence when consumer culture is criticized on theological grounds alone, it can be linked to New Age spirituality more easily, and the real mechanism of consumer culture in its relationship with religion is bypassed. Their style of attack stays on the surface of the discourse involving religion and consumer culture and never reckons with the ways in which consumer culture works below one's beliefs about it. As a result, these criticisms of *The Purpose-Driven Life*, while consistent with a general Evangelical suspicion of the self, nonetheless attempt to treat the symptom while the cause of the problem is left untouched.

An understanding of the relationship between *The Purpose-Driven Life* and consumer culture must, as Miller puts it, "attend to the nonintentional aspects of social and economic systems, how they frequently work without any supporting ideology or implicit ontology."[74] The implication that Warren is simply taking cues from marketing strategies to sell his message to the widest audience does not further our understanding of the dynamics of consumer culture.

The Purpose-Driven Life participates in the dynamics of consumer culture on a fundamental level; that it has seeker-sensitive qualities is predicated on the availability of ready-made, commodified religious products, not the other way around. Miller's deeper investigation moves us beyond a kind of culture war between those guardians of the "true Gospel" and the apologists for seeker religion—a step towards a clearer understanding of purpose, and hence towards the kind of vocation that can possibly move beyond its commodified form.

VOCATION ON VACATION

Without expressing the equation of purpose and vocation outright, it can be said that Warren's phrasing and intention of his idea of purpose mimic those found in the original idea of the Protestant vocation. Warren echoes Luther's expansion of vocations to include all jobs so long as love for one's neighbor is the fruit of labor. And like Luther, the actual job that one uses to express brotherly love is inconsequential. Having a purpose dictates that

> [y]ou are called to serve God. Growing up, you may have thought that being "called" by God was something only missionaries, pastors, nuns, and other "full-time" church workers experiences, but the Bible says every Christian is called to service. Your call to salvation included your call to service. These are the same. Regardless of your job or career, you are called to *full-time* Christian service.[75]

In addition, like a vocation, one's true purpose in life acts as a mediator between God and yourself that translates God's will into proper thoughts and actions. Instead of articulating a singular purpose that God calls us to live out, *The Purpose-Driven Life* depicts God's will as made up of five broad purposes. These purposes make up the foundation off of which human purposes are granted their own legitimacy. They are as follows: one, that humans bring enjoyment to God; two, that humans participate in God's family; three, that humans become like Christ; four, that humans serve God; and five, that humans fulfill their mission in the world. All five are general in that they apply equally to all and speak to the baseline activities that align individual purposes with God's will. For instance, the second purpose states that the tripartite Godhead reveals that God "treasures relationship," hence one of God's general purposes is to have all of creation included in the divine family.[76]

If we respond suitably to God's purposes, our own individual purposes in life are made manifest. Just as an individual's calling gains its direction from the original call from God, so too purpose is found and lived out based solely on God's purposes. For instance, Warren asserts that God's purpose in sending Jesus is so that humans emulate him.[77] Likewise, he claims that the purpose behind God's insistence that the Gospel be spread is so that humans find their purpose in mission work.[78] A purpose, like a vocation, conjoins God's will to proper human activity so that God's demands are satisfied through responsive human activity.

Purpose also disciplines the human tendency to wander off the righteous path. Recall Calvin's description of a calling as a governor of the fickle mind. Warren, too, ascribes this function to purpose.

> Knowing your purpose simplifies your life. It defines what you do and what you don't do. Your purpose becomes the standard you use to evaluate which activities are essential and which aren't. . . . Without a clear purpose you have no foundation on which you base decisions, allocate your time, and use your resources. You will tend to make choices based on circumstances, pressures, and your mood at that moment. People who don't know their purpose try to do too much—and *that* causes stress, fatigue, and conflict.[79]

It is God's plan, in both Warren's purpose and Calvin's calling, which quells the worried mind. And by binding followers to a direction in life that reliably accords with God's overall plan, Warren likewise leaves little room either to ignore the charge put before those called or to expropriate freely how God's purposes are to be fulfilled.

Yet Calvin's *Institutes* are a far cry from *The Purpose-Driven Life*. While *The Purpose-Driven Life* agrees in principle with Calvin's assertions of the total depravity of humanity and the absolute sovereignty of God, the sharp edges of Calvin's expression are smoothed out considerably by Warren. Much of Warren's modification of some of the more unforgiving theological ideas can be attributed to his desire to attract readers to the Gospel—not repel them. And when these theological ideas are enlisted in the service of aiding the reader's search for purpose in life, instead of explicitly arguing for their truth, Warren also enlists the help of consumer culture.

PURPOSE AS COMMODIFIED VOCATION

Purpose, as an ersatz vocation, is found and lived out in a purpose-driven life at arm's length from the activities of daily work and the social context that animates them. In general, Warren minimizes talk of how one's purpose in life negotiates with the socioeconomic reality. When Warren does address more tangible, concrete life situations, he abstracts from these, thereby reducing them to emotional or psychological states. He continually asserts the additive therapeutic function of purpose, as opposed to a more subtractive role of fighting off bad circumstances. For instance, purpose "gives meaning to your life," "simplifies your life," "focuses your life," and "motivates your life."[80] Purpose marshals a collection of tactics for navigating the minefield that is the world without demanding that the world inform the navigation process. Left behind is the admission that the successful search for purpose/meaning involves more than the surmounting of insidious thoughts and emotions. Or purpose enables the avoidance of the fact that troubling emotional states are tied to their material contexts.

Not that we should expect a Rauschenbuschian wrestling with social reality from Warren. However, if the purpose-driven life was informed in part by its material context, it *should* be able to account for the ability of some to find their purpose more easily or more frustratingly within the socioeconomic context in which they inhabit. Yet for Warren, finding and living the purpose-driven life can be fulfilled by all in spite of these realities.

Expectedly, when Warren does confront aspects of the world's material context, he does so superficially. The role of money in our lives is dealt with by Warren as that which competes for God's demands for allegiance. Money can stand in the way of surrendering fully to God or sacrificing one's own purposes to those of God. He focuses on the damaging orientations to the issue of money instead of the ways that money and its flow in a capitalistic economy alters the socioeconomic context in which purposes are presented to readers. The extent of his treatment of money is as follows:

> The most difficult area to surrender for many people is their money. Many have thought, "I want to live for God but I also want to earn enough money to live comfortably and retire someday." Retirement is not the goal of a surrendered life, because it competes with God for the primary attention of our lives. Jesus said, *"You cannot serve both God and money"* and *"Wherever your treasure is, your heart will be also."*[81]

Then,

> [m]oney has the greatest potential to replace God in your life.... When Jesus is your Master, money serves you, but money is your master, you become its slave. Wealth is certainly not a sin, but failing to use it for God's glory is.... The Bible is very clear: God uses money to test your faithfulness as a servant. That is why Jesus talked more about money than he did about either heaven or hell.... How you manage your money affects how much God can bless your life.[82]

Fair enough, yet in Warren's version of the God/mammon problem, he reduces the complicated issue of money down to a question on a test that must be answered correctly. Thus money becomes a symbol whereby readers merely have to tamp down its significance in their lives by merely passing this test. In order for Warren to present money in this way, actual money must be condensed to its symbolic function as it fights other symbols in a kind of spiritual warfare. The person attempting to live a purpose-driven life should just put money in its rightful place within the divine economy, while the ways that money actually operates in the world go on without interference.

On the issue of materialism—terrain that could permit Warren to state how one's purpose can plot a course between the real need for material things and the exaggerated significance placed on accumulation in a consumer culture—Warren, again, pits the issue against that which stands outside our true purpose.

> Many people are driven by materialism. Their desire to acquire becomes the whole goal of their lives. This drives to always want more is based on the misconceptions that having more will make me more happy, more important, and more secure, but all three ideas are untrue. Possessions only provide *temporary* happiness. . . . Your value is not determined by your valuables, and God says the most valuable *things* in life are not things.[83]

Materialism is positioned as an ideology that stands in stark opposition to the life guided by God's purposes. This positioning allows Warren to capture the act of acquiring material things with non-controversial descriptions and plausible criticisms. Categorized thusly, materialism is easily discredited by the vastly superior drive that is injected with purpose from God. Once overcome by a purpose-driven person, materialism is rendered symbolically powerless.

But how has materialism come to vie for our attention over God? An honest grappling with this question would force Warren into a more nuanced discussion of the difference between the legitimate need for things and the ideology of materialism, which could then impact how a purpose is lived out in the material world. Such a discussion could then lead to questions about what forces have worked to distance materialism from material need. Yet when materialism is only viewed as that which is in competition with God's will, it is the proper orientation to material things that figures into the living out of one's purpose; material things are idolatrous symbols or utterly irrelevant. When put this way, the purpose-driven life that has put materialism in its proper place is ill-equipped to challenge capitalistic institutions that benefit greatly by our materialism. Or if it is merely the *attitude* towards materialism that needs adjustment, purpose can play no role in the adjusting of the material context of the purpose-driven life.

Warren then moves from actual material obstacles, such as money and material things, to psychological and emotional obstacles to the purpose-driven life. Guilt, anger, fear, and the anxious need for approval constitute Warren's problem emotions. On fear, he states:

> Many people are driven by fear. Their fears may be a result of a traumatic experience, unrealistic expectations, growing up in a high-control home, or even genetic predisposition. Regardless of the cause, fear-driven people often miss great opportunities because they're afraid to venture out. . . . Fear is a self-imposed prison that will keep you from becoming what God intends for you to be. You *must* move against it with the weapons of faith and love.[84]

Fear is not unnatural; of course every human experiences it often. The point is that Warren contrasts the life driven by purpose with the life driven by emotions without accounting for the sources of these drives in twenty-first-century America. And therefore, his notion of purpose hovers above the social fray here too. Fear is unhinged from its possible causes as it is set up as a kind of amorphous enemy of faith and love. Then Warren deploys purpose as that which guides readers through and around crippling emotional states. When purpose is situated as such, it never has to overcome concrete aspects of a social context such as a "traumatic experience" or a "high-control home"—only the emotions that result from them. Again, purpose poses no challenge to the causes of overblown emotional states. In fact, those living a purpose-driven life can conceivably consider issues that generate emotional trouble as excuses to be offered as to why a purpose is not being lived out.

Several more brief examples are equally suggestive. When addressing globalization and the connection that American consumers have with people all over the world, Warren writes, "Probably most of the clothes you are wearing and much of what you ate today were produced in another country. We are more connected than we realize. These are exciting days to be alive."[85] Or on the subject of multinational corporations, he states, "The largest media and business conglomerates are all multinational. Our lives are increasingly intertwined with those in other nations as we share fashions, entertainment, music, sports, and even fast food."[86] When reaching out to a suffering global community is called for, prayer is sufficient. Yet the prayer (and subsequent mission work for some) is geared strictly to effecting the salvation of those who have not heard the Gospel:

> The first way to start thinking globally is to begin praying for specific countries. World-class Christians pray for the world. Get a globe or map and pray for nations by name. . . . People may refuse our love or reject our message, but they are defenseless against our prayers. Like an intercontinental missile, you can aim a prayer at a person's heart whether you are ten feet or 10,000 miles away.[87]

Again, we should not expect a leftist rant from Warren that tackles unjust business practices and exploitation of cheap foreign labor.[88] Nor should we expect Warren to downplay the importance of evangelism. But left out of his equation are the working conditions of many producers of our imports as well as the issues that stem from the coalescence of power within the multinationals. Globalization is only a neat network, nothing more.

Lastly, as we saw from the earlier quote, Warren makes clear that a purpose-driven life can be lived fully despite the nature and conditions of one's job or career. In lock-step with many later theological articulations of vocation, the actual activities of work and the material conditions that shape them fade into the background when prioritizing that which contributes to living with real purpose. As with material things, preoccupation with one's work is judged to be another orientation towards the world that is not only excessive, but also that which unjustifiably competes with the drive to align with God's purposes. It is comportment towards or approach to one's work that Warren disparages—not the actual work that one performs in a job or career.

> We become preoccupied with making a living, doing our work, paying bills, and accomplishing goals as if these tasks are the point of life. They are not. The point of life is learning to love—God and people. Life minus love equals zero.[89]

Warren's point is well taken—workaholism is certainly not a healthy way to engage work. It is, however, the contrast between work and the real "point of life" that enable such an approach. Minus a fleshing out of how one's purpose interacts with a dissatisfying job, the status of work on that job is denigrated.

Further on in the book, he lumps an exaggerated status of one's career in with more obviously trivial pursuits that more clearly do not or should not stack up against purpose. "You are going to give your life for something. What will it be—a career, a sport, a hobby, fame, wealth? None of these will have lasting significance."[90] By grouping a career in with these more inconsequential activities such as a hobby or superficial goals such as fame, by extension, Warren succinctly classifies work as a fleeting activity. Of course it is true that no job lasts forever, but significant is that the finiteness of a career is enough to relegate it to insignificance when compared to an ever-lasting purpose.

With purpose thus situated, the work that fills out a job or career has little to do with the fulfillment of one's purpose. If it is the symbolic significance of one's career (or a hobby) that matters, purpose is freed up to realize itself apart from the material details of one's career. As such, increased job volatility wrought by flexible capitalism is one such detail that cannot derail or even make contact with the purpose-driven life. Or that a growing number of employees are disengaged from partaking in meaningful decision making at work could be similarly ignored when driven by one's purpose.

It is the freeing up of purpose from the messiness of the concrete work world that contributes most heavily to its appropriation by readers as a consumer item. As the functional equivalent of vocation, a purpose cannot be found and lived out in the absence of meaningful work without manipulating its meaning. To get around the reality that the material conditions of many jobs militate against the experience of meaningfulness on the job, Warren offers the promise of a purpose-driven life that does not worry itself with such concerns. Like Campbell's hero, purpose-*qua*-vocation is salable as a commodity precisely because of its detachment from any material context.

The delivery of both the concept of purpose and Campbell's hero is necessarily preceded by the production of that which is being delivered. Like purpose, the idea of the hero is disciplined for the market through its abstraction that, in the end, can be drawn on as inspiration in the midst of hardship. Similarly, the idea of purpose functions as a commodified version of vocation through its ability to guide readers to emotional stability that is possible only if the idea has been sufficiently cut loose from a material context, not as a concept in a self-help book or a seeker-sensitive ministry. And because it is purpose that is delivered to and finally consumed by readers, the process of its commodification stands as a clearer indicator of the role that consumer culture plays in the interpretation of *The Purpose-Driven Life* than the delivery apparatus.

CONCLUSION

Purpose in *The Purpose-Driven Life* can be consumed by anyone and be applied to almost any life project. The absence of any wrestling with how purpose should engage the material realities of the readers in order to be realized suggests that it is able to flow in a consumer culture with few obstacles. It is the particular ability of consumer culture to commodify everything from actual physical objects to concepts that tighten the connection between Warren's purpose-as-vocation and consumer culture.

And yet the predominant articulation of the connection between *The Purpose-Driven Life* and consumer culture has been that of Warren's complicity in the seeker-sensitive movement. The shortcomings of such critiques are made evident by utilizing Miller's alternative way to grasp the connection between *The Purpose-Driven Life* and consumer culture. Yet Miller's project is not merely descriptive; prescriptions geared towards redressing the social injustice that issues from the relationship between religion and consumer culture necessarily follow his description.

A consequence of the success of a book like *The Purpose-Driven Life* is the effective silencing of critical responses to harmful displays of power in countless workplace environments. If we take Miller and Bauman seriously, consumer culture operates ideologically to achieve its cultural hegemony over certain aspects of religious life. And if we take Sennett seriously, consumer culture possesses the capacity to act as insulation that relieves those at the head of a corporation from responsibility for the welfare of their employees. The concept of vocation and its Warrenian permutations carry the *potential* to act as points of resistance in the current cultural sea, but only if they can engage their adherents in a non-commodified form.

NOTES

1. Rick Warren, *The Purpose-Driven Church: Growth Without Compromising Your Message and Mission* (Grand Rapids, MI: Zondervan, 1995).
2. http://www.christianpost.com/article/20070704/28293_Christian_Books_Still_Dominate_All-Time_Best-Sellers_Lists.htm.
3. Yet some do exist. For examples, see Charles Swindoll, *Simple Faith* (Nashville: Thomas Nelson, 2003); Charles Stanley, *Landmines in the Path of the Believer: Avoiding the Hidden Dangers* (Nashville: Thomas Nelson, 2007); James C. Dobson, *Love Must Be Tough: New Hope for Marriages in Crisis* (Carol Stream, IL: Tyndale House Publishing, 2007); Gary Chapman, *Hope For the Separated: Wounded Marriages Can Be Healed* (Chicago: Moody Publishing, 2005).
4. Classic examples include Norman Vincent Peale's *The Power of Positive Thinking*, and M. Scott Peck's *The Road Less Traveled*. An incredibly popular current book that exemplifies this angle of Christian self-help is Joel Osteen's *Your Best Life Now*. For a more explicit Christian example, see Joel Osteen, *Your Best Life Now* (New York: Warner Books, 2004). For one that leans more towards general New Age spirituality, see Neale Donald Walsch, *Conversations with God: An Uncommon Dialogue* (New York: Putnam, 1996).
5. Examples include any of the works of Billy Graham and the classic, *My Utmost for His Highest*, by Oswald Chambers. See Oswald Chambers, *My Utmost for His Highest* (Uhrichsville, OH: Barbour Publishing, 2008).
6. Malcolm Gladwell, "The Cellular Church: How Rick Warren Built His Ministry," *The New Yorker*, September 9, 2005.
7. Warren, *The Purpose-Driven Life*, 19.
8. Warren, 18–19.
9. Warren, 20.
10. Warren, 21.
11. Warren, 238–39.
12. Warren, 109.
13. Warren, 110.
14. Warren, 98.
15. Warren, 63, 171, 227.
16. Peter Berger, *The Sacred Canopy: Elements of a Sociological Theory of Religion* (New York: Anchor Books, 1967), 146.
17. Kimon Howland Sargeant, *Seeker Churches: Promoting Traditional Religion in a Non-Traditional Way* (New Brunswick, NJ: Rutgers University Press, 2000), 2.
18. Richard Cimino and Don Lattin, *Shopping for Faith: American Religion in the New Millennium* (San Francisco: Jossey-Bass, 1998), 68.
19. Robert Wuthnow, *After Heaven: Spirituality in America Since the 1950s* (Berkeley: University of California Press, 1998), 3–4.
20. Wade Clark Roof, *Spiritual Marketplace: Baby Boomers and the Remaking of American Religion* (Princeton, NJ: Princeton University Press, 1999), 131.

21. This argument is made tangentially by Rodney Stark and William Bainbridge. They argue that the success of Christianity is largely based on presenting appealing concepts, or "compensators," that many other competing religions do not. These compensators, such as the idea of communion with God after death, provide reassurance amidst a world that may not compensate good behavior at times. See Rodney Stark and William Sims Bainbridge, *The Future of Religion: Secularization, Revival and Cult Formation* (Berkeley: University of California Press, 1986). In addition, some recent writings on the relationship between consumer culture and religion *credit* the rise of consumer culture with the persistence of religion. For an example, see the collection of essays in John Michael Gigge and Diane H.Winston, ed., *Faith in the Market: Religion and the Rise of Urban Commercial Culture* (New Brunswick, NJ: Rutgers University Press, 2002).

22. Richard Abanes, *Rick Warren and the Purpose That Drives Him* (Eugene, OR: Harvest House, 2005), 29.

23. Abanes, 47.

24. Warren, *The Purpose-Driven Church*, 39–40.

25. Warren, *The Purpose-Driven Life*, 85.

26. Miller, 32, 73.

27. Miller, 83.

28. Miller, 15.

29. Miller focuses primarily on scholars in the radical orthodoxy tradition, such as Graham Ward and D. Stephen Long, who may not rely solely on a certain biblical interpretation for their analysis, yet still do not touch the real problem. Both Ward and Long trace the development of modern consumer desire to the seeds planted by liberal economics of the eighteenth and nineteenth centuries. The assumptions of classical economics that place the individual at the center of consumption choices perpetually connect desire with a lack that consumption cannot satiate. Miller contends that while the radical orthodox critique moves beyond mere biblical hermeneutics, it leans on the classical economic description of consumer behavior as rational in order to describe current consumer behavior. Theirs is not a useful critique because it is unable to square with the irrationality of consumer choice that is the result of the marketing and advertising apparatus that mediate consumption. The reality, for Miller, is that any straightforward historical line drawn from a set of events in the past to today is made crooked by power that asserts itself into social discourse concerning the meaning of consumer culture. See Miller, 111–14.

30. See Michel Foucault, *Discipline and Punish: The Birth of the Prison* (New York: Vintage, 1979) and *The History of Sexuality* (New York: Vintage, 1980).

31. Miller, 20–21.

32. Miller, 22–23.

33. Miller, 18.

34. Miller, 179–228.

35. Miller, 109–10; 116–21.

36. Miller, 121.

37. Miller, 121.

38. Miller, 18.

39. Miller, 30.

40. Miller, 84.

41. See Joseph Campbell, *The Hero with a Thousand Faces* (Princeton: Princeton University Press, 1968).

42. See Walter B. Gulick, "The Thousand and First Face," in *Paths to the Power of Myth: Joseph Campbell and the Study of Religion*, ed. Daniel Noel (New York: Crossword, 1990), 28–43.

43. Miller, 83–84.

44. Miller, 84.

45. The leading quote in the chapter entitled, "Sacrifice and Bliss" reads, "If you follow your bliss, you put yourself on a kind of track that has been there all the while,

waiting for you, and the life that you ought to be living is the one you are living. Wherever you are—if you are following your bliss, you are enjoying that refreshment, that life within you, all the time." Joseph Campbell, *The Power of Myth* (New York: Anchor, 1991), 113.

46. Miller, 105–6.

47. In addition to Evangelicals, Warren has garnered criticism from a wide-ranging group. For a Catholic response, see Joseph M. Champlin, *A Catholic Perspective on* The Purpose-Driven Life (Totowa, NJ: Catholic Book Publishing Company, 2006). For a more secular response, see Alan Wolfe, "The Limits of *The Purpose-Driven Life*: Can Twenty Million Readers Be Wrong?," *In Character,* Winter 2005.

48. James Davison Hunter captures both the critic and the critiqued in the Evangelical community with his claim that "contemporary Evangelicalism contains both sectarian and accommodationist tendencies." James Davison Hunter, *Evangelicalism: The Coming Generation* (Chicago: University of Chicago Press, 1987), 196.

49. Wells, *God in the Wasteland*, 101.

50. Wells, 114.

51. Wells, 222.

52. See Wells, 27, 55–56, 188–89, 212.

53. Warren, 88.

54. Warren Smith, *Deceived on Purpose: The New Age Implications of the Purpose-Driven Church* (Magalia, CA: Mountain Stream Press, 2005), 81–85.

55. "Force," according to Smith, is used by many prominent New Age thinkers such as Neale Donald Walsch and Marianne Williamson to describe a universal life energy that all living things possess as well as God. This force is divine, and hence permits an equation between humans and God as expressed in some New Age literature. See Smith, 65, 77–78.

56. Smith, 103–13.

57. Smith, 47.

58. Smith, 173.

59. Nathan Busenitz, "A Sense of Purpose: Evaluating the Claims of *The Purpose-Driven Life*," in *Fool's Gold*, ed. John MacArthur (Wheaton, IL: Crossway, 2004), 48, 60.

60. Busenitz, 59.

61. Marshall Davis, *More Than a Purpose: An Evangelical Response to Rick Warren and the Megachurch Movement* (Enumclaw, WA: WinePress Publishing, 2006), 18.

62. Davis, 70.

63. Warren participated in one of Schuller's seminars in 1984 and several others in the early 1990s when Warren's Saddleback Church was growing. Warren has said in the past that Schuller's style of ministry had an impact on his own ministry and thought about church building. Though since the publication of *The Purpose-Driven Church* in 1995, Warren has consistently denied any substantial connection to Schuller as he began to suspect Schuller's connection to New Age spirituality. Schuller's invitations to the Mormon motivational author, Stephen Covey, disturbed Warren and implied to him that Schuller was stretching the boundaries of Christianity to include those who are distant from Evangelical principles. Schuller was disturbed by this rejection and in a series of letters, asked Warren to speak at Schuller's church repeatedly in the late 1990s, the Crystal Cathedral. Warren has rejected all of these offers. From Abanes, 99–106.

64. Davis, 25.

65. Davis, 25–26.

66. Davis, 51.

67. Davis, 65–66.

68. Davis, 68–69.

69. Davis, 106.

70. Miller, 15.

71. Wuthnow, "A Good Life and a Good Society: The Debate Over Materialism," in *Rethinking Materialism: Perspectives on the Spiritual Dimension*, ed. Robert Wuthnow (Grand Rapids, MI: Eerdmans, 1995), 1–21.

72. Wade Clark Roof notes that, while an "anti-materialism" stance may not solely guide the worldviews of most seekers, materialism certainly is not wholeheartedly embraced either. Despite the fierce striving for material comfort or perhaps luxury, "there is a yearning for something that transcends a consumption ethic and material definitions of success." Roof, *Spiritual Marketplace*, 128.

73. Miller, 18.
74. Miller, 18.
75. Warren, 229.
76. Warren, 117.
77. Warren, 171.
78. Warren, 281–319.
79. Warren, 31.
80. Warren, 31–33.
81. Warren, 81.
82. Warren, 267.
83. Warren, 29.
84. Warren, 28–29.
85. Warren, 300.
86. Warren, 300.
87. Warren, 300–301.

88. Since the writing of *The Purpose-Driven Life*, Warren and his wife, Kay, started their P.E.A.C.E. plan to begin to combat the AIDS epidemic in Africa. While their efforts have directly targeted the causes and spread of the disease in Africa, the *overall* effort still echoes his statements in the book. On the P.E.A.C.E. plan website, five "giants" are identified as the primary hindrances to living a full life in countries ravaged by AIDS. Admittedly, three of these (extreme poverty, pandemic diseases and rampant illiteracy) represent a stark departure from the emotional hindrances to purpose-driven living. Yet the P.E.A.C.E. plan's overall purpose is to provide more emotional peace than political peace. See http://www.thepeaceplan.com/ (accessed January 27, 2008).

89. Warren, 125.
90. Warren, 232.

FIVE
Towards a Political Vocation

> Our aim is to recognize what Lincoln pointed out: The fact that there are some respects in which men are obviously not equal; but also to insist that there should be an equality of self-respect and of mutual respect, an equality of rights before the law, and at least an approximate equality in the conditions under which each man obtains the chance to show the stuff that is in him when compared to his fellows.
> —Theodore Roosevelt

The echoes of Weber's closing salvo in *The Protestant Ethic and the Spirit of Capitalism* that hollows out any power that a vocation truly possesses in the working life reverberate today. Yes, the charge of a calling to work hard lingers on in our lives despite disenchantment with the world despite our flagging attempts to justify its burden religiously. Yet today, instead of the "prowling" that the ghosts do in the thick of the night, they now seem to be moving around in broad daylight, if the frequency of vocation language in self-help books is any indication. As the reception of the *The Purpose-Driven Life* indicates, the need for divine sanction of our lives is prominent, relevant, and animated with serious God-talk as it is spoken loudly in the mainstream. If a calling is not truly connected to our highest spiritual values, it appears as if many have not yet received Weber's news.

And if vocation language is still prevalent, even if packaged in a self-help book, why not celebrate its attempt to capture a powerful idea in the history of Christian theology? Does not Warren's spirited portrayal of purpose bring *some* benefits to his readers despite the inattention to actual work? Is not equanimity with purpose *qua* vocation more helpful than the allowance of an unsatisfying work experience to prevent *any* participation in a vocation, as Ellul would have it? Is a decontextualized, dematerialized, depoliticized calling better than no calling at all?

While answering "yes" to the latter two questions is justifiable, it is nonetheless a conservative answer. This is not to say that Warren's book and ministry have not helped millions of people tap deeper meaning in their lives. Purpose could be strictly interpreted as a life-strategy that acts as a steady moving ship plowing through the choppy waters of ephemeral life projects and general meaninglessness. Warren himself would likely be satisfied with this interpretation as no doubt countless readers of his book have used it in this way. Yet such an interpretation foregrounds the meaning of purpose not against the backdrop of one's working environment, but against a therapeutic one. Satisfaction with or even resignation to Warren's purpose as the *best* that a vocation can now aspire puts stock in a kind of individuated and tonic confirmation that one is in line with what is believed to be God's plan. The concrete details of work do not participate in God's plan thus construed. Hence the attenuated version of a calling offered by Warren and countless other popular authors makes negligible demands on the political status quo of the modern workplace, leaving individuals at the mercy of consumer culture to work out the meaning of their calling with a self-help book in their lap. This is an unacceptable state of affairs, both in secular and religious ways, if in fact the status quo of one's workplace fosters an unfair political arrangement.

Alternatively, if we rely on Weber's vocation to address injustice in the workplace, we are left with a naked, barely justifiable duty to work hard—hardly a weapon against such structures. The vocation that Weber describes is stripped of its distinctiveness amongst other competing reasons to get up and go to work: its theological power. It is still a call from God for most. A vocation is needed that strikes a balance between the transcendence and immanence that is inherently present in the concept. Such a vocation, or a political vocation as I am calling it, cannot afford to disregard its historical tie to a divine call in order to satisfy either individual desire or the norms of market ideology. As we have seen throughout this book, a vocation also cannot *only* be an answer to a call from a transcendent God. Otherwise it is susceptible to the tampering of consumer culture which renders it impotent to pose any political challenge in the immanent realm. The vertical dimension of a vocation must cooperate with its horizontal movement if a political vocation is able to gain traction on the slippery surface of consumer culture.

PRODUCER SUPREMACY IN A CONSUMER CULTURE

Thomas Geoghegan summarizes the current situation for workers in the United States in a 2009 article:

> The Economic Policy Institute reports that, since 1972, the median hourly wage for men has remained basically flat, and has actually declined for the bottom fifth of workers. (Women saw more of an im-

provement, but that's only because women were grossly underpaid in 1972.) What is more astonishing is that in this very same period, when workers were losing financial ground, their productivity—their output per hour—nearly *doubled*. They were doing twice as much work for the same wage or less.[1]

When increased productivity does not translate into increased wages, how are we to explain it? Certainly economic ups and downs contribute to the inability of companies to compensate worker effort fairly. However, since 1972, the overall GDP in the United States has risen higher than adjusted increases in overall hourly wages. The money is going somewhere, but not into the checking accounts of workers. It is the ever-growing wealth gap between the very richest in the United States and everyone else that reveals where the money is going. Robert Reich cites that

> [s]ince the 1970s, the nation's richest 1 percent—comprising roughly one and half million families in 2004—have more than doubled their share of total national wealth. In 1976, they owned about 20 percent of America. By 1998, the latest date available, they had accumulated over a third of the nation's wealth—more than the entire bottom 90 percent put together.[2]

Unevenness between the players in a capitalistic work environment is inevitable—the primary goal of any business is to generate profit, and leadership that requires high salaries is needed to accomplish this task. However, the fact of radical disparity between the haves and have-nots at work, while worker productivity has increased, may be justified by a market ideology, but if continued, begins to impinge on the overall well-being of a society that shoulders this burden.

Or market ideology that routinely justifies the widening of the power gap between the top and the bottom can move a society to the point of injustice. Gary Dorrien provides a general way of connecting unequal power between the controllers of the economy and the controlled with social injustice, of which workplace inequality constitutes a subset of his overall concerns.

> [I]t is terribly mistaken to think that any serious challenge to existing relations of power can ignore the factors of production. We cannot significantly advance the cause of social justice by writing off the seemingly hopeless problem of inequality. Those who control the terms, amounts, and direction of credit largely determine the structures of the society in which we live. The question of who controls the process of investment is therefore no less crucial or pressing today than it was when "socialism" seemed an innocent ideal. Gains toward social and economic democracy are needed today for the same fundamental reason that political democracy is necessary: to restrain the abuse of unequal power.[3]

Many factors contribute to the situation that Dorrien describes, and the lack of power that employees are increasingly forced to accept in large corporations is most certainly one of these factors.

Even though all cultural terrain is a contested space for power, it does not follow that all participants are on an equal playing field. This assertion seems to conflict with the fact that consumer culture is considered to be a particularly fair cultural game in comparison to its predecessor, producer culture. The market, when operating in a hospitable social environment, seemingly offers an equal chance for all producers of consumer items to put their wares on the market, so long as their finances permit. And this equality of opportunity is matched by a corresponding equality amongst consumers who freely choose what they will consume and where they will work, as long as their finances permit. The cultural contest in consumer culture, when put this way, is won by the producer who produces the more appealing product and by all consumers who benefit from the producers' battle for consumers' attention and money. Therefore, the contested space of consumer culture is fought largely amongst the producers—they are engaged in a struggle with each other, and consumers receive the spoils.

However, consumer culture can also be seen as a larger battlefield that directly puts producers in conflict with consumers. The consumer may feel the need to fight for turf against the encroachment of advertising into every conceivable social space instead of thanking the corporation for the encroachment. On an economic level, by leveraging their most powerful weapon, their decision to consume or not, consumers can force producers to lower their price or change production direction altogether or go out of business. On a cultural level, consumers have attempted to regain colonized social space by using subversive tactics against corporations. Kalle Lasn, the founder of *Adbusters Magazine*, calls subversive practices against the producers of consumer culture "subvertising"—a subcategory of the overall practice of "culture jamming."

> Corporations advertise. Culture jammers *sub*vertise. A well-produced print "subvertisement" mimics the look and feel of the target ad, prompting the classic double take as viewers realize that what they're seeing is in fact the very opposite of what they expected. Subvertising is potent mustard. It cuts through the hype and glitz of our mediated reality and momentarily, tantalizingly, reveals the hollow spectacle within.[4]

Here, Lasn describes the manipulation of a purchased item or advertisement by a consumer. One example of subvertising is the alteration of a company logo on clothing by the consumer. This sends the somewhat paradoxical message that while the consumer gave money to the producer with the original purchase, the consumer then "damages" the company with a transgressive act. Culture jamming, then, is a set of tactics designed to stake out a modicum of cultural space in the hotly contested landscape of consumer culture.[5]

The ability of consumers to employ tactics of resistance as a result of consumers' freedom to take their money where they please has led some to celebrate the newfound freedom.[6] Yet the fact that it is consumers who are the ones using tactics of resistance and not the producers provokes several questions about the nature of this contested space. What is being resisted? Does the reveling of some in the triumph of consumer culture belie the reality that power distribution between producers and consumers is entrenched and not really up for grabs? Do tactics without a strategy reveal that consumers may win some battles but lose the war? And finally, are the consumers of religious items subject to the same fate as all consumers, or does the relationship between religion and consumer culture establish a different contested cultural space?

SPIRITUALITY'S SILENT TAKEOVER OF RELIGION

Vincent Miller, whose critique of consumer culture relies in part on de-Certeau's tactics as a means of resistance, takes much of the injurious effects of free market ideology into account. The act of consumption for consumption's sake is reinforced in a society that is run by the market, and the marketplace is where all consumers must return after the consumption of durable goods or lifestyle enhancements.[7] Yet this cycle can encourage extreme corporate abuses enacted in the name of consumer satisfaction and shareholder happiness. For instance, the shameless ability for corporations to push consumption at the cost of environmental degradation and the erosion of human rights is a driving concern of his.[8]

Certainly Miller does not celebrate the triumph of consumer culture. Nor does he work towards his conclusions by instrumentally using the power of consumer culture for an ultimate good, as is the case for Jane Bennett or Tom Beaudoin.[9] Yet Miller rarely takes his grievances to a fight against the executives. Consumer culture, for Miller, refers to the "cultural habits of use and interpretation that are derived from the consumption of commodified cultural objects."[10] Hence, consumer culture is viewed primarily from the perspective of the consumer, and he accordingly responds to corporate abuse by offering tactical maneuvers: the breaking of consumer habits and dispositions.[11]

His emphasis on the consumer response over the producer's role in consumer culture is certainly supplemented by his critique of corporate abuses. Miller's concerns over corporate power evoke more of an expected emotional response to the extreme examples he cites—who is not upset with tales of corporate exploitation of Chinese children working in a sweat shop? Yet tales of this sort can run cover for more subtle corporate machinations that factor heavily in the formation of the consumer mindset, which Miller largely neglects. Then the role of the producer in modifying consumer habits and dispositions is thus minimized. Or the *how* of consumer culture is answered one-sidedly. And in conjunction with the most flagrant sins of some corporations, his analysis leaves the question of the role that the corporation in general plays in fueling the mechanism of consumer culture unanswered.[12]

Alternatively, Jeremy Carrette and Richard King lay their complaints squarely at the feet of sellers of consumer items. They operate off of the same foundation as Miller: religious elements wrenched out of their material contexts expose those elements to commodification. Yet they lodge a wider, more trenchant claim that religion has been rebranded as spirituality then bought and sold by the corporate world. A though experiment is offered:

> Let us imagine that "religion" in all its forms is a company that is facing a takeover bid from a larger company known as Corporate Capitalism. In its attempt to "downsize" its ailing competitor, Corporate Capitalism strips the assets of "religion" by plundering its material and cultural resources, which are then repackaged, rebranded and then sold in the marketplace of ideas.[13]

On their way to this claim, the authors assert that the individualization and privatization of religion that occurred over two centuries in the West dovetailed with the rise of corporate capitalism. Religion, with its power to resist and critique existing injustice, could not compete with the power of corporate capitalism and hence succumbed to it. Religion survived the transition but only in its sublimated and accommodating form: spirituality.

They contrast what they call "capitalist spirituality," that which is detached from a social context in order to be fed to us by the sellers of spirituality, with an earlier version of spirituality that was engaged with modern ideals. Capitalist spirituality, then,

> represents a shift from the earlier phase of "consumer-led" spiritual enquiry, which emphasised the individual's freedom to choose his or her own pathway in life (the bedrock of modern liberalism), to a "corporate-led" consumerism that subordinates the interests of the individual to consumerist ideology and the demands of the business world.[14]

Consumer-led spirituality immediately followed what they call the "first privatization of religion," helped in large measure by the influence of William James. It encouraged an individual reckoning of one's spiritual state, thus sending religion into an internal theatre. But Carrette and King claim that the first privatization did not necessarily sever the individual's spirituality from awareness of the wider social context which includes religious and state institutions at first.

Such an orientation is clearly not in itself incompatible with a socially engaged perspective, but it becomes so once "the individual" is conceived as an independent, autonomous and largely self-contained entity within society. Such closure, establishing the impermeable boundaries of the modern, individual self, undermines an awareness of interdependence and erodes our sense of solidarity with others.[15]

This closure beginning to occur in the 1980s represents "the second privatization of religion" and was given ideological protection under neoliberalism and an unquestioned market ideology, which feed the atomistic self.[16] Hence for Carrette and King, religion becomes spirituality when individual choice is propped up and contained by the market. The result is the second and final privatization of religion which constitutes "the tailoring of spiritual teachings to the demands of the economy and of individual self-expression to business success."[17]

Carrette and King's historical sequence fastens the transition from religion to spirituality to Bauman's articulation of the shift from solid to liquid modernity.[18] The first privatization ushered in a heightened and relatively new role for individualism, but in this phase, solid social bonds, while weakening, created an accepted cultural space in which inner-directed individuals could operate. The second privatization signals the onset of a liquid society where the social context places no restrictions on what religion can mean for the individual and little protection from the market that sells this new form of spirituality.

They then move their historical analysis to the contemporary relationship between the corporate workplace and consumer religion. With access to spirituality open to any institution participating in corporate capitalism, Carrette and King claim that many corporations have strategically begun to poach and co-opt spirituality. Spirituality has become a kind of brand built largely by way of contrast to the perception of religion as authoritarian, rigid, and dated. Cut loose from institutional bondage, it conveys freedom and can be adopted according to individual and corporate wishes.

Often the motivation for the usage of a term like spirituality by corporations is to distract employees from the realities of job insecurity by shifting the responsibility of business success to the employee alone. The works of business guru Tom Peters serve as a window into such usage, as McGee writes.

> Although Peters recognizes the need for job security as a prerequisite for a motivated and flexible workforce, he asserts that to remain competitive, businesses must cut their costs by eliminating employees.... What is required, then, is some means of making employees feel secure even though they know they're not. One solution to this is to place the onus of employment security on the individual worker by making each and every worker responsible for his or her own "career."[19]

Spirituality, while McGee avoids this term, helps individuals match up their sense of purpose on the job with the responsibility that comes with finding it. It is now your spiritual life, your career, and your task alone to wed the two comfortably.

Spirituality is also used to inspire corporate executives. Everything from the idea of "God as CEO" to Voodoo to Taoism has been employed to further the success of business.[20] Laurie Beth Jones describes the premise of her book, *Jesus, CEO*, in the preface. The book is

> a practical, step-by-step guide to communicating with and motivating people. It is based on the self-mastery, action, and relationship skills that Jesus used to train and motivate his team. It can be applied to any business service, or endeavor that depends on more than one person to accomplish a goal, and can be implemented by anyone who dares.[21]

Jesus's leadership style is Jones's model for corporate leadership, and if the model is followed, the stern task-master boss, who is not getting results, is replaced with a leader who taps employees' "energies" and "passion" (read: spiritual center) in order to move a business in the right direction.

Discourses involving spirituality in the business world function as a kind of "human-centered safety valve" that "allows workers to 'let off steam' when faced with increasingly oppressive and insecure job conditions."[22] Carrette and King enumerate several ways in which this works. First, the introduction of spirituality into such things as a business mission statement, corporate retreats, and job training is intended to foster a sense of community and company loyalty amongst employees that transcends an identity as a mere group of co-workers. In turn, employees' job tasks are cloaked with an aura of spirituality, "obviating the increasingly dehumanizing environment that they find themselves in as a result of the application of purely economic or calculative rationality to their value to the company."[23]

Second, and in conjunction with the first, "spirituality provides the all-important 'feel-good' factor that is so important for improving worker efficiency and loyalty."[24] The translation of an employee's true mission of improving the company's bottom line into a kind of spiritual quest helps with worker motivation which hopefully increases efficiency and productivity. The more pressing the needs are of an employee, such as long-term job security, fair salary/pension, and equitable participation/ownership in the company, the more these needs can be subordinated to a kind of therapeutic spiritual satisfaction at work. Big issues are addressed by even bigger spiritual solutions, whether one has anything to do with the other or not.

Though Rick Warren rejects the legitimacy of the term "spirituality" out of hand, *The Purpose-Driven Life* could have been cited by Carrette and King as well. Purpose can serve the interests of employers in two ways. First, if both employer and employee are attempting to live a purpose-driven life, each has access to the fruits of living with purpose without having to question their political relationship. Both the power held by an executive and the relative lack of power held by the employee are rendered irrelevant in the actualization of the same kind of purpose-driven life. Second, if working conditions begin to cause anxiety, Warren's purpose offers a means to allay the unwelcome feelings and get back to business. The levels of social capital possessed by both employer and employee at work can stay constant as righteous indignation is never allowed to manifest in action.

Carrette and King are quick to point out that the real travesty here is that religion has been and should be able to meet the ideology of the corporate status quo head-on. The infusion of a softened spirituality into the workplace silences the prophetic element of religion when in fact a jeremiad is needed.

> Spirituality is appropriated for the market instead of offering a countervailing social force to the ethos and values of the business world. This is not to assume that we can ever escape the influence of the market, but rather to recognize that the utilisation of a "spirituality" tailored for business enterprise ignores vital aspects of those traditions upon which it relies—aspects that directly challenge the privatization and commercialization of life.[25]

Used in this way, spirituality in business has the double effect of eviscerating the political capacity of religion, thus protecting corporate ideology, as well as disciplining religion so that it can support the interests of capitalist ideologues.

Underneath this perhaps overly cynical and sometimes hyperbolic manifesto, the connection between the commodification of religion and the salutary windfall for the corporate elite is effectively made clear by Carrette and King. Specifically their treatment of the instrumental use of spirituality in the workplace identifies the status of the winners and losers unmistakably. Unlike those who neglect this crucial consequence of consumer culture as it applies to the workplace or those who are sanguine about the power differential that obtains between peddlers and consumers of commodities, Carrette and King speak forcefully. The sellers of spiritual goods to consumers stand to gain the most while they withstand consumer tactics against them. While Miller's argument never explicitly denies the uneven power in this type of exchange, the tactics he offers for mitigating problems associated with consumer culture and religion do not substantially move the battle lines. Carrette's and King's response alternatively centers on the need for religion to resist marketability via political avenues that give power back to those who merely believe and practice.

Failure to answer this call risks the permanent establishment of corporate capitalism as the legislator of *all* norms, both public and private. A similar call is issued to vocations to present their political brawn in the face of a work environment dominated by corporate capitalism. When cast in terms of the disparity in social capital that employees possess in the types of businesses immersed in flexible capitalism, a vocation has this opportunity.

But because a commodified vocation serves to maintain and even widen this gap, a non-commodified concept of vocation is needed to help realize of a kind of workplace democracy. This new notion of vocation cannot emerge *ex nihilo*; its history necessarily impinges on any current articulation. As such, the theological history of the Protestant version of the term, while primarily expressing a quietism towards actual work itself, does contain elements that can inform a more politically engaged vocation in the workplace. No one thinker supplies sufficient theoretical content to fill out a concept of vocation that can respond to the modern workplace. However, a cobbled-together theological front from relevant sources distills out the political component of the idea of vocation indispensably well.

CALVIN AND AN ENTRANCE INTO POLITICS

Ernst Troeltsch, through his reading of the history of the Christian church, extracts the social and political consequences of Calvin's treatment of vocation in ways that give it a political charge.[26] He, like Weber, uses the differences between the theologies of vocation of Luther and Calvin to do so. Interestingly, the most profound point of departure, in Troeltsch's view, that Calvin takes from Luther is found in their respective attitudes towards vocation.[27] When situated in Calvin's overall theological and social framework, his notion of vocation, while not straying too far from Luther in spirit, acquires political traction that Luther's notion does not possess. This leads Troeltsch to conclude that Calvin, while far from promoting democracy explicitly, uses the idea of vocation along with other theological ideas to turn Geneva and other Calvinist societies "in the direction of democracy."[28] Hence Calvin's theological deviations not only from the Catholic Church but also from Luther can permit a linkage of vocation to the kind of political activity needed today, however tenuous this linkage is.

Troeltsch centers on three features of Calvin's thought to make his point: the doctrine of predestination, the promotion of individualism, and his desire for the establishment on earth of a Holy Community. All three can only be understood through the prism of Calvin's fundamental theological assertion that the majesty of God subordinates all other theological concerns. And Calvin's doctrine of predestination is the supreme statement of divine will. It is unaffected by human reason or effort, stubborn, and supreme. Troeltsch elaborates:

> In entire and arbitrary freedom He lays down the law for Himself; and this law is the law of His own glory which is served both by the gratitude of the undeserved bliss of the elect and by the misery of the merited despair of the damned.[29]

Proof of justification before God that manifests itself in appropriate inward feelings of happiness or certainty is no longer valid evidence of one's justified status. Divine will acts to save or damn despite these feelings, which in turn rearranges the order of Luther's divine hierarchical qualities.

> This means that no longer, as in Lutheranism, is the idea of Love at the center of the conception of God, but the idea of Majesty, in which the impartation and influence of the Love of God is only regarded as a method of revealing the Majesty of God.[30]

With God's love acting as a means to *the* end and not an end itself, the relationship between God and humanity is accordingly reconfigured by Calvin.

> In Lutheranism the real proof and verification of justification is that happiness which the world cannot give, which reaches its highest point in close connection with the Christ who substantially unites Himself in the Eucharist with the believer in the *Unio Mystica*, in a mystical union with God. In Calvinism, with its emphasis upon the transcendence of God, such a proof could not be imagined; union with God can only be understood in the sense of surrender to the electing and renewing will of God, and as an activity of the ever active God in the believer...[31]

This distinction between the theology of Luther and Calvin "contains a wealth of implications" for Troeltsch, but most significant is that Calvin's reordering carries new implications for human action in the world. The activity of God may or may not spark feelings of joy (and for Calvin, it is sacrilegious to ponder this casuistry), but it most certainly establishes the terms of the divine/human contract that leads to Troeltsch's second point.

On the subject of individualism, Troeltsch repeats the theme of contrasting Luther's need for faith to be bolstered by inward signs of justification with Calvin's contention that Divine Will requires no such mediation.

> In Calvin's view the individual is not satisfied with mere repose in his own happiness, or perhaps with giving himself to others in loving personal service; further, he is not satisfied with an attitude of mere passive endurance and toleration of the world in which he lives, without entering full into its life.[32]

"Mere repose" translates into "mere passive endurance and toleration of the world" under Luther. The individual who properly discounts emotional confirmation or repudiation in one's standing before God is one who can then properly be used as an instrument for God's will. Certainty of one's standing, then, is not susceptible to the turbulence on a sea of emotions. Calvin's individual is one who

> knows that his calling and election are sure, and that therefore he is free to give all his attention to the effort to mould the world and society according to the Will of God. . . . His duty, therefore, is not to preserve the "new creation" in its intimacy with God, but to reveal it.[33]

Calvin, according to Troeltsch, takes one's heavenly status as a member of the elect completely out of the individual's jurisdiction; the earthly kingdom is the only remaining realm that is able to be molded.[34] Or predestination extends to one's eternal status, and finite matters of the world seem to skirt a hard, predestined order for Calvin. Yet if the molding of the world must always abide by God's will, a potential inconsistency in Calvin's thought is overcome with his unwavering emphasis on God having dominion over all reality. How, then, is the molding to occur so that God's will is done, and what should the final product look like?

Calvin answers with Troeltsch's third component that was discussed in chapter 1: the Holy Community. There, we saw individual vocations ideally fitting together to help society run smoothly. Here, the political implications for such a relationship between a vocation and society are disclosed. As noted in that chapter, for a community to be holy by Calvin's definition, it must fully reflect the will of God. However, the reflected image will be opaque if refracted through a societal filter that is made up of Christians who merely *believe*. Believing that God has graciously added you to the elect is the only way of relating to the heavenly kingdom, and action induced by belief in a sovereign God is the only way to relate the earthly kingdom.

Belief that God will transform society to accord with divine will confuses the earthly and heavenly realms. Belief alone cannot transform the world into an adequate reflection of divine will; action induced by belief can. And Luther's "belief-to-action" idea, which centers on care for one's neighbor, is expanded by Calvin to include productive, Godly work that may not directly serve one's neighbor. When work is performed in conjunction with correct belief, a Holy Community develops that begins to integrate varied forms of work into a systematic, fully functioning whole. Hence even if individual work does not directly help others, a job indirectly helps all members of a society when it harmonizes with other jobs in this way. Alternatively, if a job is performed in the service of individual gain instead of communal good, it is unholy. Luther's conception of proper Christian action can exist with indifference to the advancement of the common good; Calvin's Holy Community cannot.

Troeltsch argues that the primary conceptual instrument that Calvin uses to ensure a functioning Holy Community is his idea of vocation. Put simply, a vocation brings individual action into line with divine will. And when God's will is followed through different jobs working towards the common good of all, albeit never perfectly, a vocation has social/political import. Following Weber, Troeltsch argues that it is the Calvinist emphasis on an "ascetic self-discipline in work" that enlists work in the service of the formation of a Holy Community. Calvin encourages an "inner-worldly asceticism" that generates a dogged work ethic to be applied within a working society, not in the desert where "other-worldly asceticism" used to confine itself.[35]

Despite the cooperation between one's work and God's will that is fostered in Calvin's society, the vast distance between the value of human effort and justification before the sovereign God foments a psychological uneasiness in the individual. The un-answerability of the question, "Is my hard work a sign of my status as a member of the elect or is it all for naught?" understandably contributes to an anxiety in Calvin's adherents. Yet this anxiety only redoubles the effort to align one's work with God's will as the striving in this world is the only valve left to believers through which stress can be released, according to both Weber and Troeltsch. The Calvinist individual may have no control over his or her standing before God, but at least control over the kind of work performed can still be exerted. Calvin can thereby sanction enlistment of work in the effort to fashion a Holy Community more easily.

Luther certainly sees jobs fitting into his own version of a Holy Community. However, the human element that contributes to a functioning society is absent in Luther's community. Troeltsch explains that Luther assigns the maintenance of an ordered community

> to the wise ordering and the kindly guidance of Providence, and not to deliberate human initiative.... The individual, moreover, regarded his work, not as a suitable way of contributing to the uplift of Society as a whole, but as his appointed destiny, which he received from the hands of God.[36]

Social order is justified, then, by a pre-existent divine order and monitored by a providential eye. Hence work in Luther's system can easily be seen to fit likewise into a corresponding certain social stratum.

> This is why it was possible for the Lutheran to regard the work of his vocation in an entirely traditional and reactionary way—as the duty of remaining within the traditional way of earning a living which belongs to one's position in Society.[37]

Work, on the contrary in Calvin's Holy Community, is freed from such restrictions in order that it may continually carry out the charge laid upon it by the community. Vocations become *the* vehicle in which Christian beliefs are carried into the wider world for the purposes of establishing a Holy Community.[38] Like the nature of one's job, Calvin's idea of vocation needs to be supple enough to negotiate with the sociopolitical environment in order that a Holy Community can be achieved. Troeltsch avers:

> And since the Church as a whole could not be fully constituted without the help of the political and economic service of the secular community, it was urged that all callings ought to be ordered, purified, and enkindled as a means for attaining the ends of the Holy Community. Thus the ideal was now no longer one of surrender to a static vocational system, directed by Providence, but the free use of vocational work as the method of realizing the purpose of the Holy Community.[39]

Thus Calvin's vision for a Holy Community requires a freer conception of vocation that can do the heavy lifting in communities that are works in progress.

Yet this lifting occurs more by example than by brute force, which leads Troeltsch to state, "[T]o what extent this rationality and mobility of the conception of vocation was carried through in detail, in the presence of the opposing conception of life with its 'guild' and 'police' spirit, is quite another question."[40] In other words, Calvin's conception of vocation, while mobile and relatively expansive, is not permitted to challenge the norms of the emerging merchant guilds, even when their practices conflict with the kind of work that is calling-worthy. Societal unrest that could follow such a confrontation would only serve to fragment the delicate whole of the Holy Community. And more importantly, a confrontational vocation would upset the balance between the Holy Community and the expression of God's will.

Therefore, while Calvin's Holy Community links vocation with the social institutions that support the community, it is finally this non-negotiable allegiance to a sovereign God that restricts the political power of a vocation in such a community. The detachment of a vocation from its place in a certain stratified social layer does not mean that it is completely without tether to authority in general. As Troeltsch reminds us, the sovereignty of God cements the lot of humanity in general as limited, flawed and ultimately impotent in matters divine. Work should be politically consequential, but those consequences are subservient to divine will. When not, human depravity explains the shortcoming. Troeltsch sums it up:

> The whole social ideal of Calvinism is controlled by the sense that human beings are unequal by Divine appointment, and that the only equality which exists is that of incapacity to do any good in one's own strength, and the obligation to render unconditional obedience to the Divine Will. The result is that the main features of this social ideal are essentially conservative and authoritative.[41]

Troeltsch's open question about the confrontation between secular institutions that combat the directives of Calvin's vocation is answered with a retreat of vocation from the political front. Or the corollary of a vocation that carries political freight is that God's plan always humbles those who think that political gains actually contribute to the carrying out of the plan.[42] Vocations are embedded and significant in Calvin's polis, but their political clout cannot result in a kind of ideology of work. Such a circumstance would indicate an exaggeration of human ability to redefine the nature of the Holy Community.

Despite a political conservatism, not only does Calvin furnish the idea of vocation with components that enable an engagement with the political structures of a society, but he also identifies vocations as the primary levers that can move a society into becoming a Holy Community. This new role disallows a vocation to manifest itself merely in acts of charity which can quickly become private acts alone. Calvin's vocations are necessarily public and communal. Calvin's qualified acceptance of secular authority is relativized given his utter deference to God. And with this kind of deference, the power of a vocation to confront authorities like merchant guilds is diminished in kind. That said, Calvin does expand the scope and power of vocations when compared to Luther, and in the process, allows for their entrance into politics, however measured.

RAUSCHENBUSCH, JUSTICE, AND VOCATION

Though 350 years and an ocean separate Calvin from Walter Rauschenbusch, their overall programs do resemble each other in ways. Rauschenbusch similarly wants God's will to be reflected by society. And neither Calvin nor Rauschenbusch argues that a retreat into a Christian ghetto is the way to accomplish the goal of alignment of society to God's plan for it. Yet Rauschenbusch's vision of the ideal society along with his description of the forces that militate against his vision compels a different approach. Calvin takes his cues for appropriate social activity and for the architecture of the Holy Community from a rigid theology that posits a transcendent, sovereign God. Rauschenbusch, on the other hand, takes his cues from the state of society in early twentieth-century America, which then gradually summons him into quasi-doctrinal positions on God. Rauschenbusch's God is limited by the world in which God's will must find purchase. Hence, it is up to God's followers to prepare the world so that God's will can be exercised. Rauschenbusch's reversal of Calvin's God/world order is precipitated by what he sees as the unfair class structure and deplorable working conditions. Rauschenbusch's vocation, if able to contain any divine content, must be able to instruct us on how to rectify the world's injustices instead of merely operating in society alongside social inequity.

Rauschenbusch addresses many of the problems that stem from industrial capitalism that Marx raises yet with a very "un-Marxian" solution. Class consciousness plays a significant role in the ideological protection of capitalism for Rauschenbusch, but his ideas of the bourgeoisie and proletariat lack the kind of ontological stability that Marx affords them. Because Rauschenbusch reduces the antagonistic class relationship to "social sin;" only *religion* can supply the solution to the social crisis wrought by capitalism. His reasoning rests on the contention that capitalism has allowed a systemic form of sin to spread unchecked and damage human relationships so drastically that mere political proposals to redress the damage, such as Marx's, lack the power to get very far.

In his exposition on the present social crisis at hand, Rauschenbusch scatters blame around. The Church, the capitalists, and the government are all culpable. Still his focus never roams far from the state of work and the worker. Recall that the present crisis for Rauschenbusch is the result of a diminishing pride in one's work under the conditions of industrial capitalism. Products are often shoddy and do not reflect craftsmanship,[43] the products made in factories are not the workers' in any sense of the word "ownership,"[44] there is a constant fear of losing one's job due to capricious downsizing,[45] and working conditions give rise to excessive mental and physical deterioration.[46] All of these contribute to the alienation of the worker from work itself along with a severely weakened worker morale.

Rauschenbusch connects the loss of satisfaction with work to a moral loss, not to an economic or social one. To extract pride from the worker is tantamount to leaving her with less of a sense of right and wrong. For instance, the humiliation and despair experienced after working long hours for years on end with little to show for it often results in alcoholism, petty thieving, and even suicide.[47] It is the erosion of collective virtue bought on by working conditions and the politics that sustain them that calls out for a spiritual and moral solution to the problem.

Therefore, widening class distinctions that are the consequence of the relations between employer and employee are underneath the moral failings, not some intrinsic human weakness. His analysis is reliant on history like Marx's, yet Rauschenbusch calls for a return to a "fundamental democracy" premised on "social equality" so endemic of the American political economy—not for a revolution.[48] By social equality, Rauschenbusch means the state in which all people can meet and have real authority in the relationship. He rebuffs the naysayers that cite the impossibility of social equality because of intractable differences such as biological makeup lock people into a social stratum. Rauschenbusch offers an example to prove his point:

> In a college community there are various gradations of rank and authority within the faculty, and there is a clearly marked distinction between the students and the faculty, but there is social equality. On

the other hand, the janitor and the peanut vendor are outside of the circle, however important they may be to it.[49]

He is not calling for equality in all areas of human life; inequalities naturally and at times, necessarily exist. The student is below the professor on other grounds. But social equality dictates that two people of differing ranks relate to each other with mutual respect. It honors distinctions in rank but does not permit abuse of the power held by the ranking member of the relationship. This is so because both parties realize that they are on the same continuum as human beings. Sharing deep interests, such as academics, helps bring about this realization. Not sharing an interest in career stuff plus having economic disparity between two parties makes the realization of social equality more difficult, though a shared humanity should be enough to realize it. The reason that the janitor and the peanut vendor do not enjoy equal treatment at the university is that economic differences between classes (that have always been with us) unjustifiably frame social differences too (which has not always been the case). And the economic disparity between classes is becoming so vast that the ability for citizens that reside on lower rungs of the economic ladder to acquire social capital and hence, mobility is severely undermined.

Social equality is a necessary condition for democracy for Rauschenbusch. It is rights that link all citizens and make everyone socially equal. Then and only then can individual rights be exercised without impediment, as should occur in a democracy. Economic disparity can take a back seat to the lack of political disparity in a free democracy. Then, people from up and down the economic ladder can exercise the political power needed to underwrite and live out a democracy in the true sense of the word. Democracy, in turn, provides the conditions for Christian morality to thrive once again. "Approximate equality is the only enduring foundation of political democracy. The sense of equality is the only basis for Christian morality."[50] Or if there is no social equality between the employer and employee, the concept of neighbor is empty.

Alternatively, social inequality fosters a sense of hopelessness in the downtrodden class, which then generates an apathy towards the question of whether society is a moral one or not. Arguing for a return to Christian moral behavior, without addressing social inequality first, which Rauschenbusch accuses Evangelical pastors of recommending, is tantamount to posturing, and even worse, is complicit in the falsehoods of industrial capitalism.[51] Because falsehoods, such as "the poor are poor through their own fault" are protected by an "integument of glossy idealization," the first task of the Christian is to use the principles of faith, as delineated by prophetic Christianity, to cut through the ideological bluster.[52] A "regenerated personality" emerges which alone is able to serve as a conduit for God's will. The Christianization of society driven by the moral character of its citizens is chronicled by Rauschenbusch in a lengthy passage:

> The greatest contribution which any man can make to the social movement is the contribution of a regenerated personality, of a will which sets justice above policy and profit, and of an intellect emancipated from falsehood. . . . If any new principle is to gain power in human history, it must take shape and live in individuals who have faith in it. The men of faith are the living spirits, the channels by which new truth and power from God enter humanity. To repent of our collective social sins, to have faith in the possibility and reality of a divine life in humanity, to submit the will to the purposes of the kingdom of God, to permit the divine inspiration to emancipate and clarify the moral insight—this is the most intimate duty of the religious man who would help to build the coming messianic era of mankind.[53]

Religion and politics are mutually reinforcing, as evidenced in this passage. In order to radically alter human relations under industrial capitalism, the social equality that is only possible in democratic societies must originate in the "eyes wide open" Christian of character. And the cultivation of character is a responsibility the Church.[54] The Church can then bring institutionalized power to the table to buttress the moral behavior needed to actualize God's kingdom on earth.

How does Rauschenbusch's idea of vocation assist in this process? The reconstruction, or perhaps restoration, of vocations is by no means the only instrument that he uses for his purposes; the Church and State play essential roles as well. Yet given the accent that Rauschenbusch puts on the state of work and the repercussions for the worker, he needs an idea of vocation that is up to the task, no matter what the Church and State can additionally provide.[55]

A calling, if anything, must be able to reattach work to the well-being of the worker if it is to aid in the furthering of the common good. If a vocation is able to set a benchmark for work to meet, then it can counter the view that work in a vocation only nourishes the soul or more generally that the Church is the only institution that can mediate vocations.

> If now we could have faith enough to believe that all human life can be filled with divine purpose; that God saves not only the soul, but the whole of human life; that anything which serves to make men healthy, intelligent, happy, and good is a service to the Father of men; that the kingdom of God is not bounded by the Church, but includes all human relations—then all professions would be hallowed and receive religious dignity. A man making a shoe or arguing a law case or planting potatoes or teaching school could feel that this was itself a contribution to the welfare of mankind, and indeed his main contribution to it.[56]

Several important ideas are conveyed here. The goal is the redemption of "the whole of human life." The means that achieving this goal involves the inclusion of proper, Godly human relations within the kingdom of God. And the primary facilitator of proper human relations is work, despite the nature of the job itself, which ideally aims at the common good.

Rauschenbusch is a kind of social Calvinist here, though without the heavy authority of God's will working on society from above. His emphasis on varied jobs functioning in harmony for the kingdom of God mirrors Calvin's Holy Community. Yet Rauschenbusch's kingdom is not so much a reflection of God's will as it is *God's will itself*. When the destructive nature of industrial work is deemed social sin, working conditions and vast social inequality serve as clear evidence of the inability of God's kingdom to be realized. Calvin's concern about *how* one does a job is converted here into *what* one does for a job. And because what one does for work and its meaning for the worker is currently dictated by uneven power distribution between employer and employee, Rauschenbusch's notion of vocation is called on to repair this set of human relations.

A vocation places work under the auspices of religion which forces a new set of standards onto what is considered acceptable forms of work and business practices. Rauschenbusch's quote about the discrepancy between a calling and certain business practices bears repeating.

> If a man's calling consisted in manufacturing or selling useless or harmful stuff, he would find himself unable to connect it with his religion. Insofar as the energy of business life is expended in crowding out competitors, it would also be outside of the sanction of religion, and religious men would be compelled to consider how industry and commerce could be reorganized so that there would be a maximum of service to humanity and a minimum of antagonism between those who desire to serve it.[57]

Religion, through a calling, reorders the individual's approach to work so that it serves the common good. Therefore, both the production of shoddy goods and the selfish motives for profit fall outside the sanction of religion. A vocation, if properly lived out, will brook no such activities. Nor can professions that promote these activities ever be a vocation. If the standard of the kingdom of God demands that only true callings fill its realm, a house-cleaning will be in order.

> As soon as religion will set the kingdom of God before it as the all-inclusive aim, and will define it so as to include all rightful relations among men, the awakened conscience will begin to turn its searchlight on the industrial and commercial life in detail and will insist on eliminating all professions which harm instead of helping, and on coordinating all productive activities to secure a maximum of service. That in itself would produce a quiet industrial revolution.[58]

Vocations are enlisted in Rauschenbusch's "quiet revolution" to carry out the redemption of work by channeling all work towards the common good and away from harm. Since harm is the direct consequence of radically unequal relations between the working class and the business owners, when work is performed under harmful conditions or causes harm itself, a vocation should be able to respond.

Rauschenbusch implies that if the business world is subjected to religious scrutiny, a vocation, lived out by both the worker *and* the boss, will bring both parties closer to the point of social equality. Social equality in the work world that is predicated on workers possessing enough of a stake in a company to own their work is the desired end of a Rauschenbuschian vocation. Economic inequality will always exist, but if social inequality continues on the path cut by industrial capitalism, the kingdom of God on earth is permanently put on hold. A vocation, if applied by a critical mass of workers and employers alike, can alter the politics of the workplace, make social equality on the job a reality, and usher in God's kingdom in one fell swoop.

If Calvin opened the door for vocations to have political import, Rauschenbusch walks through it. But what kind of world did Rauschenbusch walk into? The qualities of the early twentieth century American work world most certainly differ from ours. Moreover, Rauschenbusch's appropriation of religion as it relates to the socioeconomic realm was informed by Bauman's solid modernity, not the liquid kind. Do these differences between his time and ours alter, constrain, amplify, or perhaps have no effect whatsoever on the political power of a vocation today?

Along with the shift from societies organized around production to that of consumption there came an attendant shift from manual factory work to jobs in the service industry. Hence, most jobs in early twenty-first-century America do not entail crushing physical labor—a key component of Rauschenbusch's crisis. In addition, Rauschenbusch introduces a teleology that is somewhat contradictory in nature and inadequate for all eras. He envisions an eventual kingdom of God on earth that has a kind of metaphysical reality (it, in ideal form, pre-exists the current real world) that is only temporarily camouflaged by industrial society. The signs that Rauschenbusch's kingdom is being assembled on earth have a different point of origin than those which are conditioned by modernity alone. Hence Rauschenbusch's interpretation of these signs can pass over the history of modern notions, even though he uses these notions as an interpretive grid at times. As a result Rauschenbusch relies solely on this-worldly actions to bring forth the kingdom, while he somewhat paradoxically uses religion as an entity that is to function independently of the political economy. Religion, while necessary for Rauschenbusch's argument, is more or less added *ad hoc* to the industrial society in order to redeem the human relationships that make it up. Consequently, Rauschenbusch insists that God's kingdom, not a human one, must be the end point of the alteration. And the theological confusion that results from this kind of divine/human cooperation is not sufficiently worked out.

TOWARDS A POLITICAL VOCATION

Vocation and the Common Good

Richard Roberts echoes the assertions of Miller and Carrette/King: the unhinging of religion from its origins exposes it to the powerful pull of consumer culture at a high cost. In a particularly profound passage, he states the current situation bluntly and rather pessimistically.

> The so-called free market (including the entertainment industry) colonises and extracts from every conceivable (and newly conceived) dimensions of the human and natural life-world that which may in turn be harnessed to exchange and surplus value. This is an immensely powerful and many-sided mechanism that consumes humankind and once, as is increasingly the case, the managerial imperative elides the separation of powers and provides the hinge connecting both jaws of the machine, then resistance may seem futile.[59]

Despite the dire verdict, it is not a final one for Roberts. If a vocation can check the authority of consumer culture and the free market, then it must counter the dematerialization of religion in two ways. One, if a necessary component of a vocation is the ensuring of certain material and political conditions of work, then a vocation should be able to bring together the current usage of the term (a calling brings better feelings about my job) and the political side of vocation (a calling brooks no unjust working conditions). Two, this kind of unity will not permit a commodified vocation to hold sway in the workplace. A concept of vocation must emerge that transcends consumer-based identity formation and at the same time critiques the material realities of the corporate workplace. He enlists a vocation as an instrument that can uniquely fight for social space that is gradually being lost to this "managerial imperative." The loss of any sense of a rooted vocation in the modern work world lands employees at the end of a *cul-de-sac* where identity formation is largely at the mercy of either the market or a manager or both.

> The destruction of the idea and the reality of vocation and the voyage is consummated in a managerialised modernity, especially when this paradigm is welcomed into such public sacred space as remains. This is because the obedience required of an employee or operative is in principle total: there must . . . be no "secret pockets" left for the spontaneous or the unexpected. . . . Under these conditions the ever-frustrated search for a viable, rooted identity has thus become the normal, rather than the exceptional, "vocation" of our time.[60]

Roberts's conclusions are confirmed at several junctures in my book. First, the separation of a calling from actual work that one does on a job, as seen in the Protestant theological history of vocation, begins the ceding of labor over to secular entities. Second, the shift of production to consumption robs vocation of its staying power over a career and exposes the idea to the market for sale. Third, when commodified and hence domesticated, a vocation is disciplined for the market and is ready to be sold back to the consumer by self-help authors and employers alike.

Roberts ends his book with a desperate call for the materialization of an individual identity that is able to bolster our weakened position in the all-powerful market. His diagnosis of the practical totality of managerial control of our lives through the market and the foreclosure of religious space that results directs him to suggest a genetic solution. The vocational quest for identity must go subterranean, as Roberts digs below the current cultural milieu to unearth primal sources of religion.

> If, as I believe to be the case, much main-line institutionalised religion has in reality lost touch with the primal religious function, then what must now concern us is the investigation of those dimensions of human becoming and mutual existence that precede tradition.[61]

These sources, while not explicitly identified by Roberts, need to be rediscovered and recast into modern identities despite the difficulties that inhere in a reclamation project such as this. Roberts concedes that his proposal is merely suggestive (his future work pursues this line further), but what are we to make of it provisionally? His suggestion, while the upshot of a meticulous dissection of the state of religion and theology in the modern world as well as his own personal struggle, amounts to a resignation to that world and a retreat into an a-cultural enclave where primal religion can still be retrieved and dredged up in the twenty-first century.

It is difficult to discern how Roberts's vocation challenges market ideology and the politics that result in the workplace by returning to a "primal religious function." Yes, the theology within a vocation needs to be called forth and engaged with the political environment. But this must be, at times, tempered with the realities of the immanent work world and what forms of justice are demanded.

A Political Vocation

A political vocation, on the other hand, must continually strive to strike a delicate balance between its transcendent and immanent features. If a vocation gains its steam from being a part of an immutable divine plan, it loses touch with the materiality of the immanent world of work. But if the religious component of a vocation is removed for whatever reason, it severs ties with that which provides its unique and powerful normative voice amidst a chorus of secular noise. A vocation that can engage the politics of the workplace and engage it with sustained vigor is one that is successfully negotiating the boundary between transcendence and immanence.

Yet as we gathered from the thrust of the Protestant history of vocation, the unremitting power of consumer culture, and the resonance of self-help literature, erring on the side of immanence by attending to the material facet of work is the prudent path. Otherwise, a vocation is susceptible to the kind of commodification and consumption that threatens to depoliticize it for good. In other words, the threat is on the horizontal plane, but the temptation is to go vertical in its face. A political vocation must move horizontally in the immanent plane but must also be able to exercise the option of looking upwards for direction and strength.

Along the lines of political theology discussed in the introductory chapter, the theology of a political vocation makes no universal truth claims about itself but "indicates a commitment to certain values." It is admitted that a vocation in a postsecular world can adopt the same values and accomplish the same political goals in the workplace, whether it is explicitly theistic or not. However, in what follows, some requirements of a political vocation are laid out that are less negotiable, perhaps strangely so, than God's role in vocational matters.

A political vocation must accomplish three tasks. One, it must not identify too closely with some kind of immutable divine plan that stands above culture. This is not to say that the belief that God has called one to a vocation through work or a career stands in the way of the politicization of that vocation. However, a vocation can be quickly spiritualized and then co-opted by consumer culture. When a vocation's only grounding is in the form of a divine plan, one's own desire for success and happiness too hastily becomes that which God wants and has planned. Or God's plan can rapidly become our plan, which is often guided more by what we want and desire as religious consumers. A political vocation should include, but not be reduced to, that which mediates happiness on the job. But contentment should relate to our sense of whether we are being treated fairly.

In this way, our vocation is not limited to or rejected because of the job or career that we have but is expansive because it conveys the kind of relationship that we should have to work in general. This vocational attitude that emphasizes the political automatically tamps down the shopping mentality that permeates the job market. "Will this job make me happy?" is replaced with "does this job treat employees fairly?" when searching. Yes, a search will always be involved and consumer skills will be utilized even when justice is the goal. And the potential contentment that one experiences at a job or in a career will always be a major factor in the choosing process. But if politics is included in the vocational calculus, two problems that we have encountered in our study are mitigated. One, the pursuit of a political vocation brings the search for work closer to the ground thus minimizing the susceptibility of a vocation to the meddling of consumer culture when it is an abstract idea alone. And two, if workplace justice is a part of a vocation, the temptation to leave a job or career because one loses interest can perhaps be put aside—the task of securing and maintaining fair treatment is ongoing, despite the possibility of small victories. Both functions of a political vocation are predicated on a vocation resisting commodification and consumption by a hungry group of consumers or avoiding being a vehicle for consumer happiness.

Two, a political vocation must include the push for the achievement of the common good amongst all workers, including executives. When vocations are considered private property that have been purchased like commodities, moving them into the community of any working environment for political purposes is a challenging task. Couple the "ownership" of a vocation with the drive for individual success (often achieved at the expense of others) that typifies modern corporate culture, and it is clear that a calling has little chance of furthering the collective good. This, though, is no reason to give up on the possibility that vocations can play a transformative role in bringing about a workplace democracy where all have the opportunity to benefit. Robert Bellah couches this shift in terms of a redistribution of the rewards offered at work.

> To make a real difference, such a shift in rewards would have to be a part of a reappropriation of the idea of vocation or calling, a return in a new way to the idea of work as a contribution to the good of all and not merely as a means to one's own advancement.[62]

How, then, can a vocation advance the common good instead of promoting the good of either the individual or of a small group at the top of the pyramid?

Jose Casanova's theoretical work provides avenues for the idea of vocation to do just that. The ideology of *laissez-faire* capitalism contributes to and fosters the privatization of religion. And though the autonomous market has surely generated success in many areas, it has also cultivated an unresponsiveness to collective human concerns that do not have "market value." Or the "worker as citizen" is traded for the "worker as commodity." Market culture, then, is an area of contestation that religion can and must rise up to enter for Casanova:

> [B]y questioning the inhuman claims of capitalist markets to function in accordance with impersonal and amoral self-regulating mechanisms, religions may remind individuals and societies of the need to check and regulate those impersonal market mechanisms to ensure that they are accountable for the human, social, and ecological damage they may cost and that they may become more responsible to human needs.[63]

In the name of individual gain or consumer happiness, the logic of the market does not include the common good as a part of its calculation. Therefore, more than simply reminding, there should be the "obstinate insistence of traditional religions on maintaining the very principle of a 'common good' against individualist modern liberal theories which would reduce the common good to the aggregated sum of individual choices."[64] Religion can and must possess more public authority in a postsecular society to then push self-regulating financial institutions into working towards the public good over the private. Specifically, religious norms represent

> new types of immanent normative critiques of specific forms of institutionalization of modernity which presuppose precisely the acceptance of the validity of the fundamental values and principles of modernity, that is, individual freedoms and differentiated structures. In other words, they are immanent critiques of particular forms of modernity from a modern religious point of view.[65]

A political vocation is such a concept that must stand as such an immanent normative critique of the political norms of the modern workplace.

Three, a political vocation must draw on its theological features that are unmistakably political while not completely subsuming the theological into the political or vice versa. This means that a reversal of the recent theological distancing of a calling from actual work itself is called for. As we have seen, when a calling is cast only in terms of a way to do one's job that is obedient to God's will, it is susceptible to the kind of packaging and selling that Rick Warren unwittingly does. Or when a retrieval of some long-lost concept is intended to remedy problems with the relationship between work and vocation, such as Larive's Holy Spirit or Roberts's primal religion attempts to do, the effect is the same. The theology of a political vocation should be wary of confessional theological articulations that have the tendency of overwhelming the meaning of vocation and setting it up for appropriation by corporate brass and self-help authors alike.

Hence, a political vocation rejects both Barthian calls for the role of culture to be removed from all thinking about what a vocation is and the Gilded Age conflation of a calling and financial success. In between is a vocation that is on the side of justice *by* taking the world seriously. Yet it admits that it often gains strength from a sense of the ultimate without attempting to cast itself solely in terms of it. Calvin and Rauschenbusch help us chart this middle path for a modern political vocation. Calvin's demand that vocations act to further the communal good is the starting point. Whether that community (in the workplace or society at large) is meant to reflect God's will or simply to stand as an example of moral behavior between individuals, political vocations can help create and sustain such a community. And Rauschenbusch's use of vocations to help usher in the kingdom of God here on earth theologizes the political function of a calling but with ends that correspond to secular goals of freedom and democracy. In both Calvin and Rauschenbusch, it is their theology and religious conviction that give weight to the values embedded in what a vocation should be. However, they also refuse to keep vocations in the air, as if the immanent domain has nothing to do with God's call to humanity. A political vocation, therefore, carries with it a Calvinist ticket to enter the polis and a Rauschenbuschian set of religious norms that integrate the need for social equality into the workplace to mitigate the deleterious effects of flexible capitalism.

While both would likely put political goals into the service of theological truths, we do not have to in a postsecular context. Theological aims can merge with secular ones while remaining separate in the minds of those engaging their vocation with the political environment. Or perhaps political injustice at work is already at odds with one's theology, hence the secular and the religious go hand-in-hand. The entanglement of theology and culture in a postsecular context does not destine vocations either to obedience to "worldly" forces or to the complete surrendering of its religious credibility. Instead, and perhaps ironically, a culturally attuned, politically aware vocation is uniquely capable of drawing on its history and entering the world armed with qualities that can challenge competing cultural norms while remaining amenable to change as the circumstances warrant. Whatever the case, if a vocation is to be a political one, it must draw on its theological significance to strengthen its norms while refusing to over-theologize itself to the point that its eye is taken off of the horizon and moved in a vertical direction for too long.

In line with Casanova's requirements and the insights of political theology, this new idea of vocation must also be enlisted to advance the overarching goals of modernity. If the norms that a vocation brings into the public are grounded solely on a transcendent divine authority, they cease to be public in the modern sense. Moreover, if a vocation is used as an instrument to Christianize the secular workplace, no longer is the workplace a site of genuine contestation. The winner is prefigured, and any conversation is stopped despite the success of such tactics on the ground. And most importantly, a vocation loses its capacity to combat the norms of market ideology when it becomes just another commodity in the marketplace. It is not a contest at that point but essentially two entities speaking the same underlying language: a commodified vocation like Warren's purpose and the vocabulary of the same market in which this kind of vocation gains its potency.

Instead, a vocation that adapts its long history (that meaningful work is, in fact, godly work) to the honorable objectives of modernity, such as freedom, human rights, and democracy, can enter the contested space of the work world as a desperately needed voice—it becomes political. That voice, however, is not monolithic but protean. It carries religious weight but must be willing to remain silent when anti-religious norms that also promote the common good are offered; loud when competing norms attempt to justify unjust measures. Absent the moral muscle that a vocation of this kind brings, it is difficult to say whether a self-regulating institution that is rarely questioned, like the market, would ever truly be contested.

I conclude with a passage from Zygmunt Bauman.

> The vagabond does not know how long he will stay where he is now, more often than not it will not be for him to decide when the stay will come to an end. . . . What keeps him on the move is disillusionment with the last place of sojourn and the forever smouldering hope that the next place he has not visited yet, perhaps the place after next, may be free from the faults which repulsed him in the places he has already visited. . . . The vagabond is a pilgrim without a destination, a nomad without an itinerary.[66]

If a vocation is to be the driving force behind the journey of Bauman's pilgrim instead of a handmaiden to the drifting vagabond, it must be able to contribute to real satisfaction with work and not simply color the way in which the journey is undertaken. Yet if vocations continue to be championed for their transcendent qualities and/or therapeutic value, they become mere travel guides for the cultural vagabond and fodder for the winners in the game of consumer culture who can continue to exploit it for their own gain. "The political" is merely one component of the idea of vocation. However, it is the one element that must emerge if a vocation is to leave the privatized realm of consumer satisfaction and provide work with the characteristics that render it calling-worthy.

NOTES

1. Thomas Geoghegan, "Infinite Debt: How Unlimited Interest Rates Destroyed the Economy," *Harper's Magazine*, April 2009, 33–34.

2. Reich, *Supercapitalism*, 113–14.

3. Dorrien, "Social Salvation: The Social Gospel as Theology and Economics," in *The Social Gospel Today*, ed. Christopher H. Evans (Louisville: Westminster John Knox Press, 2001), 112.

4. Kalle Lasn, *Culture Jam: How to Reverse America's Suicidal Consumer Binge—and Why We Must* (New York: Quill, 2000), 131–32.

5. Naomi Klein is skeptical of the real effects of culture jamming that alters advertisements to undermine their message. "But after a while, what began as a way to talk back to the ads starts to feel more like evidence of our total colonization by them, and especially because the ad industry is proving that it is capable of cutting off the culture jammers at the pass." They silence the protest by co-opting the protest spirit itself for its own ad campaigns. See Naomi Klein, *No Logo* (New York: Picador, 2002), 297–98.

6. See James B. Twitchell, *Lead Us into Temptation: The Triumph of American Materialism* (New York: Columbia University Press, 1999).

7. Miller, 121.

8. Miller, 16–18.

9. See Jane Bennett, *The Enchantment of Modern Life* (Princeton: Princeton University Press, 2000); Tom Beaudoin, *Consuming Faith: Integrating Who We Are with What We Buy* (Lanham, MD: Sheed and Ward, 2003).

10. Miller, 30.

11. Miller suggests using a "sacramental operation" that has a "subversive tactical value against commodity abstraction." Engagement in sacraments, communion for

instance, forces the consumption of items to reckon with the items' deep religious significance, thus reintegrating the material of religion with its symbolic value. When expanded into consumption practices, Miller desires that a "sacramental imagination" can similarly engage consumer culture as a subversive tactic against the abstraction of commodities. Miller, 188–92.

12. It must be noted that Miller did not set out to address the power differential that may exist between producer and consumer. His invocation of Foucault serves to reveal how power can disconnect what we intend by our beliefs and practices and what they actually do. Yet he does not investigate the nature and motive of the discursive regimes supplying the power. See Miller, 21–22.

13. Carrette and King, 15–16.

14. Carrette and King, 45.

15. Carrette and King, 41.

16. David Harvey defines neoliberalism as "a theory of political economic practices that proposes that human well-being can best be advanced by liberating individual entrepreneurial freedoms and skills within an institutional framework characterized by strong private property rights, free markets, and free trade." David Harvey, *A Brief History of Neoliberalism* (New York: Oxford, 2005), 2. Neoliberal advocates push for the substitution of markets for the state and consequently for the reduction of the role of government in the lives of its citizens. Critics of neoliberalism, including Carrette and King, typically claim that the political dimension of the individual, when replaced by the economic dimension (as consumer/investor), loses out. Neoliberalism protects those who stand to gain the most by the market while muzzling the voice of the only possible threat: the democratic citizen. See also Reich, *Supercapitalism*; Carl Boggs, *The End of Politics: Corporate Power and the Decline of the Public Sphere* (New York: Guilford Press, 2000); Henry Giroux, *Against the Terror of Neoliberalism: Politics Beyond the Age of Greed* (Boulder, CO: Paradigm Publishers, 2008).

17. Carrette and King, 44.

18. Bauman is not as quick to connect definitively the implications of consumer culture to a socioeconomic power dynamic that elevates corporations and subjugates consumers as Carrette and King do. He is more concerned with describing the effects of consumer culture on the *way* social relationships now function, as opposed to prescribing some kind of call to action against corporate capitalism. For Bauman, the kind of vaulted and unique ontological status given to corporations by Carrette and King would be to establish a solid institution in a liquid society. While Bauman is critical of some of the effects of consumer culture, he refrains from making categorical statements about the almost unquestioned power of corporations to dictate completely the rules of consumer culture (which Carrette and King suggest).

19. McGee, 133.

20. See Rene Carayol and David Firth, *Corporate Voodoo: Principles for Business Mavericks and Magicians* (Mankato, MN: Capstone, 2001); E. Thomas Behr, *The Tao of Sales: The Easy Way to Sell in Tough Times* (Charleston, SC: BookSurge, 2007).

21. Laurie Beth Jones, *Jesus, CEO: Using Ancient Wisdom for Visionary Leadership* (New York: Hyperion, 1995), xi.

22. Carrette and King, 134.

23. Carrette and King, 134.

24. Carrette and King, 134.

25. Carrette and King, 126–27.

26. Both Luther and Calvin address the relationship between their respective theologies and society in their writings. Yet I primarily rely on Troeltsch's reading of both theologians as opposed to the primary texts for several reasons. One, as with the use of Weber for those concerned with the economic impact of theology, more is gained from a careful analysis that has the benefit of a centuries-long hindsight. Two, Luther and Calvin are primarily concerned with establishing correct theologies, not with the political world alone. Hence Troeltsch's attention on the sociopolitical world that emerged as a result of their theologies serves as a more fruitful source than the original sources.

Troeltsch conveniently cuts out the middle man. For Luther and Calvin's own treatment of the relationship between their thought and the larger society see *Luther and Calvin on Secular Authority*, ed. and trans. Harro Höpfl (Cambridge: Cambridge University Press, 1991).
27. Troeltsch, *The Social Teaching of the Christian Churches*, 610.
28. Troeltsch, 628.
29. Troeltsch, 582.
30. Troeltsch, 582.
31. Troeltsch, 584.
32. Troeltsch, 588.
33. Troeltsch, 589.
34. Troeltsch points out that an unintended consequence of activity in the world in later expressions of Calvinism "drove the individual to the practice of self-examination and to systematic concentration on his own independent achievement"; an egocentrism that gradually drove a wedge in between God's will and achievement. Troeltsch, 590.
35. Troeltsch, 611.
36. Troeltsch, 610.
37. Troeltsch, 610.
38. Troeltsch, 610.
39. Troeltsch, 610–11.
40. Troeltsch, 611.
41. Troeltsch, 620.
42. For Calvin's fullest treatment of the relationship between religious and secular authorities, see Calvin, *Institutes of the Christian Religion*, vol. 2, 1485–1521.
43. Rauschenbusch, 193.
44. Rauschenbusch, 194.
45. Rauschenbusch, 194.
46. Rauschenbusch, 197–202.
47. Rauschenbusch, 196.
48. Dorrien, "Social Salvation: The Social Gospel as Theology and Economics," 111.
49. Rauschenbusch, 203.
50. Rauschenbusch, 203.
51. Rauschenbusch, 285, 289, 298.
52. Rauschenbusch, 286.
53. Rauschenbusch, 287.
54. Rauschenbusch, 289.
55. Admittedly, Rauschenbusch does not offer a robust notion of a calling, as do Luther and Calvin, which could more fully explicate how he sees it in operation. Still, his treatment of vocation furnishes us with enough to work into his overall vision for the kind of work that can generate social equality.
56. Rauschenbusch, 290.
57. Rauschenbusch, 290.
58. Rauschenbusch, 290.
59. Roberts, 298.
60. Roberts, 298.
61. Roberts, 302.
62. Bellah, 287-88.
63. Casanova, 229.
64. Casanova, 229.
65. Casanova, 221–22.
66. Roberts, 301–2. Cited from Bauman, *Postmodern Ethics* (Oxford: Blackwell, 1993), 240.

Bibliography

Abanes, Richard. *Rick Warren and the Purpose That Drives Him.* Eugene, OR: Harvest House, 2005.
Aldridge, Alan. *Consumption.* Cambridge, UK: Polity, 2003.
Anderson, Victor. *Pragmatic Theology: Negotiating the Intersections of an American Philosophy of Religion and Public Theology.* Albany: SUNY, 1998.
Anker, Roy M. *Self-Help and Popular Religion in Early American Culture: An Interpretive Guide.* Vol. 1. Westport, CT: Greenwood Press, 1999.
_____. *Self-Help and Popular Religious in Modern American Culture: An Interpretative Guide.* Vol. 2. Westport, CT: Greenwood Press, 1999.
Arendt, Hannah. *The Human Condition.* Chicago: University of Chicago Press, 1958.
Baldwin, Stanley. *Take This Job and Love It.* Downers Grove, IL: InterVarsity Press, 1988.
Barth, Karl. *Church Dogmatics.* Vol. III. Edinburgh, AL: T & T Clark, 1985.
Barthes, Roland. *Mythologies.* London: Paladin, 1986.
Baudrillard, Jean. *The Consumer Society: Myths and Structures.* Thousand Oaks, CA: SAGE, 1998.
_____. *Jean Baudrillard: Selected Writings*, edited by Mark Poster. Stanford: Stanford University Press, 1988.
_____. *The Mirror of Production.* St. Louis: Telos, 1975.
Bauman, Zygmunt. "The Consumerist Syndrome in Contemporary Society; An Interview with Zygmunt Bauman by Chris Rojek." *Journal of Consumer Culture* 4, no. 3 (2004): 291–312.
_____. "Consuming Life." *Journal of Consumer Culture* 1, no. 1 (2001): 9–29.
_____. *Freedom.* Milton Keynes, UK: Open University Press, 1988.
_____. "From Pilgrim to Tourist—Or a Short History of Identity." In *Questions of Cultural Identity*, edited by Stuart Hall and Paul du Gay. London: Sage, 1996.
_____. *Intimations of Postmodernity.* New York: Routledge, 1992.
_____. *Liquid Modernity.* Cambridge, UK: Polity, 2000.
_____. "Morality in the Age of Contingency." In *De-traditionalization: Critical Reflections on Authority and Identity at a Time of Uncertainty*, edited by Paul Heelas Scott Lash, and Paul Morris. Oxford: Blackwell, 1996.
_____. *Work, Consumerism and the New Poor.* Berkshire, UK: McGraw Hill Education, 2004.
Baxter, Richard. *The Practical Works of the Rev. Richard Baxter.* London: James Duncan, 1830.
Bayer, Richard C. *Capitalism and Christianity: The Possibility of Christian Personalism.* Washington, DC: Georgetown University Press, 1999.
Beardslee, W.A. *Human Achievement and Divine Vocation in the Message of Paul.* London: SCM, 1961.
Beaudoin, Tom. *Consuming Faith: Integrating Who We Are with What We Buy.* Lanham, MD: Sheed and Ward, 2003.
Beck, Ulrich. *Risk Society: Towards a New Modernity.* London: SAGE, 1992.
Belk, Russell W., Melanie Wallendorf, and John F. Sherry Jr. "The Sacred and the Profane in Consumer Behavior: Theodicy on the Odyssey." *Journal of Consumer Research* 16, (1989): 1–38.
Bell, Daniel M. Jr. *Liberation Theology After the End of History.* London: Routledge, 2001.
Bell, Daniel. *The Cultural Contradictions of Capitalism.* New York: Basic Books, 1996.

Bibliography

Bellah, Robert, et al. *Habits of the Heart: Individualism and Commitment in American Life.* Berkeley: University of California Press, 1985.
Benavides, Gustavo. "The Study of Religion under Late Capitalism, or Commodity Triumphant." *Council of Societies for the Study of Religion Bulletin* 26 (1997): 88–91.
Bennett, Jane. *The Enchantment of Modern Life.* Princeton: Princeton University Press, 2000.
Berger, Arthur Asa. *Shop 'Til You Drop: Consumer Behavior and American Culture.* Lanham, MD: Rowman and Littlefield, 2004.
Berger, Peter L. *The Capitalist Spirit: Toward a Religious Ethic of Wealth Creation.* San Francisco: Institute for Contemporary Studies Press, 1990.
———. *The Heretical Imperative.* New York: Doubleday, 1980.
———. *The Human Shape of Work.* New York: Macmillan, 1964.
———. *The Sacred Canopy: Elements of a Sociological Theory of Religion.* New York: Anchor Books, 1967.
Berry, Wendell. *Sex, Economy, Freedom and Community.* New York: Pantheon, 1994.
Bibby, Reginald. *Fragmented Gods.* Toronto: Stoddart, 1990.
Biéler, Andre. *Calvin's Economic and Social Thought.* Geneva: World Council of Churches, 1961.
Bobo, Kim. *Wage Theft in America: Why Millions of Working Americans Are Not Getting Paid—And What We Can Do About It.* New York: New Press, 2008.
Bocock, Robert. *Consumption.* London: Routledge, 1993.
Bourdieu, Pierre. *Distinction: A Social Critique of the Judgment of Taste.* Cambridge, MA: Harvard University Press, 1984.
Brown, Delwin. *Boundaries of Our Habitations: Tradition and Theological Construction.* Albany, NY: SUNY Press, 1994.
———. "Refashioning Self and Other: Theology, Academy and the New Ethnography." In *Converging on Culture: Theologians in Dialogue with Cultural Analysis and Criticism,* edited by Delwin Brown, Sheila Greeve Davaney, and Kathryn Tanner. Oxford: Oxford University Press, 2001.
Brunner, Emil. *The Divine Imperative.* London: Lutterworth, 1937.
Budde, Michael L. *The (Magic) Kingdom of God: Christianity and Global Culture Industries.* Boulder, CO: Westview Press, 1997.
Busenitz, Nathan. "A Sense of Purpose: Evaluating the Claims of *The Purpose-Driven Life.*" In *Fool's Gold,* edited by John MacArthur. Wheaton, IL: Crossway, 2004.
Cady, Linell. "Loosening the Category That Binds." In *Converging on Culture,* edited by Delwin Brown, Sheila Greeve Davaney, and Kathryn Tanner. Oxford: Oxford University Press, 2001.
———. *Religion, Theology, and American Public Life.* Albany: SUNY, 1993.
Calhoun, Robert L. "Work As Christian Vocation Today." In *Work and Vocation: A Christian Discussion,* edited by John Oliver Nelson. New York: Harper and Brothers, 1954.
Calvin, John. *Institutes of the Christian Religion.* Vol. 1. Philadelphia: Westminster, 1967.
———. *Institutes of the Christian Religion.* Vol. 2. Philadelphia: Westminster, 1967.
Campbell, Colin. "The New Religious Movements, The New Spirituality and Postindustrial Society." In *New Religious Movements: A Perspective for Understanding Society,* edited by Eileen Barker. New York: Edwin Mellen Press, 1982.
———. *The Romantic Ethic and the Spirit of Modern Consumerism.* London: Basil Blackwell, 1987.
Campbell, Joseph. *The Hero with a Thousand Faces.* Princeton: Princeton University Press, 1968.
———. *The Power of Myth.* New York: Anchor, 1991.
Carrette, Jeremy and Richard King. *Selling Spirituality: The Silent Takeover of Religion.* New York: Routledge, 2005.
Casanova, Jose. *Public Religions in the Modern World.* Chicago: University of Chicago Press, 1994.

Casey, Catherine. *Work, Self and Society: After Industrialization*. London: Routledge, 1995.
Cavanaugh, William T. and Peter Scott. *The Blackwell Companion to Political Theology*, edited by Peter Scott and William T. Cavanaugh. Malden, MA: Blackwell, 2007.
Certeau, Michel de. *The Practice of Everyday Life*. Berkeley: University of California Press, 1984.
Chidester, David. "The Church of Baseball, the Fetish of Coca-Cola, and the Potlatch of Rock 'n' Roll: Theoretical Models for the Study of Religion in American Popular Culture." *Journal of the American Academy of Religion* 64, no. 4 (1996): 743–65.
Cimino, Richard and Don Lattin. *Shopping for Faith: American Religion in the New Millennium*. San Francisco: Jossey-Bass, 1998.
Clapp, Rodney. "The Theology of Consumption and the Consumption of Theology." In *The Consuming Passion: Christianity & the Consumer Culture*, edited by Rodney Clapp. Downers Grove, IL: InterVarsity Press, 1998.
Colson, Charles, and Jack Eckerd. *Why America Doesn't Work*. Dallas: Word Publishing, 1991.
Corrigan, Peter. *The Sociology of Consumption: An Introduction*. London: SAGE, 1997.
Cosden, Darrell. *The Heavenly Good of Earthly Work*. Milton Keynes, UK: Paternoster, 2006.
Cross Currents 42 (1992): 342–56.
Covey, Stephen R. *The 8th Habit: From Effectiveness to Greatness*. New York: Free Press, 2004.
Crockett, Clayton. *Radical Political Theology: Religion and Politics After Liberalism*. New York: Columbia University Press, 2011.
Dahl, Robert. *A Preface to Economic Democracy*. Berkeley: University of California Press, 1985.
Davaney, Sheila Greeve. "Mapping Theologies: A Historicist Guide to Contemporary Theology." In *Changing Conversations: Religious Reflection and Cultural Analysis*, edited by Dwight N. Hopkins and Sheila Greeve Davaney. New York: Routledge, 1996.
_____. *Pragmatic Historicism: A Theology for the Twenty-First Century*. Albany: SUNY, 2000.
_____. "Theology and the Turn to Cultural Analysis." In *Converging on Culture: Theologian in Dialogue with Cultural Analysis and Criticism*, edited by Delwin Brown Sheila Greeve Davaney, and Kathryn Tanner. Oxford: Oxford University Press, 2001.
Davidson, James C. and David P. Caddell. "Religion and the Meaning of Work." In *Journal for the Scientific Study of Religion*, 33, no. 2 (1994): 135–47.
Davis, Marshall. *More Than a Purpose: An Evangelical Response to Rick Warren and the Megachurch Movement*. Enumclaw, WA: WinePress Publishing, 2006.
DeChant, Dell. *The Sacred Santa: Religious Dimensions of Consumer Culture*. Cleveland. Pilgrim Press, 2002.
De Vries, Hent. *Political Theologies: Public Religions in a Post-Secular World*. New York: Fordham University Press, 2006.
Dorrien, Gary J. "Social Salvation: The Social Gospel as Theology and Economics." In *The Social Gospel Today*, edited by Christopher H. Evans. Louisville: Westminster John Knox Press, 2001, 101–13.
_____. *Soul in Society: The Making and Renewal of Social Christianity*. Minneapolis: Fortress Press, 1995.
Douglas, R. M. "Talent and Vocation in Humanist and Protestant Thought." In *Action and Conviction in Early Modern Europe: Essays in Memory of E. H. Harbison*, edited by Theodore K. Rabb and Jerrold Siegel, 261–98. Princeton: Princeton University Press, 1969.
Du Gay, Paul. *Consumption and Identity at Work*. Thousand Oaks, CA: SAGE, 1996.
Edwards, Tim. *Contradictions of Consumptions: Concepts, Practices and Politics in Consumer Society*. Buckingham: Open University Press, 2000.
Ehrenreich, Barbara. *Bait and Switch: The (Futile) Pursuit of the American Dream*. New York: Henry Holt and Company, 2006.

———. *Bright-Sided: How Positive Thinking Is Undermining America*. New York: Picador, 2010.
Einstein, Mara. *Brands of Faith: Marketing Religion in a Commercial Age*. New York: Routledge, 2008.
Eldredge, John. *Wild at Heart: Discovering the Secret of a Man's Soul*. Nashville: Thomas Nelson, 2001.
Ellul, Jacques. *The Technological Society*. Trans. John Wilkinson. New York: Random House, 1964.
———. "Work and Calling." In *Callings!*, edited by James Y. Holloway and Will D. Campbell, pp. 18–44. New York: Paulist Press, 1974.
Estey, Ken. *A New Protestant Labor Ethic at Work*. Cleveland: The Pilgrim Press, 2002.
Ewen, Stuart. *Captains of Consciousness: Advertising and the Social Roots of the Consumer Culture*. New York: Basic Books, 2001.
———. *All Consuming Images*. New York: Basic Books, 1988.
Fantasia, Rick and Kim Voss. *Hard Work: Remaking the American Labor Movement*. Berkeley: University of California Press, 2004.
Featherstone, Mike. *Consumer Culture and Postmodernism*. London: Sage, 1991.
Fiske, John. *Understanding Popular Culture*. New York: Routledge, 1989.
Frank, Thomas. *One Market Under God: Extreme Capitalism, Market Populism, and the End of Economic Democracy*. New York: Anchor Books, 2000.
Freeman, Richard B. and Joel Rogers. *What Workers Want*. Ithaca, NY: Cornell University Press, 2006.
Friedman, Jonathan. *Consumption and Identity*. Chur, Switzerland: Harwood Academic Publishers, 1994.
Gabriel, Yiannis, and Tim Lang. *The Unmanageable Consumer: Contemporary Consumption and Its Fragmentation*. London: SAGE, 1995.
Gamwell, Franklin I. *Politics as a Christian Vocation: Faith and Democracy Today*. Cambridge: Cambridge University Press, 2005.
Gay, Craig M. "Sensualists Without Heart: Contemporary Consumerism in Light of the Modern Project." In *The Consuming Passion: Christianity &the Consumer Culture*, edited by Rodney Clapp. Downer's Grove, IL: InterVarsity Press, 1998.
———. *With Liberty and Justice for Whom?: The Recent Evangelical Debate over Capitalism*. Grand Rapids: Eerdmans, 1991.
Geoghegan, Thomas. "Infinite Debt: How Unlimited Interest Rates Destroyed the Economy." *Harper's Magazine*, April 2009: 31–39.
Giddens, Anthony. *Modernity and Self-Identity: Self and Society in the Late Modern Age*. Stanford: Stanford University Press, 1991.
Gillespie, Daniel. "Roaming Wild: Investigating the Message in *Wild at Heart*." in *Fool's Gold*, edited by John MacArthur. Wheaton, IL: Crossway, 2004.
Gladwell, Malcolm. "The Cellular Church: How Rick Warren Built His Ministry." *The New Yorker*, September 9, 2005.
Goldman, Harvey. *Max Weber and Thomas Mann: Calling and the Shaping of the Self*. Berkeley: University of California Press, 1988.
Greider, William. "One World of Consumers." In *Consuming Desires: Consumption, Culture, and the Pursuit of Happiness*, edited by Roger Rosenblatt. Washington, DC: Island Press, 1999.
Guinness, Os. *The Call: Finding and Fulfilling the Central Purpose of Your Life*. Nashville: W. Publishing Group, 2003.
Harvey, David. *A Brief History of Neoliberalism*. New York: Oxford, 2005.
Harvey, Van. "On the Intellectual Marginality of American Theology." In *Religion and Twentieth Century American Intellectual Life*, edited by Michael J. Lacey. New York: Cambridge University Press, 1989.
Heelas, Paul. "Cults for Capitalism? Self Religions, Magic and the Empowerment of Business." In *Religion and Power, Decline and Growth: Sociological Analyses of Religion in Britain, Poland and the Americas*, edited by Peter Gee and John Fulton. London: British Sociological Association, 1991.

―――. "The Limits of Consumption and the Post-modern 'Religion' of the New Age." In *The Authority of the Consumer*, edited by Russell Keat, Nigel Whiteley, and Nicholas Abercrombie. London: Routledge, 1993.

―――. *The New Age Movement: The Celebration of the Self and the Sacralization of Modernity*. Oxford: Blackwell, 1996.

―――. "Prosperity and the New Age Movement: The Efficacy of Spiritual Economics." In *New Religious Movements: Challenge and Response*, edited by Bryan Wilson and Jamie Cresswell. London: Routledge, 1999.

Heelas, Paul, Linda Woodhead, Benjamin Seel, and Bronislaw Szerszynski. *Spiritual Revolution: Why Religion Is Giving Way to Spirituality*. London: Blackwell, 2004.

Henry, Carl F. H. *Aspects of Christian Social Ethics*. Grand Rapids, MI: Eerdmans, 1964.

Hilkey, Judith. *Character Is Capital: Success Manuals and Manhood in Gilded Age America*. Chapel Hill: The University of North Carolina Press, 1997.

Hirsch, Fred. *The Social Limits to Growth*. London: Routledge and Kegan Paul, 1977.

Holl, K. "Die Geschichte des Worts 'Beruf.'" In *Gesammelte Aufsatze zur Kirchengeschichte*, vol. 3. Tubingen: J. C. B. Mohr, 1931.

Hollerich, Michael. "Carl Schmitt." In *The Blackwell Companion to Political Theology*, edited by Peter Scott and William T. Cavanaugh, 107–22. Malden, MA: Blackwell, 2007.

Hunter, James Davison. *Evangelicalism: The Coming Generation*. Chicago: University of Chicago Press, 1987.

―――. "Religious Elites in Advanced Capitalism: The Dialectic of Power and Marginality." In *World Order and Religion*, edited by Wade Clark Roof. Albany, NY: SUNY Press, 1991.

Hybels, Bill. *Christians in the Marketplace*. Wheaton, IL: Victor Books, 1982.

Jameson, Frederic. *Postmodernism or, The Cultural Logic of Late Capitalism*. Durham, NC: Duke University Press, 1991.

Jensen, David H. *Responsive Labor: A Theology of Work*. Louisville, KY: Westminster John Knox Press, 2006.

Jhally, Sut. *The Codes of Advertising: Fetishism and the Political Economy of Meaning in the Consumer Society*. New York: Routledge, 1990.

John Paul II. Laborem exercens. On Human Work on the Nineteenth Anniversary of Rerum Novarum. Catholic-Pages website. June 8, 2011, http://www.catholic-pages.com/documents/laborem_exercens.pdf.

Jones, Laurie Beth. *Jesus, CEO: Using Ancient Wisdom for Visionary Leadership*. New York: Hyperion, 1995.

Jones, Serene. "Cultural Labor and Theological Critique." In *Converging on Culture: Theologians in Dialogue with Cultural Analysis and Criticism*, edited by Delwin Brown Sheila Greeve Davaney, and Kathryn Tanner. Oxford: Oxford University Press, 2001.

Kavanaugh, John F. *Following Christ in a Consumer Society: The Spirituality of Cultural Resistance*. Maryknoll, NY: Orbis Books, 1991.

Kelsey, David H. *To Understand God Truly: What's Theological About a Theological School*. Louisville, KY: Westminster, 1992.

Kintz, Linda. *Between Jesus and the Market: The Emotions That Matter in Right-Wing America*. Durham, NC: Duke University Press, 1997.

Klein, Naomi. *No Logo*. New York: Picador, 2002.

Krapp, Robert Martin. "A Note on the Puritan 'Calling.'" *Review of Religion*, 7 (1943): 242–51.

Kunde, Jesper and B. J. Cunningham. *Corporate Religion*. Upper Saddle River, NJ: Prentice Hall, 2002.

Larive, Armand. *After Sunday: A Theology of Work*. New York: Continuum, 2004.

Lasch, Christopher. *The Culture of Narcissism: American Life in an Age of Diminishing Expectations*. New York: W. W. Norton, 1978.

Lasn, Kalle. *Culture Jam: How to Reverse America's Suicidal Consumer Binge--and Why We Must*. New York: Quill, 2000.

Lears, T. J. Jackson. "Beyond Veblen: Rethinking Consumer Culture in America." In *Consuming Visions: Accumulation and Display of Goods in America, 1880-1920*, edited by Simon J. Bronner. New York: W. W. Norton, 1989.

———. "From Salvation to Self-Realization: Advertising and the Therapeutic Roots of the Consumer Culture, 1880–1930." In *The Culture of Consumption*, edited by Richard Wightman Fox and T. J. Jackson Lears. New York: Pantheon, 1983.

———. *No Place of Grace: Antimodernism and the Transformation of American Culture, 1880–1920*. New York: Pantheon, 1981.

Lichtenstein, Nelson. *State of the Union: A Century of American Labor*. Princeton: Princeton University Press, 2003.

Lindstrom, Martin. *Buyology: Truth and Lies About What We Buy*. New York: Broadway Business, 2008.

Lodziak, Conrad. *The Myth of Consumerism*. London: Pluto, 2002.

Long, D. Stephen. "God Is Not Nice." In *God Is Not . . .*, edited by D. Brent Laytham. Grand Rapids, MI: Brazos, 2004.

Loy, David R. "The Religion of the Market." *Journal of the American Academy of Religion* 65, no. 2 (1997): 275–90.

Luckmann, Thomas. "The Privatization of Religion and Morality." In *De-traditionalization: Critical Reflections on Authority and Identity at a Time of Uncertainty*, edited by Paul Heelas, Scott Lash, and Paul Morris. Cambridge, UK: Blackwell, 1996.

Luther, Martin. "On Secular Authority: How Far Does the Obedience Owed to It Extend?" In *Luther and Calvin on Secular Authority*, edited by Harro Hopfl. Cambridge: Cambridge University Press, 1991.

———. "Trade and Usury." In *Luther's Works*, edited by Charles M. Jacobs. Philadelphia: Muhlenberg, 1962.

Lyon, David. *Jesus in Disneyland: Religion in Postmodern Times*. Cambridge, UK: Polity Press, 2000.

———. *Postmodernity*. 2nd edited by Minneapolis: University of Minnesota Press, 1999.

MacArthur, John. *Ashamed of the Gospel: When the Church Becomes Like the World*. Wheaton, IL: Crossway Books, 2001.

Marsden, George. *Fundamentalism and American Culture: The Shaping of Twentieth-Century Evangelicalism 1870–1925*. New York: Oxford University Press, 1982.

Marshall, Paul. *A Kind of Life Imposed on Man: Vocation and Social Order from Tyndale to Locke*. Toronto: University of Toronto Press, 1996.

———. "Vocation, Work and Rest." In *Christian Faith and Practice in the Modern World*, edited by Mark A. Noll and David F. Wells, 199-217. Grand Rapids: Eerdmans, 1988.

Marty, Martin E. "Equipose." In *Consuming Desires: Consumption, Culture, and the Pursuit of Happiness*, edited by Roger Rosenblatt. Washington, DC: Island Press, 1999.

Marx, Karl. *Capital*. Vol. 1. Trans. Ben Fowkes. New York: Vintage, 1977.

McAllister, Matthew P. *The Commercialization of American Culture: New Advertising, Control, and Democracy*. Thousand Oaks: SAGE, 1995.

McClintock Fulkerson, Mary. "Toward a Materialist Christian Social Criticism: Accommodation and Culture Reconsidered." In *Changing Conversations: Religious Reflection and Cultural Analysis*, edited by Dwight N. Hopkins and Sheila Greeve Davaney. New York: Routledge, 1996.

McDannell, Colleen. *Material Christianity: Religion and Popular Culture in America*. New Haven, CT: Yale University Press, 1995.

McGee, Micki. *Self-Help, Inc.: Makeover Culture in American Life*. Oxford: Oxford University Press, 2005.

McKibben, Bill. "The Christian Paradox." *Harper's Magazine*, July 2005.

Meeks, Douglas M. "The Future of Theology in a Commodity Society." In *The Future of Theology: Essays in Honor of Jurgen Moltmann*, edited by Miraslov Volf, Carmen Krieg, and Thomas Kucharz. Grand Rapids, MI: Eerdmans, 1996.

———. *God The Economist: The Doctrine of God and Political Economy*. Minneapolis: Fortress Press, 1989.

Meidner, Rudolf. "A Swedish Union Proposal for Collective Capital Sharing." In *Eurosocialism and America: Political Economy for the 1980s*, edited by Nancy Lieber. Philadelphia: Temple University Press, 1982.

Melman, Seymour. *After Capitalism: From Managerialism to Workplace Democracy*. New York: Alfred A. Knopf, 2001.

Michaelsen, Robert S. "Changes in the Puritan Concept of Calling or Vocation." *New England Quarterly* 26 (1953): 315–36.

———. "Work and Vocation in American Industrial Society." In *Work and Vocation: A Christian Discussion*, edited by John Oliver Nelson. New York: Harper and Brothers, 1954.

Miles, Stephen. *Consumerism As a Way of Life*. London: SAGE, 1998.

Miller, Vincent J. *Consuming Religion: Christian Faith and Practice in a Consumer Culture*. New York: Continuum, 2004.

———. "Taking Consumer Culture Seriously." *Horizons* 27 (2000): 276–95.

Mims, Ana Mollinedo. *Keeping the Faith: How Applying Spiritual Purpose to Your Work Can Lead to Extraordinary Success*. New York: Harper Collins, 2007.

Mitroff, Ian I. and Elizabeth A. Denton. *A Spiritual Audit of Corporate America: A Hard Look at Spiritualty, Religion, and Values in the Workplace*. San Francisco: Jossey-Bass, 1999.

Moltmann, Jürgen. *God for a Secular Society: The Public Relevance of Theology*. Minneapolis: Fortress Press, 1999.

———. *A Theology of Work: Work and the New Creation*. Grand Rapids: Kregel Publications, 2005.

Moore, R. Laurence. *Selling God: American Religion in the Marketplace of Culture*. New York: Oxford University Press, 1994.

Niebuhr, H. Richard. *Christ and Culture*. New York: Harper and Row, 1951.

Novak, Michael. *Business as Calling: Work and the Examined Life*. New York: Free Press, 1996.

———. *The Spirit of Democratic Capitalism*. Lanham, MD: Madison, 1991.

———. *Toward a Theology of the Corporation*. Washington, DC: AEI Press, 1990.

Peale, Norman Vincent. *The Power of Positive Thinking*. New York: Prentice-Hall, 1952.

Perelman, Michael. *The Invisible Handcuffs: How Market Tyranny Stifles the Economy by Stunting Workers*. New York: Monthly Review Press, 2011.

Perkins, William. *A Treatise of the Vocations*. London: John Haviland, 1631.

Pilzer, Paul Zane. *God Wants You to Be Rich: The Theology of Economics*. New York: Simon & Schuster, 1995.

Possamai, Adam. "Cultural Consumption of History and Popular Culture in Alternative Spiritualities." *Journal of Consumer Culture* 2, no. 2 (2002): 197–218.

Rauschenbusch, Walter. *Christianity and the Social Crisis in the 21st Century: The Classic That Woke Up the Church*. New York: HarperOne, 2007.

Redden, Guy. "The New Agents." *Journal of Consumer Culture* 2, no. 1 (2002): 33–52.

Reed, Esther D. *Good Work: Christian Ethics in the Workplace*. Waco, TX: Baylor University Press, 2010.

Reich, Robert B. *Supercapitalism: The Transformation of Business, Democracy, and Everyday Life*. New York: Alfred A. Knopf, 2007.

Reisman, George. *Capitalism: A Treatise on Economics*. Ottawa, IL: Jameson Books, 1996.

Rieff, Philip. *The Triumph of the Therapeutic: Uses of Faith After Freud*. New York: Harper Torchbooks, 1966.

Riesman, David. *The Lonely Crowd: A Study of Changing American Character*. New Haven, CT: Yale University Press, 1961.

Ritzer, George. *Enchanting a Disenchanted World: Revolutionizing the Means of Consumption*. London: SAGE, 1999.

———. *The McDonaldization of Society*. 2nd edited by Thousand Oaks, CA: Pine Forge Press, 2004.

Robbins, Jeffrey W. *Radical Democracy and Political Theology*. New York: Columbia University Press, 2011.
Roberts, Richard H. "Power and Empowerment: New Age Managers and the Dialectics of Modernity/Post-modernity." In *Religion and the Transformations of Capitalism: Comparative Approaches*, edited by Richard H. Roberts. New York: Routledge, 1995.
_____. *Religion, Theology and the Human Sciences*. Cambridge, UK: Cambridge University Press, 2002.
Roof, Wade Clark. *A Generation of Seekers*. San Francisco: HarperCollins, 1993.
_____. *Spiritual Marketplace: Baby Boomers and the Remaking of American Religion*. Princeton, NJ: Princeton University Press, 1999.
Sargeant, Kimon Howland. *Seeker Churches: Promoting Traditional Religion in a Nontraditional Way*. New Brunswick, NJ: Rutgers University Press, 2000.
Sayers, Dorothy L. "Vocation in Work." In *A Christian Basis for the Post-War World*, edited by A. E Baker. New York: Morehouse-Gorham, 1942.
Schmidt, Leigh Eric. *Consumer Rites: The Buying and Selling of American Holidays*. Princeton, NJ: Princeton University Press, 1995.
Schmitt, Carl. *Political Theology: Four Chapters on the Concept of Sovereignty*. Chicago: University of Chicago Press, 2006.
Schor, Juliet B. "The New Politics of Consumption." In *Do American Shop Too Much?*, edited by Joshua Cohen and Joel Rogers. Boston: Beacon, 2000.
_____. *The Overworked American: The Unexpected Decline of Leisure*. New York: Basic Books, 1992.
Schuurman, Douglas J. *Vocation: Discerning Our Callings in Life*. Grand Rapids, MI: Eerdmans, 2004.
Schwartz, Barry. *The Paradox of Choice: Why More Is Less*. New York: Ecco, 2004.
Sennett, Richard. "Capitalism and the City." In *Future City*, edited by Stephen Reed, Jürgen Rosenmann and Job van Eldijk, 114–24. New York: Spon Press, 2005.
_____. *The Corrosion of Character: The Personal Consequences of Work in the New Capitalism*. New York: W.W. Norton, 1998.
_____. *The Culture of New Capitalism*. New Haven: Yale University Press, 2006.
Sider, Ronald J. *Rich Christians in an Age of Hunger*. Downers Grove, IL: InterVarsity Press, 1984.
Simonds, Wendy. *Women and Self-Help Culture: Reading Between the Lines*. New Brunswick, NJ: Rutgers University Press, 1992.
Slater, Don. *Consumer Culture and Modernity*. Cambridge, UK: Polity Press, 1997.
Smith, Christian. *Christian America?: What Evangelicals Really Want*. Berkeley, CA: University of California Press, 2000.
Smith, Ted A. "Redeeming Critique: Resignations to the Cultural Turn in Christian Theology and Ethics." *Journal of the Society of Christian Ethics* 24, 2 (2004): 89–113.
Smith, Warren. *Deceived on Purpose: The New Age Implications of the Purpose-Driven Church*. Magalia, CA: Mountain Stream Press, 2005.
Sommerville, C. J. "The Anti-Puritan Work Ethic." *Journal of British Studies* 20 (1981) 70–81.
Stark, Rodney and William Sims Bainbridge. *The Future of Religion: Secularization, Revival and Cult Formation*. Berkeley: University of California Press, 1986.
Storey, John. *Cultural Consumption and Everyday Life*. London: Arnold, 1999.
Storkey, Alan. "Postmodernism Is Consumption." In *Christ and Consumerism: Critical Reflections on the Spirit of Our Age*, edited by Craig Bartholomew. London: Paternoster, 2000.
Strangleman, T. and I. Roberts. "Looking Through the Window of Opportunity: The Cultural Cleansing of Workplace Identity." *Sociology* 33 (1999): 47–67.
Sundquist, James. *Who's Driving the Purpose-Driven Church?* Bethany, OK: Bible Belt Publishing, 2004.
Tanner, Kathryn. *Economy of Grace*. Minneapolis: Augsburg Fortress Publishers, 2005.
_____. *Theories of Culture: A New Agenda for Theology*. Minneapolis: Augsburg Press, 1997.

Tawney, Richard Henry. *Religion and the Rise of Capitalism*. New York: Harcourt, Brace and Co., 1926.
Terkel, Studs. *Working: People Talk About What They Do All Day and How They Feel About What They Do*. New York: Ballantine, 1972.
Thompson, Craig J. "A New Puritanism?" In *Do Americans Shop Too Much?*, eds. Joshua Cohen and Joel Rogers. Boston: Beacon, 2000.
Tomlinson, Alan. *Consumption, Identity, and Style: Marketing, Meanings, and the Packaging of Pleasure*. New York: Routledge, 1990.
Troeltsch, Ernst. *The Social Teaching of the Christian Churches*, vols. 1 and 2, trans. Olive Wyon. New York: Macmillan, 1931.
Twitchell, James B. *Branded Nation: The Marketing of Megachurch, College Inc., and Museumworld*. New York: Simon and Schuster, 2004.
———. *Lead Us Into Temptation: The Triumph of American Materialism*. New York: Columbia University Press, 1999.
Veblen, Thorstein, *The Theory of the Leisure Class*. New York: B. W. Huebsch, 1912.
Volf, Miroslav. *Work in the Spirit: Toward a Theology of Work*. Eugene, OR: Wif and Stock Publishers, 2001.
Waldman, Steven. "The Tyranny of Choice." *New Republic* 206 (1992): 22–25.
Warren, Rick. *The Purpose-Driven Church: Growth Without Compromising Your Message and Mission*. Grand Rapids, MI: Zondervan, 1995.
———. *The Purpose-Driven Life*. Grand Rapids, MI: Zondervan, 2002.
Weber, Max. *Economy and Society: An Outline of Interpretive Sociology*. Berkeley: University of California Press, 1978.
———. "Politics As a Vocation." In *The Vocation Lectures*, edited by David Owen and Tracy B. Strong. Indianapolis: Hackett Publishing, 2004, 32–93.
———. *The Protestant Ethic and the Spirit of Capitalism*. New York: Scribner's, 1958.
Weigert, Andrew J. and Anthony J. Blasi. "Vocation." In *Vocation and Social Context*, edited by Giuseppe Giordan, 13–34. Leiden, The Netherlands: Brill, 2007.
Wells, David F. *Above All Earthly Pow'rs*. Grand Rapids: Eerdmans, 2005.
———. *God in the Wasteland: The Reality of Truth in a World of Fading Dreams*. Grand Rapids: Eerdmans, 1994.
———. *No Place for Truth or Whatever Happened to Evangelical Theology?* Grand Rapids: Eerdmans, 1993.
Wesley, John. "Sermon 51: The Good Steward." Vol. 4. In *The Works of John Wesley*, edited by Frank Baker. Nashville: Abingdon, 1987.
Williams, Raymond. *Keywords: A Vocabulary of Culture and Society*. New York: Oxford University Press, 1983.
Wingren, Gustaf. *Luther on Vocation*. Eugene, OR: Wipf & Stock Publishers, 2004.
Witherington III, Ben. *Work: A Kingdom Perspective on Labor*. Grand Rapids, MI: Wm. B. Eerdmans, 2011.
Witten, Marsha. *All Is Forgiven: The Secular Message in American Protestantism*. Princeton, NJ: Princeton University Press, 1993.
———. "'Where Your Treasure Is': Popular Evangelical Views of Work, Money, and Materialism." In *Rethinking Materialism: Perspectives on the Spiritual Dimension of Economic Behavior*, edited by Robert Wuthnow. Grand Rapids, MI: Eerdmans, 1995.
Wolfe, Alan. "The Limits of *The Purpose-Driven Life*: Can Twenty Million Readers Be Wrong?" *In Character*, Winter 2005.
Wrzesniewski, Amy, Clark McCauley, and Paul Rozin. "Jobs, Careers, and Callings: People's Relations to Their Work." *Journal of Research in Personality* 31 (1997): 21–33.
Wuthnow, Robert. *After Heaven: Spirituality in America Since the 1950s*. Berkeley: University of California Press, 1998.
———. "The Cultural Turn: Stories Logic, and the Quest for Identity in American Religion." In *Contemporary American Religion: An Ethnographic Reader*, edited by Penny Edgell Becker and Nancy L. Eiesland. Walnut Creek, CA: AltaMira Press, 1997.
———. *God and Mammon in America*. New York: Free Press, 1994.

_____. "A Good Life and a Good Society: The Debate Over Materialism." In *Rethinking Materialism: Perspectives on the Spiritual Dimension*, edited by Robert Wuthnow. Grand Rapids, MI: Eerdmans, 1995.

Zweig, Michael. *The Working Class Majority: America's Best Kept Secret*. Ithaca, NY: ILR Press, 2000.

Index

Adbusters Magazine, 144
After Sunday (Larive), 63
America, 66, 69, 83–86, 100; evangelical theology in, 69–71, 126; Gilded Age, 33–34, 35, 100, 165; twentieth century, 134, 155; nineteenth century, 32–33, 34, 85; culture, 69–73
Animal laborans, 93
Aquinas, Thomas, 46n4
Arendt, Hannah, 93–94, 103
Arminianism, 32
Asad, Talal, 119
Augustine, 46n4

baby boomers, 115, 124
Barth, Karl, 4, 39–43, 46, 52, 59, 165
Baudrillard, Jean, 87
Bauman, Zygmunt, 13, 88–93, 99, 102, 103–104, 115, 120, 136, 147, 160, 167; solid modernity, 88–90, 99, 160; liquid modernity, 13, 88, 90–91, 115, 120, 147
Baxter, Richard, 31, 49
Beaudoin, Tom, 145
Belabored self, 73–74, 75, 101–103
Bellah, Robert, 10, 164
Bennett, Jane, 145
Berger, Peter, 114–115
Beruf, 20
Bieler, Andre, 26
Blasi, Anthony J., 1
Bolles, Richard Nelson, 74–75
Brown, Delwin, 51
Brunner, Emil, 39–41
Busenitz, Nathan, 125–129

calling. *See* Vocation
Calvin, John, 4, 15, 25–30, 31–35, 37, 113, 131; Holy Community, 28–29, 31, 34, 150, 152–155

Calvinism, 27–29, 30, 32, 60, 69, 100
Campbell, Colin, 86–88, 90, 103
Campbell, Joseph, 121–122, 136
capitalism, 10–11, 13, 19, 27, 35–36, 65, 89, 103, 156; corporate, 146, 147, 150; flexible, 11, 13, 95, 103, 135, 150; industrial, 155, 157–158, 160; *laissez-faire*, 8, 164; monopoly, 35
career, 10, 74, 95, 135
Carrette, Jeremy and Richard King, 14, 146–147, 148–149, 161
Casanova, José, 7, 164, 166
Cavanaugh, William, 76, 77
Christian Coalition, 74
Christianity and the Social Crisis (Rauschenbusch), 37
Cimino Richard, 115
colonialism, 89
commodification, 5, 14–15; of religion, 110, 120, 146, 149, 163
commodity, 5, 85; production of, 84; fetishization of, 85
confession, 51, 71–73
conspicuous consumption, 85–87
consumer culture, 2, 6, 9, 13–15, 57, 66, 71, 83–88, 91, 92–100, 109–118, 120, 122, 141, 160
consumer insatiability, 86–87, 88, 90
consumer society, 88, 90, 92; and work, 93–94
Cosden, Darrelll, 56–65
Covey, Steven, 67
crisis theology, 39
Crockett, Clayton, 7–9
culture jamming, 144
cultural turn in theology, 51–55

Davis, Marshall, 126–128
De Certeau, Michel, 145
De Vries, Hent, 16n21

Dorrien, Gary, 143–144
Douglas, Richard, 22, 24, 26, 29–30

Economy of Grace (Tanner), 54
Edwards, Jonathan, 32
Eldredge, John, 68
Ellul, Jacques, 23, 32, 41–45
enlightenment, 70, 71, 88
Estey, Ken, 4
evangelization, 58

Fantasia, Rick, 4
Featherstone, Mike, 84
flawed consumer, 91–92
Fordism, 89, 106n25
formation of identity, consumerist conception, 161
Foucault, Michel, 73, 119
Franklin, Benjamin, 34

Geoghegan, Thomas, 142
Getting On in the World (Mathews), 34
Gillespie, Daniel, 69, 72, 73, 119
Gladwell, Malcolm, 111, 112
God in the Wasteland: The Reality of Truth in a World of Fading Dreams, Above All Earthly Pow'rs (Wells), 70
Gospel accommodating to culture, 68, 110, 116, 117–118, 123, 124–126, 127–130
Great Awakenings in America, 32–33

Habits of the Heart (Bellah), 10
Harvey, David, 168n17
Hauerwas, Stanley, 53
Hilkey, Judith, 33–34
Holy Community, 28–29, 31, 34, 150, 152–155
Holy Spirit, 1, 2, 44, 59, 63, 64
Homo consumens, 83
Homo faber, 93
humanism, 22

individualism, 32, 147, 150, 151
Industrial Revolution, 46
industrial society, 41
industrialization, 35, 62, 71

James, William, 146

Jensen, David, 58–61, 63–65
Jesus, CEO (Jones), 148
Jones, Laurie Beth, 85, 87, 148
Jung, Carl, 122

Klein, Naomi, 167n5
Klesis, 20

labor, 6, 12, 32, 44, 55, 58, 60, 61–63
Laborem exercens, 62, 63, 64, 165
Larive, Armand, 63–66
Lasn, Kalle, 144
Lattin, Don, 115
Lears, T.J. Jackson, 81n60, 84, 100–101
Leo XIII, Pope Leo, 62
liberal theology, 41
liquid modernity, 14, 88, 90, 99
Luther, Martin, 1, 11, 20–24, 25, 26–27

Marshall, Paul, 22, 24, 25, 32
Marx, Karl, 21, 32, 37, 77, 85, 89, 93, 105n8, 155–156
materialism, 119, 129, 133, 140n72
Mathews, William, 34
McGee, Micki, 73, 74–75, 101–102, 113; consulting, 97–98
McLuhan, Marshall, 117
Miller, Vincent, 14, 110, 118–123, 128–129, 129–130, 138n29, 145–146, 149, 167n11, 168n12
Moltmann, Jurgen, 76
More Than a Purpose: An Evangelical Response to Rick Warren and the Megachurch Movement (Marshall), 126
motivation literature, 3. *See also* self-help
Moyers, Bill, 122

nationalism, 89
neoliberalism, 8, 147, 168n17
neo-orthodox, 39, 41
Niebuhr, H.R., 71
No Place for Truth or Whatever Happened to Evangelical Theology (Wells), 70

outsourcing, 6

Patterson, Eugene, 124

Paul II, Pope John, 62
Peale, Norman Vincent, 126
Perkins, William, 30
political theology, 7, 8–9, 16n21, 76–79, 163
Possibility Thinking (Schuller), 124, 126
postsecularism, 3, 7–8, 9
pre-industrial labor, 65
privatization, 8
producer society, 2, 13–14, 37, 39, 52, 76–77, 83–86, 88, 89–90, 91, 144–145
Protestant work ethic, 27, 35–36, 96, 103, 152
psychological angst, 26
public policy, 76
Puritan, 29–34, 45
purpose as vocation, 131–136

radical democracy, 8
Rauschenbusch, Walter, 15, 35, 37–42, 49, 52, 131, 155
Reformation, 10, 34, 45, 71, 83
Reich, Robert, 143
religious commodification, 120
repoliticization, 8
Rerum Novarum (Pope Leo XIII), 62
Rieff, Philip, 107n57
Riesman, David, 100
Robbins, Jeffrey, 8
Roberts, Richard, 161–162, 165
Robertson, Pat, 74
Romantic era, 87
Roof, Clark, 115
Roosevelt, Theodore, 141
Rorty, Richard, 53

Saddleback Church, 116–118
Sayers, Dorothy, 35, 38
Schmitt, Carl, 77
Schuller, Robert, 124, 126
Scott, Peter, 76, 77
secularism, 8, 9, 13–15
secular humanism, 70
secular politics, 76, 77
seeker, 101, 114
seeker-sensitive method, 115, 123
self-help literature, 6, 66–68, 73–75; Christian, 51, 68, 78; Christian criticism of, 69; as commodifier, 67; in *The Purpose-Driven Life*, 109, 110–112
Self-Help, Inc. (McGee), 73
self-referentiality, 27, 32
Sennett, Richard, 11, 13, 17n29, 94, 95–99, 136
Siegel, Bernie, 124
Simonds, Wendy, 66
Slater, Don, 104n4
Smith, Ted, 52, 53
Smith, Warren, 124–125, 126
social capital, 97–99, 148, 150, 157
Social Gospel, 36, 37, 39
social sin, 155, 159, 160
solid modernity, 88–90, 99
spirituality,: of seeking, 115; New Age, 123, 124, 126, 129; as capitalistic, 146–149
success manuals, 33, 35

Tanner, Kathryn, 54
team-based work model, 96–97, 98, 103
Technique, 43, 102, 109, 115, 117
teleology, 41, 160
The Heavenly Good of Earthly Work (Cosden), 56
The Hero with a Thousand Faces (Campbell), 121
The Power of Myth (Campbell), 122
The Protestant Ethic and the Spirit of Capitalism (Weber), 35
The Purpose Driven Life (Warren), 4, 68, 109–136
The Seven Habits of Highly Effective People, The 8th Habit: From Effectiveness to Greatness (Covey), 67
The Technological Society (Ellul), 41
Troeltsch, Ernst, 27, 28, 49, 150–154, 168n27
Turkel, Studs, 1

unemployment, 38, 58, 92
Unio Mystica , 151

Veblen, Thorstein, 85–87
vocation: democratization of, 1; as political, 12, 14–15, 142, 162–165; Reformed notion of, 20–30; Puritan notion of, 31–32; and the self-made

man, 32–34; as a problem, 2–3; as a sentry post, 25; as a gift from God, 26
Volf, Miroslav, 4, 41
Voss, Kim, 4

Warren, Rick, 3, 14, 109–136
Weber, Max, 1, 12, 27–28, 29, 35–36, 73–77, 141–142, 152
Weberian Triangle, 94–95, 97, 98
Weigart, Andrew J., 1
Wells, David, 70–75, 123–124
What Color is Your Parachute? : A Practical Manual for Job Hunters and Career Changers (Nelson), 74
Wild at Heart (Eldridge), 68
Williams, Delores, 53
Williams, Raymond, 10
Wingren, Gustav, 23
Woolf, Virginia, 84
work: as ideology, 39, 41, 43, 44; theology of, 56–66; as co-creation with God, 62, 66, 80n38
Work in the Spirit (Volf), 43, 44
workplace democracy, 6, 150, 164
World War I, 52
Wuthnow, Robert, 115